Tempests
into
Rainbows

Managing Turbulence

ROBBEN W. FLEMING

Ann Arbor

THE UNIVERSITY OF MICHIGAN PRESS

Copyright © by the University of Michigan 1996
All rights reserved
Published in the United States of America by
The University of Michigan Press
Manufactured in the United States of America
∞ Printed on acid-free paper

1999   1998   1997   1996   4   3   2   1

A CIP catalog record for this book is available
from the British Library.

Library of Congress Cataloging-in-Publication Data

Fleming, R. W. (Robben Wright), 1916–
    Tempests into rainbows : managing turbulence / Robben W. Fleming.
    p.   cm.
Includes index.
ISBN 0-472-10674-0 (alk. paper)
    1. Fleming, R. W. (Robben Wright), 1916–   . 2. University of
Michigan—Presidents—Biography. 3. Corporation for Public
Broadcasting—Presidents—Biography. I. Title.
LD3275.F54A3   1996
378.1'11—dc20
    [B]   95-46711
                                                                          CIP

To Sally,
our children,
and our grandchildren,
whose love I cherish

Preface

I began this memoir for our children and grandchildren in order that they might learn about a part of my life with which they were unfamiliar. As I wrote, memories of the years after they came on the scene kept flooding through my mind, and I continued.

Now, at age seventy-eight, I am largely retired. My story is, in a sense, the story of so many others of my generation. We were born in small towns, suffered the loss of siblings whom modern medicine could now save, endured the economic depression of the late 1920s and 1930s, worked our way through school, and got out just in time to enter the armed services during World War II. For us, marriage was either delayed or a cause of being long parted until the war was over, and we had to start over once we returned. My entry into the academic world was an accident of the time, but it was a career that I loved, even though it included a difficult period of student unrest.

There are those who believe that, despite any hardships our generation endured, these were the golden years of our country's history. Whether or not that is true, only time will tell, but they remain in my memory as mostly happy years.

I owe a great debt to Sally for encouraging me to go ahead, to the readers and staff of the University of Michigan Press who corrected errors and made many useful suggestions, and to our dear friends, Roger and Esther Heyns, for reading the manuscript and greatly improving it.

Finally, I remember with affection the support and cooperation the governing boards, the faculty, the students, and the alumni at the Universities of Illinois, Wisconsin, and Michigan gave to me in the course of our common endeavors.

Insofar as there are errors in anything I have said, the responsibility is, of course, mine.

Robben W. Fleming

Contents

Chapter 1

In the Beginning: 1916–34

In American folklore the place to be born and to spend your childhood is in a small town. If that is true, my birthplace, Paw Paw, Illinois, fit the description perfectly, and I arrived on the scene on December 18, 1916. The town had about five hundred residents, many of whom were either merchants or retired farmers. It is located in that wonderfully rich and fertile farmland of northern Illinois, and its grain and livestock were shipped via train to Chicago, which lay about eighty miles straight east.

Like every other small town in the Midwest, Paw Paw had a main street that extended for about two blocks, along which all the local stores were located. Off the main street were the railroad station, two grain elevators, and a stockyard. There was no mail delivery, everyone being expected to pick up mail at the post office.

The town had no fire department, but it did possess a non-motorized cart and hose that volunteers would haul to the site of a fire. Water was readily available from a large tower that stood in the midst of the town. There was always good-natured jesting after a fire as to whether the fire or the firemen had done the greater property damage. The enthusiasm of the firemen was not always matched by their knowledge of how to fight a fire, but it was reassuring to have them available.

By the same token, there was no police force, although we did have a single policeman who, if my memory is correct, was paid something like seventy-five dollars a year for his efforts. In truth, there wasn't much need for a policeman. No one ever locked a house door even when out of town. The exception that proved the rule was my uncle, the postmaster, who always locked his door and then hung the key on a nail right outside the door. I once asked him why he did this and his answer was, "Someone might need to get in." Maybe he simply wanted our volunteer firemen to be able to get in without knocking down his door!

There were three churches in town, all of them Protestant—Baptist, Presbyterian, and Methodist. Since none of the congregations was large, there was always some talk of merging, but this never came about largely because of doctrinal differences. There were a few Catholics in town, but not enough to support a church and they had to go to another nearby town. There were, to my knowledge, no Jewish residents. We were what would now be called a WASP community. A major event of the year in our Presbyterian church was the Christmas Eve service at which Santa Claus would make an appearance at the end of the program. The evening would end with a quiet singing of "Silent Night," and we would all walk home through the snow to await the arrival of the real Santa Claus sometime during the night.

The entire school system, from first grade through high school, was housed in a single building on the east side of town. Consolidated school systems and busing came along later.

Except in the winter, Saturday nights were always the big night in town because all the farmers came to town to sell their produce, replenish their supplies, and gossip with their neighbors. From 7 to 10 P.M. the street would be filled with people. To a lesser extent, Wednesday nights would draw people to town to hear a band concert played by local musicians.

The quality of life was quite different than it would be today. There were still a number of privies that stood in backyards, and electricity in the home was not universal. There were very few water heaters, and bathing was therefore less frequent. Coal was the universal fuel for hand-fed, mostly hot-air furnaces. Since the furnace was not tended during the night, it was always cold when one got up in the morning.

In my early youth there were no refrigerators in town, but in the summer the iceman would circulate, selling chunks of ice that fit into a lead chest at the top of an icebox. Perishable food was then stored in the lower part of the cabinet. The system worked quite well and was great fun for children, because a slow-moving horse-pulled ice cart would come along accompanied by a well-muscled man with a rubber sheet over his shoulder. He would take orders, cut the ice accordingly, and carry it in a pair of tongs to the chest on the back porch. By the time it melted, he would reappear for another sale. The stock of ice had been cut from frozen ponds during the winter and stored for use in the summer. The enterprise was carried on by the local lumberyard, and the chunks of ice were stacked in sawdust in a large, frame icehouse.

Telephones were available in most homes but the system was a very different one. The phone was part of a wooden cabinet that hung on the wall. On one side of the cabinet was a handle. To make a call, one went to the phone, cranked the handle, and then took the receiver off its hook to find that an operator had answered, asking for the desired number so that she could then make the connection. She could also listen to the entire conversation or any part thereof. She was, therefore, the best-informed person in town! Some of the lines, particularly in the countryside, were so-called party lines on which everyone on the line could listen. This was often a form of entertainment for people who were either lonely or curious. In addition to her other duties, the telephone operator also triggered the noon signal from the siren and gave a special series of blasts on it when there was a fire or when the water was about to be shut off for one reason or another. If a fire occurred at night, it was a frightening thing to wake up to the wail of the siren.

Radio was the major source of entertainment, and even people without electricity often had battery sets. The earliest sets I remember required the use of earphones and, since there were rarely enough to go around, people experimented with ways of augmenting the sound. It sticks in my memory that I heard the 1924 World Series that way. My father took a sauce pan from the kitchen, put two sets of earphones in it, and then turned up the volume. The sound was miserable but we could understand what was going on. Later, the speaker radio became a big part of all our lives. All summer long the big league afternoon baseball games were on. In the fall came the football games, and the air was also filled with some of the greatest comedians the country ever had. There were also soap operas filled with wonderful ethnic characters whom we can no longer hear because it is considered demeaning to other cultures. In short, radio often furnished far better images in our imaginations than television does today.

There was no movie house in town, but we did have a regular Saturday night movie in a hall used for other purposes. The first shows were silent with subtitles, and, since we had no basis for comparison, we thought they were wonderful. The *Our Gang* series, which is still occasionally shown on cable, was in its prime. The *Perils of Pauline* featured an intrepid woman who was always involved in a hair-raising adventure from which she could escape only the following week, just in time to become enmeshed in another like episode. Jackie Coogan was the winsome child star, Rin Tin Tin was the greatest dog performer of the day, and Rudolph Valentino was the idol of the adults. The fee for each session was, I believe, a nickle for children and a quarter for adults. Popcorn was the staple food at movies, just as it is today. The difference was that a small sack cost a nickle and a large sack a dime.

Social life in small towns of that era was limited, but there were two big town picnics each year with ballgames, races, and entertainers. There was also a march by schoolchildren from the school to the cemetery on Memorial Day. The band led the parade, all the children carried a flag, and one uniformed Spanish-American War veteran rode a great white horse. On reaching the cemetery, the people would surround a World War I artillery piece while a squad from the American Legion post would fire a three-volley salute to their fallen comrades. At the conclusion of that ceremony, everyone would proceed to a stage where some chosen individual would read Lincoln's Gettysburg Address. It was a solemn occasion over which hung an air of sadness but also of camaraderie, as if we all needed each other. There was also a sense of history about it for, in addition to other war veterans, there were still a few Civil War veterans who spoke only of the Great War in which they had participated. Indeed, it is recorded that ninety-five men from the Paw Paw area volunteered for service in September, 1862. They fought at Perryville, losing 50 percent of their members. Ultimately, only twenty-seven were left to be discharged at the end of the war.

To this day, the perfumes of lilacs and iris remind me of Memorial Day in Paw Paw, for those were the flowers with which we decorated the graves.

Finally, the town had its "characters," some of whom I remember clearly. The first of them was "Jim-Jim the Democrat." We would today recognize him as a retarded individual, but he was perfectly capable of performing such unskilled jobs as driving livestock to the local stockyard for shipment to Chicago. Paw Paw was at that time a fiercely Republican town. There were only one or two Democrats, one of whom, horror of horrors, was a banker. The other was my maternal grandmother, whom I dearly loved. She was a strong-willed woman who was undaunted by the fact that her husband and all her children were Republicans. Anyway, "Jim-Jim" apparently got it through his head that there was something wrong with being a Democrat, a view that many Republicans hold to this day! Thus it was that a generation of children came to know that if they shouted "Jim-Jim the Democrat" at him when he passed he would become enraged and chase them. He wore a drooping mustache and was little, portly, poorly coordinated, and short of wind, so there was never any chance that he would catch them. It was years later before I realized that what seemed like good fun to us was, in fact, very cruel to this poor man.

Then there was the town drunk who managed to acquire alcohol despite the Volsted Act. In those days drinking was not viewed as a disease, but as a lack of character or discipline. Fortunately, this man drove only a horse and buggy and the horse knew its way home, so he could slumber while riding home. Since he was never violent, he posed no problem and was, in at least one way, quite a useful citizen. Each year a religious revivalist would come to town and occupy a big tent during revival sessions. For the truly religious, this was a great event, but for many others in town it was also entertainment at a time when there were not many other things to do. Moreover, some of the revivalists were quite famous, Billy Sunday among them. A former big league baseball player who once played for the Chicago White Sox, his preaching featured great athleticism. As he warmed up he would progressively remove his coat, vest, and tie, and climb over the furniture, including sometimes standing on the pulpit. He always drew a big crowd, partly because a big league ballplayer was someone to be reckoned with and his fiery delivery entertained some people who were not convinced by his message. After a revivalist had thundered hellfire and damnation for a week, the time would come for asking those who had been saved to come forward. Not many did this, but our drunken friend could always be relied upon to advance. This was comforting to local people who were themselves uneasy about not coming forward and who clearly felt that the minister deserved some reward for his efforts. Since the same revivalist seldom returned, our local stalwart could be relied upon to represent us in future years without his past performances being known.

During all the years of my childhood the extended family was the center of my universe. Three aunts and uncles lived in Paw Paw, as did the mothers of both my parents (neither of my grandfathers was living). We can trace my mother's family back to the marriage of Tomys Swartwout and Hendricksen Olser Barents in Amsterdam in 1631. They apparently arrived in New York in 1652 where, on landing, "they were greeted cordially by Director General Stuyvesant." On my father's side, I can go only as far back as my own grandfather, Peter Fleming, who was born in Renfrewshire, Scotland, in 1822. What strikes me most about all this is how short the history of our country really is. Peter

Fleming, my own grandfather, was born in 1822 when James Monroe, the fifth president of the United States and a Founding Father, was still in office. My maternal grandfather, Beniah Wheeler, was born in Bangor, Maine, in 1836 just as the seventh president of the United States, the redoubtable soldier-statesman, Andrew Jackson, left office. Grandfather Wheeler went west in the late gold rush of 1859. My maternal grandmother, Cale Wheeler, told fascinating stories of the "banditti of the prairie" (horse and cattle thieves) who plagued the Illinois prairie in her youth, and of the *posse comitatus* that was formed to chase them. She also had a clear memory of seeing the train carrying Lincoln's body as it came through Illinois on that last sad journey. Thus, in three generations, from my grandfathers' time to my own, we have spanned the life of the country through the terms of all but the first four of our forty-two presidents.

The family that surrounded me in my youth was largely on my mother's side. Her sister, Addie, lived in an adjoining house with her husband, Ed Guffin. They had no children, but my grandmother lived with them. She was sixty-five when I was born and had broken her hip so that she had to wear a brace and walk with a cane. I loved her dearly. Her mobility was limited, so she sat for long hours in her favorite rocking chair by a window through which she could see people pass up and down the main street. I spent hours talking to her about things past and present.

Our own immediate family consisted of our parents and three boys. The oldest was Teddy, and he was only thirteen months older than I was. Then came Jack who was five years younger than I was. Teddy and I came so close together that we were almost twins, particularly because he was of a somewhat slighter build than I and we were about the same size. We did everything together, even to celebrating our birthdays at the same time although they were really slightly different.

The benefits of living in a small town were evident during our early years. Our nearby neighbor ran a garage and he had children our age. Behind the garage, in the old but occasionally still used hitching yard, were parked old and abandoned cars. All of the boys had an interest in tinkering with these cars. There was little harm that we could do, none of the cars could be started, and we could devote endless hours to playing in them and in taking various parts off and putting them back on. Even the grease that we accumulated on our clothes was a satisfactory price to our parents for the hours of diversion we enjoyed. The grease, incidentally, was augmented by oil that was sprayed on the dirt roads in the summer to keep the dust down.

Throughout all those years we always had a dog. The first and the best of these animals was a collie named Princess. We got her when our parents answered an ad in the *Chicago Tribune.* It came from a city man who said that he had a beautiful collie he wanted to give to a country family with small children. He invited applications and Mother promptly wrote to him, enclosing a picture of her small boys. Shortly thereafter the dog arrived by train and proved to be an absolutely ideal pet. She could ride on the running board of the cars of that time, she would tolerate pummeling without reprisal, and she could even guard us when crossing the street, although crossing a street in Paw Paw at that time could hardly be classified as a hazardous enterprise. Dad had a little harness made for our wagon so that Princess could pull us around. And then one winter day when we were on a walk, she was poisoned and died almost immediately. She probably ate some poisoned meat designed to dispose of some varmint. It was our first encounter with death, and we were devastated. To console us, another dog was promptly procured, and thereafter we always had a dog in our household.

Our parents were marvelous in both their patience and their tolerance for the constructive though bothersome things they would permit us to do. There was, for instance, an unused door to our bathroom that opened at the far end of the living room. During the winter, when we were likely to be confined inside in the evening, we were allowed to open this door wide, leaving a space behind it over which a soccer ball could be thrown. After dinner we would take off our shirts, strip our long underwear to the waist, and then play a rough-and-tumble game of basketball in the living room. Naturally, this was not the best thing for the wallpaper, the ceiling, the nearby lamps, or the composure of our parents. Nevertheless, they tolerated it while huddling at the far end of the room with their reading.

Our parents only rarely entertained guests for dinner, but when they did we were allowed to be present at the table. We loved dill pickles, and anytime Mother bought them we were likely to consume them before they could be served. On one occasion she had hidden them, which caused her to proudly tell her guests how she had managed to outwit us. Turning to us, she said, "I finally managed to keep the dill pickles out of your hands until dinner." To this, Teddy casually responded, "Oh, we found them but we just licked them off!" Since some of the pickles had by then been consumed, there was a certain amount of queasiness among the guests.

As we got a little older, Mother decided it was time to introduce Teddy and me to the world of work. Mowing the yard seemed to be a good place to start, since whatever portion of it we did would to that extent relieve Dad. We liked things mechanical but we shortly discovered that pushing the mower was hard work. The result was that we went through endless preparatory measures, such as finding a large jug we could fill with water in order to slake the inordinate thirst that came upon us every time we started mowing. Imbibing this amount of water quite naturally led to other pauses while we went to the bathroom. Mother nevertheless persisted, despite the fact that it was doubtless more trouble for her to keep us going than to do it herself. We were presumably learning that we had some responsibilities at home.

It must have been about that same time that Mother decided it was time to give us a preliminary talk on sex. It was her nightly habit to come upstairs with us for a little chat and our prayers before we went to sleep, so on this occasion she decided to launch into the subject of sex. We apparently found it so uninteresting that we went to sleep while she was talking. She never mentioned the subject again, a fact that, in my mature years, she explained by saying that she talked about it once and that we didn't pay any attention so she assumed we were not interested!

Early in our lives Mother, who had been trained as a teacher and had taught in Montana before marrying Dad, began our education. She bought a little red table and two chairs that she placed in the bay window of our house. Here we had lessons each morning. Teddy proved to be a more apt pupil than I, and was far less distracted by what was going on outside.

The thing I remember best about those sessions was that Mother always read to us, and this we both loved. The books were for children, but they were on various subjects, some of which were substantive and some were pure fiction. Among the latter were the adventures of Tom Swift. Tom was an enterprising soul who got involved in an unending series of threatening situations from which, quite naturally, he escaped. Some of these were quite scary and I would flee to the other room until

Mother finished that part for Teddy and then called me to say that all was well. She tried to explain to me that this was all make-believe and that the series could only continue by having Tom escape, but I preferred having her solve the difficulty before I returned.

There was another way in which I was a particular problem to my parents. I quite easily got sick when riding in an automobile. This could be alleviated if I sat in the front seat with the window wide open. It wasn't so bad in the summer, but it was also necessary in the winter. That gave the rest of the family the sensation of riding in a ski lift. They were as reluctant to take me anywhere in a car as to leave me home, so we all struggled with it for years.

While Mother was our primary caretaker, Dad was always very interested in us, though the fact that he was a storekeeper with long hours made it difficult for him to spend much time with us. He was himself not in any sense athletic, but he managed to encourage our interest in sports in many ways. We had regular, nightly track meets in the summer. Included were races around the house (accompanied by our current dog who almost always won), pole vaulting, high jumping, broad jumping, and shot putting with a medium-sized rock. The pole vaulting was accomplished by the use of two two-by-fours that Dad mounted and drilled with appropriate notches for pegs on which a light bamboo pole rested. The poles, both for vaulting and for the crossbar, were obtained from the local furniture dealer who received them inside rugs that were shipped to him. Sometimes we would be joined by neighboring boys, but for the most part Teddy and I most enjoyed each other's company. Our brother Jack was still too young to take part.

As we grew big enough to travel a little, Mother decided to take us to Chicago via train. Doing so by car would be far more time consuming and over uncertain roads, besides which taking me anywhere in a car was an unattractive option. Paw Paw still had a daily train that went to Chicago fairly early in the morning and returned in the evening. It wasn't many years later before the daily train became what the locals called a triweekly—it came in one day and tried like hell to get back another day. A train ride was a great treat to us and we enjoyed it immensely. Once we were in the city, Mother would take us around Chicago's Loop in the famed El train and we would then go shopping. At that time, I handled all my shopping through the Sears Roebuck catalog and it involved sporting goods or hardware. In short, I was vastly uninterested in the kind of shopping that Mother had in mind.

The result was that I would soon get lost in the big city. Once Mother discovered that I was no longer with them, she would hurry ahead on the theory that, since I was not interested in the window displays, I was probably plowing straight ahead. She always found me, usually unaware that I was considered lost but doubtless also pondering how much longer I had to wear those dreadful city clothes and listen to all that noise. After the first experience, she equipped me with a note stating my name, address, and telephone number in Paw Paw.

Since Teddy and I were not angels, we were occasionally involved in episodes that did not please our parents. On one of those occasions we had, under the tutelage of some older boys, discovered that if one took the generator out of an old telephone and hooked it to some wires, it could be made to deliver an electrical shock to some unsuspecting recipient. We promptly drummed up a social club into which a new member could be initiated only through grasping wires that connected with the generator in another room. We then selected a male cousin of mine to be the first new club member. He didn't think the shock he received (which was sharp but not dangerous) was funny and promptly went home and told his mother. She, in turn, called our mother. I don't think she took the matter quite as seriously as her counterpart, but she confined us to the yard that afternoon unless we apologized to my aunt. Teddy decided he would stay home and read, but I had a ball game that seemed very important to me. Accordingly, I delivered one of the shortest apologies on record. When my uncle (Mother's brother) heard of the incident, he laughed it off, which made us feel better.

A far more serious incident occurred later. On a Sunday morning after Sunday School, we had gone to another boy's home to play during the church hour. We ended up in the basement, where someone found an old .22 rifle. Since most of us were not allowed to have guns, this rifle intrigued us. The gun ultimately ended up in Teddy's hands and he pulled the trigger. It turned out that there was a bullet in the chamber and the gun fired. The bullet hit a wall, ricocheted, and then went through the hand of one of the boys. Blood gushed forth, he screamed, and there were no adults in the house. We rushed to the church, got one of the adults, and he summoned the doctor. As it turned out, the bullet had gone through the fleshy part of the link between the thumb and the index finger so that no serious wound resulted. It was, nevertheless, a frightening experience and one that left all of us far more careful in handling guns.

Despite these occasional aberrations, our childhood was very comfortable. We were never wealthy, but we were, prior to the Great Depression, very contented. I am not sure that Dad ever had a net income of more than $1,500 to $2,000 a year, but prices were low, food was cheap, housing was inexpensive, and taxes were very modest. On top of it all, there was that wonderful and supportive extended family around us.

When it came time for Teddy to go to school, our parents decided to hold him back a year so we could start together. Mother could continue our lessons at the little red table and the idea of keeping us together seemed sensible, so we did start together the following year. Within a month the teacher paid a visit to our house and told Mother and Dad that the first grade was the wrong place for Teddy. He should not only be put ahead, but should actually skip two grades and go directly into the third grade. Meanwhile, they thought the first grade was just right for me! To my parents' credit, they acceded to the teacher's request and allowed Teddy to advance. Fortunately, it did not seem to bother either of us.

In the early 1920s Dad started a new business. With one or more partners he constructed a gymnasium-sized Quonset-hut type of building that could serve as an indoor recreational facility suitable for basketball, roller-skating, and dancing. Roads were still not good enough to encourage widespread travel and people in small towns still tended to find their pleasures in their own towns and villages. The sale and distribution of liquor was still prohibited, but there was a soda fountain available. For a short time, even the big bands of the era could be attracted to one-night stands in small towns, and some of them came to Paw Paw. Teddy and I were allowed to spend an hour or so watching the dancing before we were sent home to go to bed. The most interesting part of the dancing, even to our young eyes, was a local belle who enjoyed twirling in a fashion that caused her skirt to fly up even with her waist. The women found this objectionable, but none of the local men were heard to complain. Perhaps it was part of the reason that Teddy and I usually got sent home early!

In the fall of 1926 a series of events, which would extend over the next eight years, shattered our elysian life. In that year, just as Teddy was about to be eleven, he was stricken with spinal meningitis. There was at that time no remedy for it. His illness lasted only a couple of weeks, and then he died. The last time I saw him his speech was slurred and I asked Mother why he couldn't talk right. She hustled me out of the room. I remember how hard I prayed each night that he would get well, promising God that if only Teddy could recover my behavior would be forever beyond reproach.

Teddy's funeral was held at our house with the same pastor who had married my parents officiating. They thought it would be easier for me if I did not attend, so I was sent to the home of a neighbor who had a son my age. Teddy's death was, of course, devastating to me, and I don't think my parents ever quite recovered from it. Mother died at eighty-six and to her dying day she spoke of Teddy. Now, more than sixty-five years later, tears still come to my eyes when I think of him. Trying to understand that he was gone and that he would never come back was a crushing experience. He had always been our leader, he was wonderfully bright, and I idolized him. How could it be that he would never grow up?

Out of my sorrow came an idea that would survive through my graduation from college. Teddy's full name was Edmunds Wheeler Fleming, while mine was Robben Wright Fleming. Both of our middle names began with a *W*. It occurred to me that if I took his middle name instead of mine it could be my way of assuring that we would continue to grow up together and that we would never be separated. No legal change of names ever took place, but I did carry his name all the way through law school, and it appears on my college diploma. Only much later, when I entered the Army during World War II, did the name discrepancy catch up with me and I resumed my legal name. Perhaps this is the place, incidentally, to explain the origin of my somewhat original first name. My maternal grandfather was named Beniah, and my mother's brother was named Robert. My mother simply put Rob and Ben together and derived the name Robben. To my surprise, a visiting Dutch scholar told me recently that I had a Dutch first name and he wondered why. I told him my version of the story, and said that though the name Robin was fairly common, I knew of the name Robben elsewhere only in connection with the island off the coast of South Africa where political prisoners, like Nelson Mandela, had been held. He then said that the word *robben* in Dutch means seal and that the island was inhabited with seals and was therefore really, in our language, Seal Island. I accept this explanation of the Dutch word, but I am sure, despite her own partial Dutch origin, that Mother chose the name for another reason.

Teddy's death turned out to be only the start of a difficult period for our family. The Great Depression came shortly thereafter and this, along with better roads and automobiles, shattered Dad's business. There were no more profitable dances or roller-skating parties. People had easier acccess to bigger cities. The enterprise had to shift gears, and it became a grocery store and soda fountain. Even so, it wasn't long before it had to remain open on Sundays in addition to every night of the week. Dad worked almost all of these hours, though Mother and I helped out during lunch hours and on busy evenings. I recall that on one of the occasions when I was working, our local alcoholic friend drove up in his buggy and came in to buy a bottle of vanilla extract. He asked for a particular brand that, as it turned out, we did not stock. I noted that we had several other kinds, and he then asked, "What is the content?" This inquiry was meaningless to me, so he asked to see the various bottles. Finally, he chose one and went out to his buggy. As I watched, he promptly opened the bottle and took a swig. This was, to me, a novel use of vanilla extract, which I had supposed was used only in baking. Only when my father returned and I related the story to him did I learn that vanilla extract had a substantial alcohol content and that the level varied with different brands. Our friend was apparently a close student of the "content." After he had imbibed, his faithful horse started for home.

In January, 1932, in the middle of the Great Depression, my beloved maternal grandmother, whom we called "Buma," died. She was eighty-one, her life had simply run its span, and she died after a very brief illness. Nevertheless, her death was a great blow to me because she and I had always had a special relationship. I am told that she was quite upset when I was born because Teddy was only thirteen months older and she thought my mother was having children too close together. As luck would have it, I turned out to have blue eyes and my grandmother was the only other member of the family with blue eyes. That sold her on me, and through all my growing years she would tell me stories of the Illinois of her youth and of the family as they spread across the country. She had some money of her own and she would help me acquire sporting goods that I needed. Another time, somewhat to my embarrassment, she bought me two pairs of silk shorts and tops, one in blue and one in orange. I loved the feel of them because I could never stand scratchy cloth next to my skin, but the idea of wearing silk under-wear seemed very feminine to me and the thought of wearing them in a locker room or where I might be seen by other boys was terrifying. So I wore them discreetly. I am sure she purchased them because she knew I loved soft cloth, and it probably never occurred to her that boys might make fun of me.

The following year, in June, 1933, Dad died of tuberculosis. He was a very heavy smoker, he worked enormously long hours, he got little exercise, and his health had been going downhill steadily. When he was identified as having tuberculosis and could no longer work in the store, the store had to be sold. His death, while a blow to all of us, was not like Teddy's. There was at that time no hope for recovery, he was embarrassed because he could no longer support his family, and he knew that his care was a burden to us.

During the years of Dad's struggle with tuberculosis, there was a natural concern about whether other members of the family might contract the disease. The county health authorities kept an eye on us and we were required to come in for periodic testing. I hated that experience with a passion. We had to go to the county seat, which was about thirty miles away. We were then seated in a big waiting room and remained on call until our turn came. At that point a very impersonal doctor who showed no understanding of the fear that Jack and I might have examined us. We knew that our father was incurably ill, we knew that we were exposed to the disease, and we knew that we might contract it. For the doctor to then mumble to his colleagues in medical jargon that we did not understand made matters worse. After Dad died, I don't think we ever went back, but in medical examinations since then I have been told that my lungs show some scar tissue that apparently healed over.

I never knew just how we survived during Dad's illness, but I am sure it was through the intervention of neighbors and members of the family. Even after my grandmother died, the family members would gather at Aunt Addie's house on Sunday evenings. Most of the aunts and uncles were there and they were a kind and generous lot. They liked each other, they all had a sense of humor, and they argued all the issues of the time. All but the youngest uncle were still Republicans, but the closing of the local bank during the bank moratorium and the depression in the farm economy worried them. I was the only teenager present, and my participation consisted largely of listening and eating from the plentiful snacks that were provided. I learned a lot from the conversations, but more than anything else I felt the support of a loving family. I think of that often in these days of fractured families.

After Dad died in 1933, Mother found a job as a country school teacher. It was five or six miles out of town, and it was one of the last of the old-time country schools. She had about a dozen students in all the grades. The building was heated by a woodstove that she had to start each morning. She drove an old car back and forth to school. This was a new acquisition since we had given up another old car and our telephone during the depths of the Depression. She was paid something like $85 per month, and, while that doesn't sound like very much, it was like manna from heaven to a family that had been without any income and had for years huddled around a single lamp at night in order to hold down the cost of electricity. It was also a tremendous tribute to my mother who, like her own mother, was indomitable in the face of both sorrow and economic distress.

By the time all these events had taken place, I was almost through high school and was beginning to think of college. That part of my life is another story.

Chapter 2

The School Years

I was in the fifth grade when Teddy died. In our grade-school years we had gone through all the childhood diseases, including measles, chicken pox, scarlet fever, whooping cough, and a mild form of mumps. This was at a time when the health authorities quarantined the homes of victims, and since we rarely came down with the disease at the same time, Mother spent some of the winters largely under quarantine.

Perhaps because I tried for many years to live both Teddy's life and my own, my academic performance, which had always been good but not outstanding, improved and I did very well. Still, my greatest outside interest was in sports, principally basketball and baseball. Mother was happy to have me involved in athletic ventures, but the school also offered a number of programs in music, theater, and speech, and she insisted that I participate.

Music was the area in which I had the least talent. She had, during my grade-school years, sent me off to piano lessons, followed by the guitar and then saxophone. At the piano I became known as the only pupil who kicked the piano with his feet while playing and managed to do so without synchronizing the two activities. The guitar did not improve my performance, and while I learned to play the saxophone well enough to participate in a trio, my errors were covered by the others. I could, on the other hand, take part in the glee clubs without embarrassment, even though I did not have a very good voice. We sang for various local occasions, and in the spring of the year we would participate in state-sponsored contests that led up to a state final.

Because Mother had been a speech specialist in her teacher training, she was particularly interested in getting me involved in forensic activities. I had little enthusiasm for the idea, but I did understand how much it meant to her. By that time Dad was gone, life had been very hard for her, and I could not in good conscience refuse. On looking into the possibilities, I came to the conclusion that I ought to enter the extemporaneous speaking event. The description indicated that all I would have to do was read some prescribed articles and then be pre-pared to stand up and talk about something for about five minutes. While I was not accustomed to public speaking, I did like to read and from that reading I had a good vocabulary. Extemporaneous speaking sounded like the path of least resistance. The only obstacle was that the coach was the English teacher, and I did not like her. The fault for this was probably more mine than hers, but I thought she treated us like little children and this annoyed me. Since she needed contestants, and I needed to please Mother, we eventually reached an agreement that I would participate but that I would not practice. Though this was an unlikely way to proceed, it did take place. I won the district contest by default because there were no other contestants. I then won the regional contest against other contestants, and proceeded to the state finals, where truth and justice finally prevailed and I won only a ribbon.

Mother was immensely pleased, and learned only later that I had never practiced. My teacher was pleased because the statistics showed that one of her pupils had done well, and I was pleased because Mother was happy. In short, it all worked out very well!

My high school also offered a play or musical each year and be-cause it was a small school, it was easy to get a part. I had no great talent, except that I could learn lines easily. The teacher was fun, it was a diversion from our normal activities, and I suspect all of us have in us a thespian desire. It also involved both boys and girls, while most of my activities were athletic, which at that time meant only boys. Girls were an unknown and somewhat mysterious quantity to me since our family had only boys. Because I was shy with girls, the opportunity to partici-pate with them in something like theater, where the contacts were part of a routine, was good for me.

If school and its activities occupied most of my time, there was also the fact that the economic depression had left our family in a very precarious position, and I needed to find as much work-for-pay as I could. In his last two or three years, Dad had not been able to work, and if I could make enough money to buy most of my clothes and my school books, it was helpful. Like most small-town boys, I knew how to fix many mechanical things, and I could paint, mow, work in a store or on the farm, and do odd jobs of all kinds. We had no factories in Paw Paw. In the summer, I could work in the fields during the day, and then come home and work in the stores on a Wednesday or Saturday night. I could also pick up odd jobs, like helping a carpenter with roofing or distributing utility bills. I remember the latter because, at a time when first-class postage was three cents, the utility found it cost-efficient to hire a local boy at two cents apiece to distribute utility bills in small towns. I could do this in a day, and I treasured the job. Somewhat to my bewilderment, Mother queried me about whether a nice looking local woman who lived alone ever invited me in. She never did, but I liked her because she was always friendly in greeting me. I was about fourteen at the time, and I learned only later that some people thought she entertained men in a more mature way.

The pay for doing most of these jobs was not very good, but it was appropriate for the time. I once bought twelve pairs of socks for a dollar. The elastic in them wasn't very good so they fell down, but I wore them out. I usually got fifty cents for mowing a lawn, and most of the lots were large because there is no shortage of land in small towns. Pay for working in the fields or in a store was usually thirty to thirty-five cents an hour.

We could not afford vacations, and we did almost no traveling outside a radius of fifty miles.

Curiously enough, our economic status never dampened the common expectation within the family that I would go to college. I had graduated as the valedictorian of my class, and though it was a small high school it had a good reputation. I was also well enough known for my athletic skills to strengthen the possibility that a scholarship would be forthcoming. Mother had a very small life insurance policy from Dad, and she thought she could help me a little if I could find a way to support myself fully after the first year.

In many ways, the logical place for me to apply was to the University of Illinois in Champaign-Urbana. There was a teachers' college nearer home, but I did not want to be a teacher. I was also fearful of going to a huge university. The result was that, after looking around a good deal, we settled on Beloit College, which is just across the Illinois-Wisconsin line. It was, and is, one of the fine small liberal arts colleges in the country. It offered me both a scholarship and a board job that would pay half of my board cost. I could also have a job working for the college. With that much help, and with the contribution that Mother could make, I was confident that by the end of that year I could find a way to finance myself in the succeeding years. And so it was that in the fall of 1934, I set out for Beloit. I was not quite eighteen years old, I had never been away from home, even at a summer camp, I didn't have the social sophistication of young people from larger towns, yet somehow I never had any doubt that I could survive and even prosper.

As it turned out, Beloit College was ideal for me. The courses were good, well taught, and based on the liberal arts. I took German, math, English literature (after testing out of the freshman composition course), and political science the first year and ended up with a major in political science. It isn't clear to me just why I took German rather than French, which was more popular at the time, but the choice proved to be wise when, some years later, I ended up in Germany during World War II.

One of my jobs turned out to be mopping the floors of Middle College at 6:30 each morning. It wasn't a hard job, but I disliked getting up so early in the morning. My board job consisted of waiting tables or working in the kitchen of one of the boys' dormitories. It was not time consuming because I would have spent most of that time eating anyway.

There were both fraternities and sororities at Beloit, and I rushed along with other students, but with no intention of joining since I had no spare money. Beta Theta Pi succeeded in pledging most of my new friends and invited me to join, but when I explained my circumstances they simply invited me to take part in their social life anyway. This continued throughout my college career, though in my senior year, through the generosity of one of my uncles, I did manage to join and live in the house.

The thing I missed most at the outset was participation in some form of intercollegiate athletics. I could not play football because of a knee injured in high school, and basketball did not start until a month or two after the beginning of the semester. Meanwhile, I had to be content with intramural sports.

My social life was very limited that first year, partly because of the lack of money, but perhaps more because I was still shy with girls and the main social activity consisted of dances sponsored either by the college or by the Greek houses. Dancing had never been allowed in my small high school, and I had only learned to dance, and not very well, when Mother got one of her young friends to give me a crash course just before I went to school!

In the years when I was there, Beloit required chapel attendance about three times a week at noon, and on Sunday afternoons at 4 P.M. There were proctors who recorded attendance and very few absences were allegedly tolerated. In fact, there were some students who rarely attended. The weekday services were not primarily religious, rather there were speakers on some subject of general interest. The Sunday afternoon meetings were religious, founded in the Congregational tradition of Beloit's origin. I rather liked them, because few of us went to Sunday church in the city, there was a good choir, and the speakers were generally good. As I sat there and looked at the stained glass windows with the late afternoon sun streaming in from the west, the world somehow seemed a better and kindlier place.

By Christmas of that first year I was comfortable in my new surroundings. I had made the freshman basketball team as a regular, I was doing very well academically, and I was secure financially in the sense that I could pay my bills if little more than that.

The summer of 1935 was the last one I would ever spend in Paw Paw. I had to have a knee operation, which kept me partially immobile, but it did help and I continued to play basketball and to run on the track team throughout my college years. In track I was a sprinter. I ran the hundred-yard dash in ten seconds flat, which was fast enough to place, but not win, major competitions.

When I returned to Beloit for my sophomore year I had found a solution to my financial problems. My scholarship would continue, I could have a full board job waiting table in the dorms, I could have a room free for doing odd jobs at the Faculty Club, and I could retain my previous job for incidental expenses. I would also thereafter always find a summer job that would pay my other expenses. The "room" in the Faculty Club may be worth explaining. It was an unfinished and unheated attic that I shared with a fellow student whose financial situation was like mine. There was a skylight for a window, and, if we happened to leave it open in the winter, the snow would come in. Since the room was as cold as the air outside, the snow didn't melt and we could just sweep it off the beds. Actually, this wasn't as much of a hardship as it might sound. There was a heated bathroom right across the hall from us and there was always hot water and a shower handy.

Though my social life in the first year at Beloit was minimal, in the second year I met the girl who has now been my wife for more than fifty years. Aldyth Louise (Sally) Quixley came to Beloit as a freshman in the fall of 1935. She lived in Rockford, Illinois, which was only fifteen miles away, and her older sister was already at Beloit. Her father was a purchasing agent for a machine tool company in Rockford, and her mother was a musician who gave piano and voice lessons. Besides the older sister there was another younger sister at home. Having two girls in college at the same time required that they work part-time, and Sally was a waitress in the same dorm in which I worked. She was a beautiful, dark-haired, slender girl of five feet six and was in many ways everything that I was not. She had been brought up in a family of three girls, whereas my family had three boys. She played the violin beautifully, she sang in the choir, she loved music, she won the poetry reading contest her freshman year, and she was a very good swimmer while I had all the buoyancy of a rock. She was not greatly interested in sports, except for swimming. She thought baseball was the height of boredom, and football followed close by. Basketball did hold some interest for her.

Sally and I came to know one another while working in the dining hall along with a group of other men and women. We were all good friends long before she and I dated. That was an ideal introduction because it was free of any romantic context and we simply enjoyed one another. I was very leery of being involved with any girl because I had no money and I had law school in mind after college. Nevertheless, our relationship progressed, though each of us occasionally dated someone else. We parted that summer when she went to work up in northern Wisconsin and I worked at a different resort near Delavan. I had great fun, working with other Beloit friends and enjoying the companionship of other college students from elsewhere. Sally had a less satisfying experience. Girls were expected to work as hard as boys but were paid less and at the time all of us accepted that practice without thinking much about it. Part of it was an outgrowth of the depression years when it was considered unfair for both a man and wife to have jobs when there was so much unemployment. It was also encouraged by the prevailing view that men were the breadwinners and the place of women was basically in the home.

In the remaining two years of my undergraduate days, Sally and I went together steadily. In the summer between my junior and senior years, I had a job in Rockford, working in the Greenlee Brothers machine tool plant. It was procured for me by my cousin, the daughter of my father's sister. They also provided me with free board and room so that I could save the money I made for school. Once more my extended family had come to my aid. It was, of course, an added bonus for me that Sally was at home while working that summer, and we saw each other constantly. The factory experience, incidentally, was a real education for me because I had never before worked in that kind of a job. It helped me in later years when I spent time trying to settle industrial disputes between unions and companies.

By the spring of my senior year in college, I had to make a decision about whether to look for a job or go to law school. The job market wasn't very good in 1938, and anyway I always thought I would like to go to law school. Exactly why this was so, I am not sure. No member of my family had ever been a lawyer, and there had been but one lawyer in Paw Paw whom I did not even know. Probably it was my interest in government and the fact that so many lawyers seem to be involved in it.

If I did go to law school, I knew that I would be wholly reliant on my own resources. That meant going to either the University of Illinois or the University of Wisconsin where, in both cases, I could perhaps claim residency and thereby benefit from the lower, in-state tuition. As between the two, I now felt closer to Wisconsin because I had lived there throughout my college years, and anyway it was nearer Beloit where Sally would still be for another year. Accordingly, I applied to Wisconsin with the full support of some of my professors at Beloit. I had missed Phi Beta Kappa because of my preoccupation with work and other activities during my last year, but I still had very respectable grades and was later made an honorary member. The Wisconsin Law School had few scholarships at that time, but I was offered a job in the law library that, along with my summer earnings, would permit me to enroll. Once that decision was made, I went back to Delavan for summer work.

The immediate logistics of where I would live in Madison when law school opened were solved when my former Beloit colleague, Dave Dupee, who was now at Wisconsin, invited me to come and live with him and three other friends in an apartment. We pooled our resources and ate at the apartment, aided greatly by the fact that one of the roommates had a father who ran a restaurant from which we were furnished with frequent supplies.

My first year in law school was Sally's final year at Beloit. Madison and Beloit were only fifty miles apart, but we saw almost nothing of each other during the school year. My job in the law library called for manning the main desk from 6 to 11 P.M. every day, including Saturdays and Sunday afternoon. That was more hours than a student was officially allowed to work, but part of it was done under the name of another student who only wished to work part-time. He received full pay, but turned the difference over to me. The job was not as onerous as it may seem because it was an open-stacks library where students got their own books. I could sit in peace at the main desk except for giving out information or finding less-used books. The pay wasn't very good, but living conditions were cheap. During my last two years in law school I found a room within walking distance of the university for which the rent was $2.00 per week. It was a small room, with just space for a cot, a desk, and a tiny closet, but it was big enough for me. I never studied there because, with my access to the library, I could leave all my books and my typewriter down in the stacks and do my studying there during the day. My room was strictly a place to sleep. One could also buy a meal ticket at one of the local restaurants or at the Student Union, for $5.00 per week. The meal ticket was worth $5.50 in trade. Breakfast of milk or coffee and a sweet roll was ten cents, and both lunch and dinner were thirty-five cents. If I skipped breakfast on Sunday mornings, I could eat on $5.00 a week, and the meals were good. At both lunch and dinner there was always an appetizer, such as soup or juice, a main course that included meat, a vegetable, a drink, and dessert. The latter might be jello or bread pudding, but I had grown up on such things and thought they were fine. Tuition was cheap and I could pay it out of my summer earnings. Since I had little time for either entertainment or travel, I had almost no expenses for either. When I did travel, I hitchhiked, and in those innocent days hitchhiking was both quick and easy. Most people would pick up a college student and I found I could often exceed the speed of a bus between two points. Still, I had almost no chance to see Sally because of my work schedule, and we had to content ourselves with writing and seeing each other during vacations.

I had hardly gotten started in law school when an event took place that almost ended my enrollment. A note from the university directed me to come in and see one of the officers. When I got there, he told me that he had been reviewing student files and found that I was not really a resident of Wisconsin, but rather of Illinois. He read the Wisconsin statute to me. It said that one had to be an *adult* citizen of Wisconsin for one year before enrolling, and since I would not be twenty-one until December, I did not qualify. I would therefore be classified as an out-of-state student and would have to pay the higher tuition. Since I had no money for such an expenditure, the news was devastating. We then talked a little about how I had lived in Wisconsin for the last three years and had paid all my own expenses, whereupon he suggested that perhaps I could claim to be an "emancipated minor." I had no idea what that meant, but he explained that if I could prove that I had been self-supporting, as I said I was, he could then declare me to be an emancipated minor and a resident of Wisconsin. He directed me to get some affidavits to this effect, which I proceeded to do. The matter was then settled, and I continued through law school as a Wisconsin resident. Many years later I returned to Wisconsin as chancellor of the Madison campus, and Neil Cafferty, the man who had helped me, was in high office. I reminded him of the incident, and he remembered. Actually, my case was not unique. Over the years, I have observed that university officials generally try hard to help a needy student stay in school.

I liked law school from the outset. It was hard, and it was different from anything I had previously experienced. One's grades depended not nearly so much on memory as on reasoning. I was impatient with procedure courses, which seemed to me to thwart justice in favor of technicalities, but that was changing as common-law pleading declined. I didn't care much for property courses, but I loved all the public law courses, such as constitutional law, trade regulations, anti-trust law, municipal corporations, labor law, etc.

Like all law schools, Wisconsin had among its faculty some well-known characters. Leading all the others in that respect was William Herbert Page. He was at that time perhaps sixty years old, a little bit of a man, feisty, a bully in class, and an authority on the subjects of contracts and wills. The stories about him are legion, but I will limit myself to two.

The Law School was located right next to the Music School. Neither building was at that time air conditioned, and in the spring or early fall the windows of both buildings would be open and one could hear music students practicing. Professor Page would sit at his desk on an elevated platform peering out at students as he prepared to call on some one. On one occasion when he selected a victim, the individual replied, as he was required to do if this were the case, "Unprepared." With glee, Professor Page patted his head, stamped his feet under the desk, and said, "My boy, my boy, why didn't you go to Music School?"

Another time, in the same circumstance, he said, "You remind me of the squadron of men in the desert. They asked the captain in the morning how far they had to march, and he said twenty-five miles. They asked again at noon and at the end of the afternoon and the answer remained the same, and one of the men said, 'Well, we are holding our own, anyway.' That is like you. You didn't know anything when you came into this course, and you don't know anything now. You are holding your own."

The dean of the Law School was Lloyd K. Garrison, a descendant of the famous abolitionist. He was a strong supporter of President Roosevelt and the New Deal and was tied into many government operations, both in the state and in Washington. Willard Hurst, the distinguished historian of Anglo-American law, was then young and newly arrived on the faculty. He was the finest teacher I ever had. His own learning was so great that even poor students were embarrassed to ever say, "Unprepared." I worked for him as a research assistant. At that time, he was looking into the workings of the Territorial Legislature in Wisconsin and one of my duties was to go into the archives and search through the bills that were introduced in order to pick out those that were of special interest to him. With the consent of both the library and Professor Hurst, I could do some of the research while working at the main desk, thus increasing my earnings while working the same hours.

Professor Nathan Feinsinger taught labor law when I took the course. He was involved in working on labor legislation both in Wisconsin and at the federal level. At that time, labor law was essentially the law of collective bargaining between unions and companies. The Wagner Act, which gave unions the right to organize and bargain collectively free from employer interference, was not upheld by the United States Supreme Court until 1937. Though I had no knowledge whatsoever of unions, I found the course fascinating. Professor Feinsinger was a provocative teacher. He knew so much more about it than I did that he could take either side and best me in an argument. Nevertheless, I would sometimes emerge with the feeling that I was really right but that I simply had to learn more about the subject so that I could better compete. That was, of course, exactly what he wanted. In the years after I was out of law school, and after my army days were over, Nate was largely responsible for bringing me into both the university and the field of labor-management arbitration. More of that later.

Between my second and third years at Wisconsin, I remained in Madison, worked in the library, and went to summer school. Wisconsin had a somewhat unique statute (though there are a few others around the country) under which if one graduated from an accredited law school in the State of Wisconsin, of which there were only Marquette and Wisconsin, one could be admitted to practice in the state without taking the bar examination. There was another provision, however, that said that to qualify for this you had to either serve a three-month apprenticeship in a law office or take an additional summer school with prescribed hours. Law offices would not at that time pay an apprentice, hence my choice had to be to go to summer school where I could work many hours, make enough money to come back for my final year, and still take enough classes to meet the requirement. Dave Dupee, who was also taking summer school, shared a room with me in the dorms that summer, and I then returned to my regular room in the fall.

During my second and third years in law school I had an opportunity, as did other students, to engage in a Legal Aid program that taught me an early and very important lesson about trial work. Under the auspices of the local Bar, students were allowed to handle rather simple cases involving charity clients. On one occasion, an unemployed painter came in to tell me that he had been evicted from his apartment. As the tale unfolded, it turned out that when he became unemployed his landlord had told him that if he would paint other apartments in the building the landlord would forgive his rent. This arrangement was undertaken, but, as is so often the case, the parties did not agree on a system of accounting that would record how much time he spent painting or at what rate. When they eventually became unhappy with one another, the landlord evicted the client.

In what I hoped was a very professional manner, I probed further and found that after the landlord evicted the tenant, he added another charge that the man wasn't a good painter in the first place. I concluded that the heart of the case was whether my client was, or was not, a competent painter. He was not a union member, and I would have to rely on what other people had to say about his work. He assured me that he could produce plenty of evidence when we came before the Justice of Peace who would conduct the trial. On the day of the trial he brought with him an attractive, middle-aged woman who said he had done an excellent job for her. I put her on the stand and she was articulate and sincere. Her testimony was faultless. It was, in fact, so good that I ventured a final question, which was: "And so you would say that Mr. So and So is a very competent painter?" She replied, "Of course, my brother always does good work!" Her married name was different from that of my client, they did not look alike, and neither of them had mentioned their relationship. Since she was our only witness, the trial ended swiftly and detrimentally. I had violated rule number 1 of a good trial lawyer, I had asked a critical question of my own witness without knowing that she was related to my client. It was a lesson I never forgot.

Meanwhile, Sally graduated from Beloit at the end of my first year in law school. She had taken a major in sociology and had found a job shortly thereafter working as a case worker on one of the federal programs. Her schedule required her to move around central Illinois interviewing people who were eligible for federal benefits. Though she would be in several cities during any given week, the schedule was predictable and she would tell me each week where she was going to be. I would then write to her in that city in care of General Delivery and she would go to the post office and get the letter. To the amazement of her colleagues, it worked like clockwork and we kept in regular touch. Incidentally, the people who came to see her in one city found themselves in an overheated room, and since they reeked of garlic, she has since that time found it one of her least favorite perfumes.

By my last year in law school, Sally had left her casework and was working in an office in Rockford. Because of my work schedule, I couldn't go down there much, but she could and did come to Madison on occasion so that we managed to see each other more often.

By 1939 World War II had started in Europe and all of us were apprehensive about the future. America was not then ready for war and the favorite remark around law school was that the British would be pleased to fight to the last American. Even so, all of us were coming to realize that Hitler was a brutal despot and that America's involvement in the war was probably inevitable. I recall waiting up late one night to hear President Eduard Beneš make his plea from Czechoslovakia just before the Germans invaded his country. The anguish and desparation in his voice were stunning.

With the passage of time, we moved ever closer to war. The draft was in effect, I was registered, and I knew that it would not be too long before I would be called up. I hoped to have as much as a year before going so that I would not have to come back a few years later never having held a professional job.

As the school year ended, I had to think about a job, however temporary. Law firms would not be anxious to hire me, knowing that I would shortly have to leave. Anyway, I had a hankering to go Washington, where the New Deal programs seemed so exciting. The liberal climate in Wisconsin, fostered by the LaFollettes, attracted me, and my conservative roots from Illinois were fading away. Accordingly, during spring vacation of that year I went to Washington. The dean and other professors armed me with strong endorsements and with suggested points of call. I knew some former Wisconsin students now working in Washington, and I got in touch with them and arranged for a place to stay. I then took a train to Chicago and boarded the coach of the Baltimore and Ohio for the trip to Washington. My memory is that the roundtrip from Chicago cost $50.00.

I had never been to Washington—indeed, I had hardly been anywhere outside the Middle West. I was met on arrival at the lovely old Washington Station and was immediately awed by the sight of the capitol building across the way. Washington was still a rather sleepy southern city, and my friends took me to a rooming house not far from the White House. It would be cheaper than a hotel.

My next few days were spent job hunting. Because of my letters of introduction, I had no trouble getting interviews. My preference list included, as a first priority, something in either trade regulations or labor law, but it turned out there were no openings in those fields. The Securities and Exchange Commission offered me a job in the corporate reorganization division, and, while this was not something I really wanted, I decided to take it with the idea that I might change later if I didn't go into the army too soon. I could at least go back to Madison with a job assured. In my remaining days in Washington, I had time to visit some of the sights, including the Capitol, the Washington Monument, the Lincoln Memorial, Lee's home and Arlington Cemetery, and the Supreme Court. I was enormously impressed. The city was beautiful, the buildings were awesome, there was excitement in the air, and I was delighted with the prospect of living there. My starting salary would be $2,000, which was the beginning rate for lawyers!

In June, 1941, I graduated from law school and was admitted to both the Wisconsin and federal bars. Mother insisted on being there, and she came, along with Sally. I had been elected to the Order of the Coif, which is the Phi Beta Kappa of law school, and I had about two hundred dollars in my pocket. I was proud of both, the money because I needed it to get started, and the academic honors because it gave me confidence that I could compete in any market.

My very last night in Madison, I slept in the Law School lounge in order to avoid another week's rent in my regular room. One wasn't supposed to sleep in the Law School, but I figured that since I worked until 11 P.M. in the library no one would be around to see what happened to me after that. My supposition was right and no one bothered me.

I was to report to Washington around mid-June. Meanwhile, I went home to Paw Paw to see the family, and then Sally and I had a little time together. It was hard leaving her, but neither of us had any money and young people at that time still thought they ought to have some money before they married. We thought she might be able to come to Washington shortly and find a job. I boarded the Baltimore and Ohio in Chicago and once more rode the coach to Washington. My friends had arranged for me to stay at their boarding house.

I transferred my draft registration to Washington and was aware that it would not be too long before I was likely to be called up. Pearl Harbor had not yet taken place, so the imminence of my entry into the army was not as evident as it would be in December of that same year.

And so ended my school years. It never occurred to me that I might some day return to the academic world, nor had I harbored any aspirations in that direction.

Chapter 3

From Washington to the Army

By mid-June, 1941, I was firmly settled in my job as a junior attorney in the Corporate Reorganization Division of the Securities and Exchange Commission in Washington, D.C., and I had a room with some Wisconsin friends in a rooming house on 19th Street NW, near Dupont Circle.

Before long it was apparent that the job was not going to be very interesting. They had hired several young attorneys, just out of law school, but, as of that moment, there was not any great need for their services. I thereby learned one of the great truths of public employment. Because it is hard to add new personnel when an agency really needs them, it is dangerous to give up positions when the work load is down. The obvious option is to preserve the positions against a future day of need, and this becomes standard operating procedure. Added to this are other, less justifiable motivations, such as a department head who understands the Civil Service system well enough to know that the importance of the position can be enhanced by enlarging the staff. I shall never forget the department head who asked his staff, of which I was a member, to think about how many additional counterparts we would need when we went into regional offices around the country. We were already overstaffed, but we dutifully calculated that one might (at the maximum) need ten additional people elsewhere in the country. When we presented our conclusions to him, he looked thoughtful for a moment and then said, "Good, why don't we just round it off to twenty!"

One good thing did happen while I was at the Securities and Exchange Commission (SEC). There was then pending in New York City a major utility fraud case, much like the earlier Samuel Insull case in Illinois in which modest operating properties had been pyramided into a paper empire that had then collapsed. My division was not taking an active role in the case, but it did want to keep a close eye on it and I, as a junior attorney, was assigned to cover the case and to make regular reports to my boss. The task gave me something to do, and turned out to be quite educational. I got to know the city of New York, I saw some first-class attorneys at work in a major trial, and a very interesting judge, then retired from the New York courts, was hearing the case as a Special Master. Since he was somewhat hard of hearing, he wore a hearing aid of a now primitive type that had a volume control dial strung around his neck. Whenever he found the lawyers too verbose on any given subject, he would simply reach up, in full view of everyone, and turn down the volume dial so that it was apparent he was unable to hear what was being said. From my point of view, this had a very salutary tendency to shorten the proceedings!

If my work during that period was not very interesting, the city of Washington was. Moreover, it was possible to sublet an apartment in Arlington for a month, during which I could have Mother and my aunt and uncle, the Guffins, come for a visit. I owed a great deal to all of them, they had not done much traveling, and the opportunity to visit Washington was exciting for them. While I was at work during the day, they could roam the city and visit Congress, the Supreme Court, or the many museums. On weekends we could take more extended trips, including boat tours down the Potomac River to Mt. Vernon or a visit to Arlington National Cemetery.

While Mother was still in Washington, Sally came down to look for a job so that we could both be there. She quickly found a secretarial position in an insurance company, and came to Washington to live. When Mother left, we gave up the apartment, and both Sally and I returned to the rooming house on 19th Street. We thought of that many times in later years when there was such a fuss about coed dorms at universities. In our rooming house, the second floor was all women and the first floor was all men; there were only about a dozen of us, and we did a good deal of socializing as a group. Only two of the people had cars, so most of our trips were within the city by bus or the then existing electric streetcars. We also occasionally went to such nearby places as the Naval Academy in Annapolis, and Harpers Ferry, which was made famous by John Brown and the Civil War.

A favorite spot for us was always the site on the Potomac River behind the Lincoln Memorial where the evening waterfront concerts were offered. We still have a picture of such an evening at which, during the intermission, we are clearly visible with Mrs. Franklin D. Roosevelt, who was seated nearby.

The summer and fall of 1941 passed joyfully, and Sally and I were both saving some money with the idea that we would soon be married. My entry into the Army was still pending, but we were not at war and it still seemed probable that it might be many months before I was called up. Then came Pearl Harbor and all our lives were changed forever.

Like so many others of our generation, we remember with clarity where we were on that fateful Sunday afternoon. With another couple, we had gone to a movie in downtown Washington. When we came out, newspaper vendors were shouting about the attack on Pearl Harbor. It seemed incredible, but we headed for the Japanese Embassy, which was, I believe, still on Massachusetts Avenue. American security forces were already surrounding the building in anticipation of angry mob action against the building, but no serious incidents took place. Within the grounds we could see staff members burning documents that they presumably feared might be taken from them.

For the rest of the evening we listened to the radio, learning that President Roosevelt would address Congress the following morning and would ask for a declaration of war against Japan, to be followed shortly thereafter by a similar action against the Axis powers in Europe. From that moment, there was no doubt in any of our minds that we would be at war for the next several years.

On Monday morning we listened to President Roosevelt deliver his somber message and heard Congress confirm our entry into the war. As we came to work that morning there were soldiers patrolling the tops of some of the government buildings. I remember that they were wearing World War I–type steel helmets that could only remind us that our military supplies were not wholly up-to-date.

At Christmastime, Sally and I became officially engaged when I gave her a diamond ring while standing in LaFayette Park across from the White House.

Despite the increasingly obvious fact that I was going to be in the Army within a few months, I wanted very much to find a new and more interesting job. The Securities and Exchange Commission was being moved out of Washington as a part of the decentralization effort designed to make room for the defense agencies, and that alone would pose a problem because it would mean that Sally and I would have jobs in different cities.

With the declaration of war came a raft of new government agencies. Wage and price control measures were deemed necessary in order to contain inflation. The Supreme Court had ruled in 1937 that the

Wagner Act was valid. It required companies to bargain with unions duly selected by their employees. This had been a hotly contested issue for some years, and unions were anxious to take advantage of the new law. Strikes would nevertheless imperil war production, therefore a National War Labor Board (NWLB) was established in an effort to settle labor disputes without strikes. When I learned that some of my Wisconsin law faculty members (Dean Garrison and Professor Feinsinger) would be involved, I got in touch with them in the hope that I could qualify for some junior position with the NWLB. With their help I did obtain a job as a panel assistant to more senior people who were brought in to work with the parties on the settlement of disputes that threatened war production. This proved to be one of the great turning points in my career. I met some wonderful people who have been lifelong friends, I learned an enormous amount about dispute settlement and how people act under tension, and I was happy to find a job in which I felt useful.

My new job was to start early in April of 1942. Meanwhile, I was still attending the trial in New York on behalf of the SEC. Sally and I had been looking for a time when we could get a few days off and get married, and the Easter trial recess offered that opportunity. The Special Master announced the week before Easter that he would recess the hearings on Wednesday of Easter week, and would not resume until the following Monday. As soon as I knew that, we decided that I would return to Washington on Wednesday night, we would be married on Friday morning, and then go back to New York, where Sally had never been, for our weekend honeymoon. She would have to make all the arrangements in Washington, because I had to return to New York for the first three days of Easter week. Meanwhile, I would get tickets to the theater, including a performance of *Blithe Spirit,* and make our arrangements in New York.

With modest complications, the scenario worked out as planned. We had attended the First Presbyterian Church on New York Avenue on occasion. The pastor there was Peter Marshall, whose wife wrote a series of popular books about his work. He later became Chaplain of the Senate. When Sally approached him about marrying us, he said that he didn't like to marry people without having a number of counseling sessions in advance. She told him this would be impossible and explained the reasons. She pointed out that her parents had long been active in the church during her youth, and that we had known each other a long time. Perhaps because it was already apparent that young couples in our situation would be married whether or not the usual church procedures could be pursued, he relented and agreed to marry us on Friday morning, April 3, 1942, in the Lincoln Chapel of the church. (Exactly fifty years later we celebrated our Golden Anniversary in Ann Arbor with our predecessors in office at Michigan, Harlan and Ann Hatcher. They had been married on the same day, in the same year, and had taken a trip to New York where they also saw *Blithe Spirit!*)

During my few days in New York that week, I acquired tickets to a number of theater performances, including a movie at Radio City (*Reap the Wild Wind*) and the then very popular dancing Rockettes, the play *Blithe Spirit,* written by Noel Coward and starring Clifton Webb, and George Gershwin's *Porgy and Bess.* During the day we could wander around New York, visit Staten Island to see the Statue of Liberty, and view the great French liner, the *Normandie,* which had sunk on its side in New York harbor. We would stay at the Governor Clinton Hotel, across the street from Penn Station. The hotel offered a special rate to government employees, and I had often stayed there in connection with my SEC work. It was well located for our purposes.

We particularly enjoyed the theater, but one funny incident took place during the performance of *Blithe Spirit.* As the story unfolds, there is one scene in which the theater is darkened while a seance takes place. In the darkness, one of the actors rapped on a table to call forth the spirit world. Unfortunately, an inebriated spectator promptly yelled, "Come in!" This was repeated a second time when further rapping took place. At that point, the theater lights were brought up, and Clifton Webb came to the front of the stage and said, "Will the ushers please remove that member of the audience." Ushers promptly moved forward, the man was ejected without a struggle, the lights were brought back down and the play resumed. It was the one and only time we have ever seen such an event in the theater, though there must have been many times when the cast would have liked to get rid of members of the audience.

Besides arranging for the wedding, another of Sally's chores had been to find us a place to live. This wasn't easy in wartime Washington, but she performed superbly. Somehow, she located a small apartment in a private home at 1630 Upshur Street NW. It consisted of a bedroom, a living room, a kitchen large enough for a table for two, and a private bathroom. It was in a new brick home and had been designed for one of the owner's mother, who unfortunately died before ever occupying the apartment. The price was $60 per month, a figure that then seemed quite proper and would now seem incredible.

Because of both the expense that would be involved and wartime restrictions on travel, none of our family could attend the wedding. Present were only about ten of our friends from the rooming house. The ceremony went quickly, and immediately following we went to Pennsylvania Station to take the train to New York. Enroute we stopped in Philadelphia to see Constitution Hall and the Liberty Bell. There was a guest register at Constitution Hall, probably to prove to budget officers how many people visited that shrine during a year! It was the first place that we had ever signed our married names. Years later we returned for another visit only to find that the registers were destroyed quite regularly and our names were lost forever.

We had a wonderful time in New York, but the time passed very quickly. I had one more week to serve the SEC before moving to the National War Labor Board, so I had to remain in New York to continue with the trial. Meanwhile, Sally had to go to Washington on Monday in order to be there for work on Tuesday. This was hardly the ideal arrangement, but we accepted it knowing that it would only last one week. We had already gone shopping to acquire the limited furniture we would need for our unfurnished apartment, and it was in place awaiting Sally's return.

As it turned out, we would have only about five months together in that apartment because, by the end of the summer, I would be in the Army. Nevertheless, in that short period of time I had a marvelous job experience that served me well all the rest of my life. For those who have no experience in the field of labor-management relations, it is perhaps necessary for me to explain why the work of the National War Labor Board was so exciting.

Unions were, of course, not a new phenomena at the time of World War II. Indeed, there had been an organization similar to the National War Labor Board for dealing with disruptive labor disputes during World War I. Most of the well-established unions had been craft unions, that is, those that included a single craft, such as plumbers, carpenters, or electricians. With the growth of such mass production industries as steel, autos, rubber, or chemicals, it was difficult to organize those workers on any kind of a craft basis. What was needed, in the eyes of union organizers, were industrial unions to which almost all of the workers in the plant would belong regardless of what they did. John L.

Lewis, the formidable leader of the coal miners union, had succeeded reasonably well in organizing miners. Just as the craft unions had joined together in a federation under the name of the American Federation of Labor (AFL), Lewis and others saw the need for a Congress of Industrial Organizations (CIO). This could not be accomplished at that time under the AFL banner, hence the formation of the CIO and a split in the House of Labor that would last for many years.

One of the lessons the federal government had learned in earlier times, including World War I, was that, in a democracy, it is not possible to simply ban strikes and expect that ban to be obeyed. If unions defy the law, as they are likely to do under strong leadership such as Lewis's, the government's option is to obtain a court injunction requiring the employees to return to work or to use the police or the Army to clear a path for replacement workers who are willing to walk through picket lines. Neither approach is likely to be very successful. A court order may be defied since the Constitution forbids involuntary servitude. In this case, the judge can choose to imprison the union's leadership or fine them if they refuse to order a return to work. Imprisoning the leadership will only make them martyrs in the eyes of their members and strengthen their future role in the union. Fining them may not work because the union may maintain only a very small treasury. Violence may occur, with or without the approval of the union leadership. And, in any event, workers feel very strongly that it is unfair to deny them the right to use their collective strength against the far greater economic power of the company. The Wagner Act, when passed by Congress, gave the unions the right to organize and use their collective strength in the course of collective bargaining, and the Norris-LaGuardia Act restricted the power of the federal courts to issue injunctions in labor disputes.

In this context, any hope that labor unrest could be contained during wartime was dependent upon obtaining a no-strike pledge from the unions in return for some kind of government agency that would have the power, backed by the president, to impose settlements if the parties could not agree. Industry, on the other hand, would not want to participate in any such arrangement unless it could at least take part in the decisions that were to be made. The result was that there was created a tripartite board consisting of four public, four labor, and four management members. The president appointed all the members after consulting with labor and management organizations on their personnel. Top labor and industry personnel agreed to serve, and they had alternates so that the burden would not be too heavy on any one individual. The four public members deserve special attention because they were an extraordinary group who interacted beautifully. The chairman was Will Davis, who was a very dignified and imposing patent lawyer from a prestigious New York law firm. The vice chairman was George Taylor, from the Wharton School at the University of Pennsylvania. He was a short, stout man with a great deal of experience in dealing with labor-management matters. A third member was Wayne Morse, who was then dean of the Law School at the University of Oregon and later a senator from Oregon. Finally, there was Frank Graham, then president of the University of North Carolina, and also later a senator from that state. He was one of the kindest, gentlest men who ever lived.

I was one of a group of rather young people hired by the board. Above me on the totem pole were men, and a woman or two, who were a few years older. My peer group were all about the same age. Most of us were lawyers, some were more experienced than others in the field of labor law, and practically all had been drawn to Washington by the charisma of Franklin D. Roosevelt and the New Deal. All of the staff were lively, devoted, highly intelligent, innovative, and hard working. Because the staff had not yet grown large enough to cope with all the business, those of us who were both junior and inexperienced were given opportunities that would not have come our way for years in normal times. That is why I always thought I gained about three years of experience in my five months of employment.

For purposes of dealing with the disputes that came before the board, ad hoc mediators were called in from across the country to work with the parties toward settlements. Those of us who were panel assistants served as staff for these individuals. We were to provide advice on board procedures, keep board members posted if things started to go wrong, and give the mediator the benefit of any experience we had. The mediators were mostly out of the academic world and were not equally talented. In one of my early cases, the mediator, after hearing the initial presentations from the union and the company, said to the union, "That is probably the stupidest presentation I ever heard!" At the time of the noon break the two parties took me aside and said, "You have got to get rid of this man." I, of course, had no such power, so I promptly went in to see the chairman. He told me to give him a few minutes to talk privately to the representatives of the two parties. He returned very soon and told me to have the parties request an adjournment for a week during which he would quietly get rid of the mediator. This was done, and that particular individual never returned.

If and when our cases had to go to the board for settlement or approval as being within the terms the board could allow, we panel assistants were brought into the meeting. That gave me the opportunity to watch the board work. On some occasions, when one or another of the parties was obdurate, they would be called in to meet with the board. It was great fun to watch what happened. Will Davis would open with a dignified statement about the need for cooperation in wartime, and George Taylor, who was the master mediator of them all and the theorist of the board, would follow with a well-thought-out analysis of the case. Wayne Morse was the tough-talking slasher and he would attack whomever was giving the greatest resistance. Then, in conclusion, would come Frank Graham, the gentle, wise idealist. Not many parties could resist this combination. For those of us who were learners, this was a fascinating scene to witness.

Because of the work load, some of the younger staff members were soon assigned to go out across the country in an effort to settle disputes in the field. Later on there would be regional offices to deal with such problems.

My first such assignment sent me to Connecticut, to the Wright Aeronautical plant where two unions, the United Automobile Workers (CIO) and the Machinists (AFL) were both trying to organize the plant and were seeking increased benefits for the workers. I was twenty-five years old, I had never even been at the site of a labor dispute, and certainly I had never tried to settle one on my own.

There were initial difficulties over whether I would meet with the UAW or the Machinists first. Since the UAW had been first on the scene and the two unions refused to meet together with the company, there was nothing for me to do but make a choice. I told the Machinists that I would not pull out of the meeting with the UAW, but I would meet periodically with them. For whatever reason, the Machinists accepted and I then went ahead with the UAW.

The next problem was that there were about fifty UAW members who wanted to join the meeting with the three or four company representatives. Customarily, a mediator meets with only a few select representatives of each side and relies upon them to sell their colleagues on the proposed settlement. I suggested this, but the UAW members would have nothing to do with it. Since I didn't want the case to blow up without ever having a chance to see if I could settle it, I suggested that we go into a nearby company room where the leaders would sit with me at a head table and the rest of them would be seated out in front where they could see and hear but could not talk. This they agreed to.

After a certain amount of time, we seemed to be making some progress. Then we took a short break, and, as we did so, a big Irishman in the audience stood up and blasted me, the company, and even his union colleagues. He then subsided and I was dismayed, thinking that every bit of progress we had made was now lost. But when we returned to the discussions, both sides acted as if nothing had happened. At each succeeding break, the same Irishman delivered the same philippic— and nobody paid the slightest attention! That taught me another lesson I never forgot. In the course of controversial discussions, one must not be diverted by what individuals who are not in charge may say. It is frequently just a way in which the leaders allow their members to let off steam, perhaps sometimes hoping it may intimidate somebody. Whether it is accidental or planned makes no difference. It will not destroy the negotiations.

We settled the case on the second day. At the conclusion, my Irish friend came up and warmly congratulated me. I felt like telling him that he had taught me a good deal more than I had taught him!

After that I went on a number of other cases and enjoyed a good deal of success. In all fairness, I think it should be said that, under wartime pressure, the parties really wanted to settle and any reasonably able mediator could have done the same thing.

In my remaining few weeks, I did learn some other worthwhile lessons. At that time, some of the CIO unions were Communist domi-nated. Though this was proven only later, it was widely believed to be the case at the time, and those of us who worked on disputes involving such unions knew it. My experience was that they were very tough negotiators but if they made a deal they would stick to it. After Hitler broke his alliance with Russia they were easier because they wanted to throw the full might of the American war effort on the side of Russia. I remember one negotiation in which the first day was filled with acrimo-nious debate, including insulting aspersions to the lineage of the repre-sentatives of the other side. Within the next day two events took place. The Justice Department disclosed that it was suing the company for fraud in connection with the testing of the war products it was producing and, at about the same time there was a tense battle between the Germans and Russians. The following day both sides behaved like lambs. Their motives for settlement were quite different, but their objective was the same—settle the dispute. That was another lesson I tucked away in memory. It isn't always the merits of a dispute that bring about a solution.

While this was happening, my draft board was making it clear that my time had come. There was some talk of asking for a deferment for me on the ground that I was essential in the role I was playing, but that was not acceptable to me nor did I think there was any merit in the claim. The young men of my generation were going into the service, and I could not in good conscience stay out. Much as I hated the idea of war as a device for settling differences, Hitler did seem to me to be a monster who could not be stopped in any other way. I hold that same view today.

My few months at the NWLB had given me one other asset. I got to know, although in a very junior way, many of the leading labor and management figures of the time. After World War II, many of the staff members of the NWLB became professional mediators and arbitrators, and they are only now retiring after having been the leading force in the field for almost fifty years. My mentors at the board remembered me and helped me get started in the field when I returned after the war.

Sometime in August, 1942, I got my Army induction orders. I was to report in Washington and then be shipped to Camp Patrick Henry, Virginia, for assignment. When the day finally came, Sally and I took the bus downtown together. She went to work and I reported to the induction site dressed in casual clothes and carrying only a small bag in which I could send those clothes home. Later that same day, as I put on my GI uniform and shoes, I sent the other clothes to Sally, feeling as I did so that the change in clothing epitomized the great change in our lives, and suggested that we were not likely to see much of each other in the years immediately ahead. This was a very hard thing for both of us although we had accepted it as inevitable. We had known and loved one another so long, we had held off our marriage until we could make a little money, we were happy in our little apartment, and, though we never spoke of it, we both knew I might never come back.

So off I went to Camp Patrick Henry. We had hoped that I would be sent for basic training to some place in the East where we could see one another, but I found myself enroute to Ft. Riley, Kansas, within a week.

It was, I was told, the exact geographical center of the United States. In any event, it was a long way away!

Before I left we had agreed that Sally would remain in Washington until I completed basic training. At that point we might know a little more about where I would be and, if it was not possible for us to be together, she would return to Rockford, Illinois, and live with her parents until the war was over.

It turned out that at the time I was inducted there was an order to send lawyers to the military police, and Ft. Riley was the base for training in the military police. It had long been a cavalry post and still had units of the armored cavalry.

Basic training for me was, I suspect, the same as it was for most inductees. We had marching drill, weapons training with the M-1 and carbine rifles, pistols and revolvers, mortars, machine guns, and the bayonet. We even had some training directing traffic in Junction City, which was much smaller than Ft. Riley, and where there was so little traffic that our signals only befuddled drivers. We saw every sunrise and sunset for the next three months. The weather changed from sweltering hot to frigid, though the Army changed from summer to winter clothes by date regardless of the weather! We had a parade every Saturday morning. We were free Saturday afternoon and Sunday, and even though Kansas was a dry state our sergeant managed to be drunk by three o'clock every Saturday afternoon. For this he was periodically "busted" to buck private, but he would rise again because he was very good when sober. Late in the war, when we were in Germany, I ran across him again at a road block. He was once again a buck private.

I was in good physical condition, so the training didn't bother me. Still, I probably learned more about the American people in basic training than I ever did thereafter. My life had for so many years been among college graduates that I tended to think of the average American as a college person. I learned that we had in our battalion one company of illiterates who spent part of their time learning their ABC's. My next door bunkmate in the barracks was a bootlegger from the hills of West Virginia. He could hardly read, so when he received letters from his common-law wife he would often ask me to read them to him. On one occasion, when she was quite explicit about the nature of their most intimate relationships, he asked me if I would mind "reading that one part again." Despite his lack of formal education, I discovered when we were firing on the range that he was an expert shot. Given the line of work we were now in, I concluded it was better to be alongside him than someone with a Ph.D.

We had another character in our barracks who had impregnated a girl in his hometown in Minnesota and was given the alternative of marrying her or going into the army. I never knew the girl, but he chose the army. He was totally incapable of keeping in step while marching. Each Saturday he would dress for the parade, and each time he would be called out of the ranks at the last minute and ordered to put on his fatigue clothes and swab the barracks. Our company commander was not about to have his company spotted in the parade with one soldier who could never keep in step.

My favorite memory of that period is that when we had night hikes the cook would have freshly baked sugar doughnuts and coffee waiting for us. Once, when winter came and we had been out in the snow on maneuvers, the orders got mixed up and both companies thought they were on the defensive, as the result of which nothing happened. That was when the doughnuts were particularly soothing. I remember that I was also doing guard duty the night before Thanksgiving. Walking around an area carrying an unloaded rifle had little to do with security, but quite a lot to do with discipline. Fortunately, my beat included a Mess Hall and the smell of roasting turkey reminded me of home and the many wonderful occasions on which our extended family would gather at that time of year. Those memories made the night go much faster.

Basic training ended in December. Sally had planned to come out to see me and she was to arrive by train on Christmas Eve. Her train was supposed to come in just before midnight and I could house us in the camp's guest house for a night or two. I went in early to meet the train because the camp was a few miles out of town and one had to take the bus when it was scheduled to make the trip. I expected to have to sit and wait for her, but she had gotten on an earlier train and had just come in. She hardly recognized me in army clothes because I had a very short hair cut and a winter coat that was too big for me.

Just before she came I was told that I was being sent to Ft. Custer, Michigan, to attend Officer Candidate School for the next three months. Enroute I would have a few days' leave and could go to Washington. Thus we had a few days at Ft. Riley before she had to return to Washington, and within a week or ten days I had my orders for a leave and then assignment to Ft. Custer.

Since we had no way of knowing where I would go from Ft. Custer, we decided that Sally should remain in Washington until I was commissioned and we knew what the next assignment would be. It was evident that the road was going to be long and that we were unlikely to be together very much of the time.

Chapter 4

Fort Custer to the War in Germany

I attended Officer Candidate School at Ft. Custer, Michigan, for the first three months of 1943. It was a largely uneventful time. Since we were now disciplined in the ways of the Army, there was less emphasis upon marching, although we still did a good deal of hiking. There was more weapons training, and for the first time we heard that we were going to be something called civil affairs officers. We weren't quite sure what that meant, but we realized that, as the Army moved through enemy territories, there would be great devastation, including total collapse of the government and probable destruction of the utilities. This would obviously cause hardships for the residents of the area, but it would also be hazardous to the troops. It would be important that immediate steps be taken to get the captured areas functioning again. Senior officers (major and above) were being trained at Charlottesville, Virginia, to constitute the key executive officers, and we, the junior officers, would be the staff. It turned out that some of the seniors were given little or no military training, which led to some interesting byplay among us later.

Sally was able to visit me over the Easter weekend, at which time we concluded that I was probably going to be shipped somewhere overseas within a relatively short time and that she might as well start making plans to return to Rockford, Illinois.

Meanwhile, the Army had to find something to do with a batch of newly commissioned second lieutenants, so we were given various assignments around the post. I taught fingerprinting for a while, a subject about which I was totally ignorant and could only stay one short step ahead of the students. Ted Shannon, one of our classmates and who would later join me on the University of Wisconsin faculty, was shipped off to Algiers. Ted was of Lebanese-American parentage and had learned to speak Arabic as a child. His destination suggested that the rest of us might soon go to North Africa, probably as a staging point for going into Italy.

Having made the decision that Sally would return to Rockford, it was an easy next step to see if we could find an apartment in Battle Creek, near Ft. Custer, where we could share whatever time was left. She arrived and, with her usual skill, found us a little apartment, where we were able to stay from about June until early August of 1943. At that point, a number of our group were placed on orders to go to Algiers, and we had a good-bye dinner for them. It was a very nice affair, but the following morning the orders were changed and a new group of officers, of which I was one, were substituted for the original list. We were ordered to be in Washington within forty-eight hours.

Sally went with me to Washington and we stayed with good friends for a few days while I was being processed at the Pentagon. She gave me a daily diary that, for the only time in my life, I kept faithfully all the time I was overseas.

On August 14, 1943 I left by train for Camp Patrick Henry, Virginia. We remained there until August 25, when we were taken to the Norfolk area to board ship. It turned out to be a left-over flat-bottomed transport from World War I. On board we had thirty-four officers and enlisted men plus what was described as a cargo of sugar that smelled suspiciously like gasoline! We were part of a convoy of some eighty-odd ships that were assembled. Surrounding us were a few destroyers to guard against German submarines that were still quite active in the Atlantic. We knew that our destination was Algiers, and though the war in Africa was over by that time, the Axis powers still held France, more than half of Italy, and Spain was not thought of as very friendly. We heard on the ship's radio that Italy had surrendered on September 8, but this meant that once we reached the Mediterranean we would still be fair game for hostile aircraft.

Movement in a convoy is slow and, though we set out on August 27, we didn't reach Algiers until September 17. There was nothing to do on the ship, although we spent a little time studying Italian and looking at various military government manuals that told us about the governmental system in Italy and how we were to perform. Some of the senior officers who had trained at Charlottesville were aboard and we began an acquaintance with them. That was when we first learned that they had had no weapons training. Our confidence was not improved when we got to know one former member of Congress who was among the senior group. He made no secret of the fact that he wanted to go to Italy, obtain a Purple Heart (which was awarded to those who were wounded in battle), then get his discharge and return to his home state to once again run for Congress as a war hero. Naturally, he preferred that the wound be minimal. Sometime within the next year we heard that he had received a Purple Heart in Italy. The story was that he fell out of a Jeep and was modestly injured. Still later he did run once again for Congress from his home state and, to the everlasting glory of the people of his state, he was defeated.

When we anchored at Algiers we assumed we would disembark because our orders all read that this was our destination. In the wonderful way the Army and Navy sometimes work, however, they took both us and the cargo on east to Bizerte. That beautiful port loomed up and we disembarked to a tented camp set up in the hills above the city. The camp was filled with olive trees and I couldn't help but wonder how many wars that grove had seen over the centuries. We had hardly settled in when orders came in mid-evening that we were to go to the railroad station where a French train would take us back to Algiers! We finally boarded the train about 3 P.M. the next day. It moved so slowly that one could almost walk ahead of it.

By the time we got on the train I was suffering from something like the flu. In the course of the second day, we stopped near an American air corps camp and a doctor came aboard to find that I had a temperature of 103 degrees. They promptly took me off to the hospital, where I remained for several days. They thought at first that I had malaria, but this seemed unlikely since we had only been there a day or two and had been taking antimalaria medication all the way across the ocean. They never did decide what was wrong with me, but the temperature went away and I was released.

The Army did not deal in individual travel, it dealt in troop movements. That meant that, though I was released from the hospital, I had to find some way to get to Algiers and report for duty. I strongly suspected that if I just disappeared no one would ever know that I was lost. But where would I go? The best advice I got was to thumb my way via military vehicles to the nearby air base and wait for a military plane going to Algiers with room for me. This I did and, after waiting a second day, found a small cargo plane that would take me. The pilot told me I would have to go get a parachute because they couldn't take anyone without a parachute. The supply office provided a parachute and I climbed aboard. As I did so, I said to the pilot, "I never put on one of these things, so you'd better show me how to use it." He replied,

"Oh, don't bother. Just throw it in the corner. We fly so low in order to avoid radar that you couldn't use it anyway!" That was a comforting thought.

Once in Algiers, I found the appropriate headquarters and was told that my outfit was in a place called Tizi Ouzou, which was in the hills to the east. I managed a day or two in Algiers first, and then reported in Tizi Ouzou. We were housed in tents outside a school building in which we ate and had some offices. The nights were very cold, but it was warm enough to take a shower outside during the daylight hours.

The hardest part about being in the Army, aside from actual combat, is surely just waiting. We had been sent to North Africa in anticipation of going on to Italy, but when Italy surrendered and a new government loyal to the Allies was in place the picture changed substantially. Nowhere near the number of civil affairs officers that had been anticipated were needed. Some of the earlier arrivals went to Sicily, and then on to Italy. But, despite the Italian surrender, the Germans held everything in Italy above Naples, and were holding on to it very firmly.

We remained at Tizi Ouzou from September 27 until December 11. Finally, we were put on an LCI (Landing Craft Infantry) and taken to Naples. We were promptly transported to a monastery in Vico Equense, which is near Mt. Vesuvius. The Jesuits had vacated a part of the building, and we occupied it. During that time we performed only occasional duties, spending some time in Naples helping cope with some of the problems that arose out of the destruction that had taken place during the departure of the Germans. A new beachhead was mounted at Anzio by American troops, but the Germans held firm and it didn't make a lot of progress. Planes pounded Cassino, where the Germans were holed up in an ancient monastery, but it likewise held out for a long time. Meanwhile, pressure for another Allied invasion in Southern France was mounting, and the question arose of whether a land battle for Rome was worth the cost in lives and destruction.

And so we waited once again, doing relatively little. The Germans continued to raid Naples on occasion, or throw some shells into the city, but it was more for harassment than military purposes.

On February 4, 1944, we were told that we were going back to England for the invasion. We didn't in fact go until March 5 and, in the interim, Sol Barsy (another old friend from OCS days) and I decided to hitchhike down to Brindisi to see his brother, who was part of a bomber crew flying over Romanian oil wells. It was not hard to get a few days off since we were not doing much anyway, and we started out. Our progress was so slow that we soon realized we could not make the round-trip as quickly as we thought. In the best tradition of an entrepreneurial army, we reassessed our position. Sol was always a better and more convincing entrepreneur than I, so we went to the British transportation office, told them that we had an important mission to Brindisi, and asked if they had a vehicle. The clerk very kindly said that while they didn't have a Jeep they did have a weapons carrier we could have for the trip. Since officers did not normally drive, he also gave us a driver. We set off promptly, before the clerk thought to ask to see any orders, and ultimately arrived in Brindisi via Foggia. We didn't want the driver to know that our real mission was for Barsy to see his brother so we agreed that they would drop me off at the Military Headquarters in Brindisi where I would conduct our "official" business. I had no official business and intended to simply look around the city while waiting for Barsy to return. I left them, went in the front door of the building, waited a couple of minutes and then reemerged from the same door. It turned out that Sol's driver had missed a turn and was now recircling the block just as I walked out. They could hardly miss seeing me, so the driver stopped, thinking I might need a ride. Even as I wondered to myself how I was going to explain this curious coincidence, I heard myself tell him that the officer I was to see was out and I would have to wait until later to see him. They then left, and I proceeded to look over the city.

We boarded the Dutch transport *Tegelberg* on March 4, 1944, for the trip to Gurroch, Scotland. Sally kept me supplied with books while I was away, and I read Charles Beard's *Rise of American Civilization* during most of the trip.

Scotland was a very welcome sight to all of us. Gurroch was not badly damaged as far as we could see, the fields were green, and the people were speaking a language we could understand. My paternal grandfather had come from that city and I could therefore tell my family where I was by stating that fact.

From Gurroch we were promptly shipped by train to Shrivenham, which is west of London and is a permanent military base in England. While there we went through the same old routine, except this time the language was German and the manuals focused on Germany. I had had two years of German in college, and though this experience was now about eight years old, I did know a fair amount of German and could handle modest conversations. On weekends, while in Shrivenham, we could hitchhike around the nearby countryside or take the train. We were used to hiking, so a ten-mile walk around the little villages was always an option.

We stayed in Shrivenham until May 9, at which time some of the American officers, including me, were shipped off to Eastborne to become a part of an Anglo-American team of civil affairs officers that would go to France. Eastborne is on the southeast coast of England, the nearest spot on the coast to France, and is largely a resort city in peacetime. The old hotels had all been taken over for troop use, and we were housed in the Grand Hotel.

We were still in Eastborne on June 6 when the invasion of France started. I wrote the following entry in my diary for that day.

> This is it! All night long planes were overhead. This morning as far as the eye could see the channel was filled with a bridge of ships. It looked almost like one could walk across from one ship to another. Fighter planes darted in and out in the sky, and by tonight the Mosquito bombers were winging back. Eisenhower, Churchill, and De Gaulle were all on the radio.

Some of our colleagues who were still with the American forces went in that day. The big event of the summer for us was the advent of the German buzz bombs. These pilotless rockets first started coming right over our hotel in mid-June, soon after the invasion. My diary is filled with mention of them.

> June 15: Had an air raid alarm last night and the ack-ack (antiaircraft fire) opened up. The firing was at a very low angle which looked like it would come right in our window. Raid didn't last long, though we had a couple of other alerts during the night. We just stayed in bed.
>
> June 16: During the day the air raid alarm rang several times. The secret is now out. Jerry [the Germans] is now using a radio-controlled pilotless plane. Barsy said he saw three of them this afternoon with Spitfires [British fighter planes] chasing them trying to shoot them down. He says the rocket has square wings well back on the fuselage, and a square tail. It is said to go 200 miles per hour and carries 2,000 pounds of high explosives. They are directed towards London.

The buzz bombs continued all summer. We were in "buzz bomb alley," which is to say that though the bombs were intended for London we were on the direct route. Rocketry was not then very sophisticated then, so the exact landing place of the bombs was not precise. Moreover, the Spitfires, which began to patrol the coast, could shoot them down though they never got all of them. The problem was that when a rocket was shot down one could never tell the exact route it would take. They might come straight down, circle and then come down, explode in the air, or explode on impact with the ground. In the military sense they were not very effective, but they did a lot of damage in London and they certainly kept the population on edge. The rocket made a roar like a tractor, so you could hear it coming at a considerable distance. It didn't fly very high, which is why ack-ack in a populated area was difficult. It had to be fired at such a low angle that it might hit distant buildings if it didn't hit the rocket. When the rocket neared its target the noise would stop. With a kind of morbid humor, we used to say that if you were still alive a minute after the noise stopped you were OK because it was landing somewhere else!

The Germans were so precise in their timing that the rockets used to start flying over around 11 P.M. Knowing that they were intended for London, we used to go up on the roof a little before 11, put on our steel helmets (because fragments of ack-ack would be falling), and watch the show. On June 25 I wrote the following diary entry.

> Just now, the first rocket came over. One was just shot down on Beachy Head, which is a half-mile away. The concussion almost knocked our windows out. During the night one came right over the hotel, very low. It gave us a bad few minutes. Then another one went over up towards Hastings. We could see ack-ack.

During all this time, Sol Barsy and I used to take the train to London on weekends. Though the city was totally blacked out at night, the streets were alive with people. There was a good deal of damage from the earlier air raids and from the rockets, and we would probably have been wiser not to risk the landing of the rockets, but we were bored with life in Eastborne and London offered a welcome respite. The Red Cross ran centers where one could get an overnight billet, there was an officers' mess hall at Grosvenor Square at which we could eat, and between British and American entertainers we could always find something to do. Our old friend, Ted Shannon, was at SHAEF (Supreme Headquarters Allied Expeditionary Force) out at Bushy Park and we saw him frequently. A number of the rockets fell on London while we were there, one of them on a billet we had stayed in the night before.

On August 1, 1944 (while still with the British), we all received what the British called a 48-hour notice before shipping overseas. It was intended for British personnel and provided that if you lived within x distance of the post you got two days of leave and if you lived further away you got three days. The Americans all claimed that we were more than x distance from home and that we were therefore entitled to three days away. Our requests were granted, so Sol and I set off for Scotland. We took the Royal Scot train out of London and spent the first night in Edinburgh. We then went to Glasgow. We had no reservation for a trip home and would be absent without leave (AWOL) if we were not back by the end of the third day. Oddly enough, this was not an enormous worry to us. We worked our way out to the big airfield at Prestwick to see if we could hook a ride on a military plane back to London. It turned out there was no space on a flight to London, but we could fly to Ireland and then on to London provided we didn't get bumped by more senior officers. We thought if we were going to be AWOL, we might as well be in Ireland, so we took the first leg of the trip and, as luck would have it, were able to complete the flight and catch a train back to Eastborne that night.

The 48-hour notice of departure turned out to be a little premature. Paris was liberated on August 23, but we remained in England. The Free French, under General DeGaulle, promptly returned to France and Le Grande Charles was not anxious to have Allied Civil Affairs officers active in his territory.

Finally, on September 3, we were taken to London, where we boarded a British transport and exited England through the Straits of Dover. There was still some shelling in that area, and our boat drifted out into the Channel rather than using its motor. We were told this was to avoid raising magnetic mines that were lying at the bottom of the Channel. Despite the relatively short distance, we didn't disembark until September 6. It was raining, the accommodations for receiving us were poor, and there were some 3,000 German prisoners of war penned up in an outdoor, fenced area.

After all this time, a decision was made to separate the Anglo-American teams. Later it was determined that once the conflict was over, Germany would be divided into four zones held, respectively, by the British, French, Americans, and Russians. In the meantime, we would return to our own armies.

On September 8 we were trucked to an American encampment on the grounds of the Chateau Rochefort Fondiere, which was approximately 180 miles from where we landed. It was an all-day trip in the back of a one-and-a-half-ton covered truck. If you sat near the back you were exposed to a good deal of truck exhaust, which didn't promote good health. By the time we arrived it was late at night, we had had nothing to eat since morning, and it was raining.

The chateau was a tremendous place. The Germans had just vacated it and there were still many signs in German on the grounds. There was an artificial lake and lots of statuary around the grounds. Except for the Army brass, we were housed in pup tents that we carried with us. The water was not working, so I remember sponging off in the lake the first morning we were there. Paris was only 28 miles away, but we were forbidden to go there. Our only food, as of that moment, was K rations bound in small packages that we brought with us. While we were at the chateau, I learned that it was built around 1900 by an Austrian, and had in subsequent years been used as a club for wealthy, expatriate Americans, then for a school, then for a fashion museum, then once again for a school, and finally purchased by a wealthy individual from whom the Germans expropriated it.

Because the rest of the civil affairs officers were still being gathered, we remained in the chateau area for almost two weeks. The fighting in Germany was continuing, but France and Belgium were free, and we were sent to Huy, near Namur, in Belgium on the German border. The first night there we bedded down in the city market area. The next morning we found that Huy had been liberated on September 15 and the people were still celebrating. Food was short, but the stores appeared to be otherwise well stocked although we were told that before the Germans left they ransacked many of the stores.

By noon of the next day we moved on to Liège, Belgium, and then to Verviers where we were housed in permanent Belgian military barracks in the city. The front line was then 15 miles away and we could hear the big guns firing. The destruction was not so bad in the area, but all the bridges had been blown up. Sappers were exploding mines around the city, so there were many explosions. Hundreds of Allied planes were flying over, pounding German cities.

While we were holding in Verviers, one of the funny (if dangerous) incidents that marred the relationship between the senior and junior civil affairs officers occurred. The commanding officer decided he was going to have a pistol inspection, so he lined up our company out in the quadrangle that was used for such formations. It was in the middle of a ring of barracks and some of the Belgian workers who had cleaned the barracks after the Germans left got up on the roof of one of the barracks in front of us to watch. Pistol inspection, like most Army drills, is done by the numbers. On the count of one, the officer removes the pistol from his holster and raises it to shoulder level with the muzzle pointing up. On the count of two, the slide (the barrel) is pulled back where it catches and remains until the next count. On the count of three, you must remove the cartridge clip, otherwise when the slide goes forward it will put a bullet in the chamber. The final count is to pull the trigger since the gun is now cocked. If you have done it right, there is no bullet in the chamber and the officer who is inspecting your weapon is safe. If, however, you didn't take the cartridge clip out, the gun will fire when the trigger is pulled.

Since we junior officers knew that some of the senior officers were untrained in weaponry, we always made it a point at such formations to get in the back row lest a bullet go whizzing by our heads. On this occasion, to the dismay of the commanding officer (who was regular army), a shot was fired. He was furious, and the Belgians who were watching from the roof were in the line of fire. They promptly decided that the customs of the American Army were not for them and they scooted for cover. Fortunately, no one was hit, the junior officers restrained themselves from breaking out in laughter, and there were no more pistol inspections.

Though there was still some optimism that the war might end during 1944, it was fading every day. The Germans were still fighting hard, Liège was bombed continually, and we first heard about the new German rocket—the V-2. Its predecessor, the V-1 buzz bomb that we had seen so much of in England, was still used, but it was the V-2 that now gained everyone's attention. Unlike the V-1, the new rocket was a high-angle missile that could not be seen and made no observable noise. One neither saw nor heard it coming, it simply suddenly exploded. In a way, this was easier to bear than the V-1, which one could see and hear coming, then listen for the noise to stop, and then only wait in anticipation to see where it was going to land. The unanticipated hazards of war were always present and everyone understood that, hence a new, unobservable rocket was simply one more problem but not one that any of us could do much about. Fortunately, the rockets of that era did not have either the accuracy or range of today's missiles, therefore they were not as much of a military weapon.

Some progress was being made in the invasion of Germany. Aachen was about to fall, as were some of the smaller towns in the Fatherland, but German resistance was still strong.

For the rest of the fall, clear up to Christmas, we stayed on the boundary of Germany, moving as far south as Luxembourg, and engaged in various and sundry activities having to do with efforts to restore civilian life in areas the Germans had occupied. We were in Bastogne when it was in Allied hands, but on December 18 it would be the center of the last German attack in what became known as the Battle of the Bulge. Later, some of us were in Esch-sur-Alzette, and then across the border into France at Audon le Teche in connection with the flooding of the mines in that area, and in trying to get food in. We visited a German factory at Thil that produced Messerschmidt fighter planes and V-1 bombs and was two to six hundred feet below ground to protect it from air attacks. It had only recently been vacated and it contained millions of dollars of undamaged machinery. We were told that it employed 5,000 people, many of them Russian women who were kept in a nearby camp. In the camp was an ominous crematory.

Soon after the Luxembourg experience, those of us who had been up north were ordered back to Verviers. These changes were accounted for by the fact that civil affairs officers were attached to armies, and we belonged to the Ninth Army. We were on loan to the First Army and, as things changed, we went back to the Ninth. This meant that we were in Verviers at the time of the Battle of the Bulge.

A tense week followed, largely because the Germans had mounted a massive attack and were aided by weather that prevented the Allied planes, which had total supremacy in the air, from attacking. The Army troops in Bastogne fought valiantly, holding their ground until General Patton arrived with the Third Army and all its armor. Thereafter, the Germans were pounded mercilessly in retreat and the Third Reich began to fall apart. Even so, it would be another six months before the war ended.

On January 3, 1945, our civil affairs team was ordered into the city of Stolberg, Germany. Our entrance to Germany involved a passage through the outer ramparts of the Siegfried Line (the counterpart of the famous French Maginot Line) with its rows of concrete dragon teeth. When we went through Aachen, one could ride for blocks and miles within the city and never see a single building that had completely escaped damage.

In peacetime, Stolberg had about 30,000 inhabitants, but it was now nearer 10,000. Hitler had ordered the people to evacuate, but many refused and were thereafter more concerned about the consequences of a German return than about our presence. About half the city was badly destroyed, but the remainder was so badly booby-trapped that many civilians lost their lives in the rubble months after the fighting was over.

For a billet we took over a stone house that was only slightly damaged, except that a shell had gone through one wall. (When we had the shell hole fixed, the workmen managed to wall themselves in so that another hole had to be made to rescue them!) The home had belonged to a wealthy manufacturer who, with his wife, committed suicide just before the American entry. He had refused an order from the Germans to blow up his plant and he feared their revenge.

Since the front was only seven miles away, we could only deal with temporary problems. There was no electricity, except for a small generator that supplied the hospital, no gas, water in only portions of the city, no stores were open, and the factories were doing only maintenance work. There was also no food except what people had stored and what could be brought in from the countryside. Communal kitchens were set up to feed one meal a day to a large portion of the city. There was a strict curfew from five in the evening until seven in the morning, no civilian traffic was allowed on the main road, and the only amenity was that there were huge stockpiles of coal in the town and most people could keep warm. The law by which the city was to be governed was Military Government Law in accordance with ordinances that we published in both German and English.

Our commanding officer, John Hall, was an experienced city manager in the states. The rest of us had varied experience. I was responsible for labor supply, legal services, and public health. At the outset, the labor supply problem was largely one of supplying the American troops with manpower to restore utilities and bridges. We did this by rounding up people in a central place at eight o'clock in the morning. Our military units would then take the number of men they needed. Under international law, enemy civilians cannot be required to work on projects, therefore all the labor had to be voluntary. An incentive to those who worked was that they would receive a meal at noon, and food was in short supply. There was never a problem of getting enough laborers.

Since food was a major problem, we shortly had women and children coming in asking for the remains of our own meals. We were forbidden to give food to the Germans, yet even the hate that war engenders never totally succeeds in persuading the troops that women and children should be allowed to starve. Therefore, there was a good deal of surreptitious help given in such cases.

Closely allied with the food problem was the public health situation. The death rate of infants under the age of one had doubled in the previous four months, and tuberculosis was on the rise. Desperately ill cancer patients could not be moved to larger hospitals. Unborn babies did not know that they must not be born during curfew hours lest there be no one to help the mother during the delivery. These were the day-to-day practical problems that we had to work out in the midst of a deadly war surrounding the city.

Abortions were another part of the pregnancy problem. Under Nazi law, women from eastern Europe who were brought in for slave labor could have an abortion. Presumably this was to prevent the birth of "inferior" people. However, in this case the only available hospital was run by a Catholic order that was opposed to abortions. Previously, such patients had been taken to Aachen, but this was now impossible. When a local doctor came to us with a case of this kind, we concluded we had enough problems without demanding that a Catholic hospital, which would probably defy our order, permit the operation. What happened as a result of our decision we never knew.

Along with these more-or-less routine and ubiquitous problems came an unusual task. As the fighting continued, our troops had no camouflage white clothing to help conceal them against a background of snow. The Ninth Army, therefore, wired all military government detachments to collect all of the white bedsheets in the community, except for hospitals, so that they could be used for camouflage. We used the civilian police, which we were organizing, to go house-to-house with our tactical troops. People were told that they must surrender every sheet they owned, including those that were on beds. A record was made of the number of sheets and the people from whom they were obtained. Ultimately, the list would be turned over to the German government for payment as an expense of the war they had started. Naturally, there were protests, but combat soldiers who are getting shot at every day have little sympathy for the mere loss of sheets. No one who has ever been close to war ever said it was a tea party.

Probably the most difficult problem we had during the early months of occupation, and until the war was over, was with the so-called nonfraternization law promulgated by Allied Headquarters. The purpose of the law was to forbid service personnel from associating with German civilians. Given the devious uses to which Hitler had put his people and the incredible annihilation of those who differed with him, it was understandable that, at least while hostilities continued, soldiers should be kept as far away from civilian contacts as possible. In practice, however, this was unworkable. Furthermore, no one quite knew what the law meant. General Patton, in his own inimitable fashion, was said to have told his troops that they could do anything they wanted to with civilians so long as they didn't talk while doing it! That our soldiers were not spending all their time fighting was later confirmed when a local doctor came in to ask me what we proposed to do about German girls who became pregnant by American soldiers. He stated that his confidential poll of other local doctors indicated that there were already thirty-six such cases. We passed his report on to higher headquarters with the observation that the nonfraternization laws did not appear to be entirely effective!

In the midst of all this chaos we did manage to gradually restore the utilities, set up an interim local government, and get food to the people. It turned out that the Germans had stored a spare supply of generators in the giant bunkers of the Siegfried Line, which our engineers were about to partially destroy. The Line contained massive rooms with a citylike structure far below ground, thus protecting the supplies from bombing. We requisitioned some generators from that stock and restored enough electricity to serve essential needs. Getting food in from the countryside was an even greater problem, because the German transportation system was destroyed and ours was devoted to military purposes. With a patchwork of local transportation and a certain amount of freeloading on military vehicles traveling in the right direction, we set up a communal kitchen where, at noon each day, a meal consisting of soup and bread was dispensed. The price was very low and those who could not afford to pay anything were fed anyway, paid for out of a city relief fund. Aside from this ration, people were dependent on what they had in their homes. The city doctor estimated that 75 percent of the local residents were completely dependent upon this diet, 20 percent could supplement it in some fashion, and about 5 percent were not dependent on it at all. Stored supplies had been depleted because troops fighting through the city had often eaten rations that they took from homes, and evacuees from other places had come into Stolberg and put a further drain on supplies.

Since our team of civil affairs personnel was small and was designed to move on to other, newly captured cities after restoring modest order in the one we were in, we were destined to leave shortly for a more advanced base. We would be succeeded by another group of civil affairs officers who would remain longer. Before we left, however, a novel nonfraternization case came up that turned out to have a good deal of bearing on what would happen to that ill-starred regulation. That is part of a larger story that remains to be told.

Chapter 5

War's End, the Occupation, and Return Home

Since I was the only lawyer on our team of officers, the legal problems inherent in the occupation fell in my bailiwick. Most of them were not very complicated, but they were difficult to deal with. When we imposed a curfew, there were bound to be violations because the everyday events of life do not permit people to be totally confined to their houses from five o'clock in the afternoon until seven o'clock in the morning. Emergencies like fires will take place. Moreover, the Germans had brought in a great deal of slave labor, most from other countries that were now allied with us. Once a town was liberated, those nationals assumed that they were free to do as they pleased. From our standpoint, the problem was that the front was only seven miles away, it would be easy for the Germans to infiltrate the city at night, and our troops were likely to shoot those who were out after curfew no matter who they turned out to be.

It was the curfew that ended up testing the nonfraternization law. One night after a fresh snowfall the Military Police found footprints from Army boots leading to a civilian home. They followed the footsteps, went to the home, and entered. There they found a few American soldiers sitting in a room listening to music with a German family. They promptly arrested the men, and they were then disciplined by their commanding officer for violation of the nonfraternization rule. Since we were attached to the infantry division, of which the colonel was in command, we were also subject to his orders. Having penalized his own men, the colonel then demanded that we try the civilians for violation of the law. We explained that, in our interpretation, this was a rule that applied to the Army but did not include civilians. He was adamant and insisted that we proceed with the trial. We were confident that our interpretation of the law was correct but, since his order was not patently improper, we had no alternative but to follow it and rely on an appeal to reverse his position. Because I was the only lawyer on our team, we decided I should defend the case in order to build a proper record on appeal.

As I looked into the case, I found other examples of fraternization that would serve our purposes in interpeting the law. Once while Stolberg was being fought over, some German civilians, seeing our troops pinned down in the doorway of a store, went around to the rear of the store and showed them an escape route. Was that also fraternization? On another occasion, an American soldier lay wounded in the street and a civilian rescued him by coming out and stemming the flow of blood from a wound that might have been fatal. In still another case, a German civilian had entered a booby-trapped building in Stolberg in an attempt to rescue an American soldier who already lay wounded in that building. Another explosion occurred and the German was killed. What about the German woman who did some laundry for soldiers in return for a couple of K rations? Were these examples of fraternization on the part of civilians, and, if so, did we wish to isloate ourselves from such help?

The trial was held in one of the German courtrooms with one of our officers presiding. The courtroom was full of Germans. The testimony was translated so that everyone could understand. There was no claim of any improper activity other than soldiers being in the same room listening to music with the German family. I argued that the law did not apply to civilians but only to our troops. I used the preceding examples to demonstrate how shortsighted it would be to say that we wanted no help from German civilians and that we would punish them for such activity. The judge duly ruled that the defendants were not covered by the law.

To my knowledge this was the only case ever tried in such circumstances. It was plain that the German audience was impressed with what they perceived as the fairness of the outcome, and, not long thereafter, SHAEF (Supreme Headquarters Allied Expeditionary Forces) ruled that the nonfraternization law did not apply to civilians. On August 6, 1945, General Eisenhower formally ended the entire nonfraternization policy by saying to the German public, "Members of my command are now permitted normal contacts with you." In point of fact the policy had not been enforced for a long time. Like Prohibition at home, it proved to be unenforceable.

The day after the trial I received orders to report at once to SHAEF in Versailles, France. I hated the idea. I was finally doing something useful, I was away from all the brass, we were a highly compatible team, and we were headed for another, larger city in Germany. I knew that my good friend, Ted Shannon, who was at SHAEF, had to be behind the order and that he thought he was being helpful. He knew how unhappy I had been doing so little for so long, and he set about getting me to Paris where I would be busy, although surrounded by all the complexities of a high command.

One does not disobey legitimate orders in the Army. So I headed for Paris, though with a heavy heart. I wondered if the German civilians in Stolberg would conclude that having just won a case excluding them from the coverage of the fraternization law I was now being banished!

As usual, to get from one place to another, one went to the nearest Army transportation center and sought a ride going in the proper direction. It was February 2 before I could find a ride, and the journey to Paris was long and cold. I got there about 8:30 P.M., but didn't find a billet until 11:30 P.M. I was housed in Versailles at the Hotel Votel. When I got to my room I found there was no heat at all and that the water pipes were frozen; there was no water and no plumbing.

The following morning I sought out Ted Shannon and found that he was, as I suspected, the inspiration for this move. I told him I really wanted to return to my team because, unbeknownst to him, it was, from my point of view, just the right place to be. He was not in a position to change the order, but we had other friends higher up who listened sympathetically and promised to try to get me back in Germany "as soon as possible." That date didn't prove to be very soon. I remained at SHAEF until March 14. While there, I read a lot of classified cables, channeled them to the right people, compiled the War Diary for the office, and wrote a weekly summary of what was happening. Paris was close and transportation into the city was simple. Our offices were in what had once been the grand stables of the Versailles Palace, and I had lots of opportunities to visit the grounds. Though Paris was still under blackout, the streets were full of people at night. Daylight visits convinced me that Paris was one of the most beautiful cities in the world, and that view has never changed. Once, toward the end of my time in Paris, I flew the daily courier route to Reims. We were in a little Piper Cub–type plane, with only the pilot and myself. We both wore .45 caliber pistols, which served as the plane's only armament! Coming back the pilot flew right over Paris at low altitude. This would not normally be permitted, but this was wartime and the rules were different. The city looked as gorgeous from the air as it did from the ground.

Being at SHAEF was mildly interesting, and certainly I enjoyed Paris and the surroundings, as well as once again seeing many of my old friends. But it was a relief to be heading back.

In order to locate my team, I had to go to Maastricht, Holland, which was the headquarters of the Ninth Army, to find out where they were. That meant finding another ride in an Army vehicle going in that direction. At the Transportation Office I was told that there was a supply truck going out on March 14 in which I could ride. I arrived at the appointed hour and checked in. The clerk said that the truck had been requisitioned by another group, but that there was a Jeep going in that direction I could have if that would be all right. Sensing that he had made a mistake, but far preferring a Jeep to a ride in the back of a truck, I agreed to accept this alternative provided we could leave right away. I knew that if we waited the mistake would be discovered. The clerk thanked me for my accommodating nature and off we went. I learned later that, as I suspected, the Jeep was really for someone else, but when this was discovered I was long gone. Perhaps I should have felt guilty about it, but in a way it seemed to me poetic justice to have the Jeep as compensation for having fulfilled an assignment I never wanted.

The week before my departure from Versailles, two major changes in the battlefront had taken place. On March 7 the city of Cologne was taken and, on March 9, the First Army captured a bridge across the Rhine (at Remagen) before it could be blown up. Troops were quickly sent across, thus constituting the first breach of the Rhine River and saving many lives in what would otherwise have been a difficult assault. From then on the end of the war was in sight.

On March 16 I rejoined my former team in Übach, Germany, which is situated just above Aachen and barely across the line from Holland. The town had been badly destroyed and there was no water power, but we had electricity. It was there that we first encountered the many serious problems that would flow out of the presence of displaced persons in Germany. In this case it was Russians, some of whom were captured civilians, who were brought to Germany for slave labor, and others were captured soldiers. They were now free, they had been very badly treated, and they wanted revenge on the Germans. Though many of them were in camps just across the Dutch border, they thought it was appropriate to raid and loot German homes in Übach. However great their justification for doing so, we could not permit it and that was not easy to accomplish.

Our residence in Übach was temporary, it already having been determined that our next objective was Solingen, the fine-steel center of Germany situated just across the river from Cologne. Since Solingen was not yet in Allied hands, we were in a holding action. We used the time to see what the problems were in the area. Going in the direction of Mönchengladbach and Krefeld, we saw the evidence of a battle just over. Horses lay bloated in death, trees along the highway had been cut and felled across the road to slow the Allied advance, and buildings were blown to pieces. We also learned that mines in the area were flooding because pumps were not operating.

During this waiting period I was suddenly ordered to report to Ninth Army Headquarters, where I was told that I was going to be the defense counsel for two sixteen-year-old German boys who had been caught spying behind American lines. Their penalty, if convicted, would be death. I had one day in which to prepare the defense. In civilian life, such a time limitation would, of course, be totally unacceptable, and even in the Army it was not an assignment I relished.

As I looked into the case, the facts were fairly simple. The boys were members of the Hitler Jugend (youth) corps, and in the final stages of the war Germany was down to using young boys. Their assignment was to cross Allied lines, spot the artillery placements, and report back on the sites. They were captured before they did any harm. They confessed, giving all the details, including the fact that there were any number of other Hitler Jugend engaged in the same kind of missions.

In the face of their confessions, there was little I could do but enter a plea for mercy in view of their age and the likelihood that the war would soon be over. My feeling was that even if they were convicted and sentenced to death there would have to be an appeal to higher headquarters and that this would take enough time for them to be pardoned. As it turned out, I was wrong on both counts. The war did not end until early May, and a determination had already been made that, in view of the continuing German use of young boys for these missions, decisions could be made at the Army level and not appealed further.

The trial started before a Military Court composed of American officers. The prosecution put in its case in the morning. It was a dark, cold day and we were operating by candlelight because there was no electricity. Everyone was armed, including counsel.

I put in the defense in the afternoon. It turned out that Eric Severeid, one of Ed Murrow's CBS correspondents in Europe and later one of the best-known CBS reporters in the States, had found out about the trial and was there to cover it.

When all the evidence had been introduced and all the arguments ended, the court took a recess to decide the case. During that period the rest of us also took a break. I remember Severeid saying to me that he thought my plea for mercy would be granted, but I didn't think so. This was not the only case of its kind. To the extent that such missions were successful our troops were endangered, the Germans had been merciless in their treatment of people, and there was a strong feeling in the Army that an example had to be made.

When the court was ready, we were called back into the courtroom, but I was told to remove my pistol. I knew that this meant they did not want either of the defendants sitting next to me to make a grab for my gun, and that this in turn meant that the death penalty was going to be imposed. It was.

There was an appeal to the Ninth Army that I was directed to prepare in the next few days. For this purpose, I visited the boys in prison. Neither had been defiant, but this time one of them had obviously been crying. There was little to be said that I did not already know. I asked each of them to prepare a written statement for me. One of them said that he didn't think he ought to be shot because his father had already been shot by the Germans for black-market violations.

The appeals were submitted. They were promptly rejected, and the boys were shot. The penalty was then made widely known in the rest of Germany as a warning of what would happen to others who engaged in this practice.

I understood the rationale for the decision, and could accept the fact that success in their spy mission could have cost many American lives. Still, they were only sixteen years old, the war was almost over, and it seemed a pity that they had to be a last-minute casualty of the war. I thought of sixteen-year-old American boys and what a tragedy it would be to have their lives cut short by the mistakes of their elders. My spirits were very low.

After the trial I handled one or two more cases of a lesser nature, and then returned to my team. For the next couple of weeks we lived around Haltern, Germany, still waiting to go into Solingen. Displaced persons were present by the thousands, moving along the roads going somewhere or nowhere. They wanted revenge on the Germans, and everyone was short of food. A Russian DP (displaced person) acccidentally let a hand grenade go off near a Dutch sergeant who was with us and almost blew his legs off. The Poles had taken over a big house and were running it in a disciplined way with rules for their residents. Their problem was food, which we could temporarily supply, but for how long? Our Army took over many of the habitable buildings, which, of course, only complicated the problem.

On April 11 we were finally ordered into Solingen, though it was still not clear that it was in Allied hands. As we moved up, we received news of Franklin D. Roosevelt's death on April 12, and it saddened all of us that, with the end so near, he would not live to see it.

One of the surprises of war, when you are in it, is how often you do not know exactly where the line is between the enemy and your own troops. As we moved toward Solingen we reached company level before we could find out who was in the city. Meanwhile, my notes show that I used a Jeep to take a small German boy, who had a bomb splinter in his eye, to a hospital that he could not otherwise reach. I wondered if the Germans would do a similar thing for us if the situation were reversed.

On April 16 we were able to enter Wuppertal, which is very near Solingen. It had just been taken and we thought we could enter Solingen the next day. We heard the BBC broadcast that night from London and it said Solingen was in Allied hands. But since information was still scarce, we sent a couple of Jeeps out the next morning to test out two of the entrances to the city. I took an enlisted man in one of them, and when we reached a bridge that we would have to cross there was an American soldier there who told us not to cross because the bridge was mined. At about the same time some American planes flew over and drew ack-ack fired from the other side. We thought that was reasonably convincing evidence that the Germans were still in Solingen.

This part of the assault was in the Ruhr area and our troops were now surrounding the German army. The noose was tightening and they knew it. We finally got into Solingen on April 17. It was badly damaged, but about 100,000 people were still there. It was without water or electricity, but when we reached the center of the city the government buildings were largely intact and our army was taking them over. There were relatively few Americans around when we first came in. As we stood there making plans for what to do next, an entire company of German soldiers, with a white flag flying on the lead vehicle, marched down the street. They stopped when they reached us, saluted, and asked where they could surrender. They could easily have over-powered us since there were so few of us present, but they knew they had nowhere to go if they did. We had no capacity to take them at the moment, so we instructed them to leave all their vehicles and drop all their weapons in a pile. This they did. We then instructed them to come back the next day! We knew if we did this many of them would don civilian clothes and disappear, but we also knew that the war was almost over and that they were now without weapons.

Whenever we entered a new city, we had both maps and informa-tion from Army Intelligence about leading Nazis in the city and also about people who were thought to be reliable. Since we always had an immediate need for reliable German personnel who could take over the local government and who could serve as interpreters, one of our first tasks was to locate such people. In this case, the Bishop of Aachen had already been contacted and he had given us the name of the ranking Catholic deacon in Solingen. Armed with this information, we set out to find the deacon. Much as one would in peacetime, we simply looked around for a telephone directory, found his residence, and promptly went there. He was not at home when we arrived, but came soon thereafter. We explained our need for help, pointed out that the city could only return to normal if we got help from civilians, and made it clear that we could not take anyone tainted with Nazism. He thought a bit, and then said that he would take us to the homes of some individ-uals. Our first stop was the home of a couple with four daughters. They were just coming up from their basement, where they had taken shelter and where they had stored some of their things. The father was a railroad man who had refused to join the Nazi Party and had forbidden his daughters to do so. For his attitude, he was sent to France and had only recently returned home. One of the daughters was a concert violin-ist who spoke English quite well. The presence of the priest reassured them. The daughter agreed to come work for us, and she showed up the next day. She ended up working for me, and we have kept in touch over the years since the war. Our next stop was the home of a lawyer who had a wife and two children. Both parents spoke English fluently. When he refused to join the Nazi Party in 1933, he lost his right to continue to practice law. Instead, he chose to open a small scissors factory, which had maintained the family. He immediately raised the question of the Wehrwolf, a group Hitler had promised would annihilate anyone who collaborated with the Allies. We argued that if Germans who had hated the old regime refused to help us, Germany would be a long time in recovering from the war. He finally turned to his wife and said, "Do I have your permission to do this work?" She answered, "I can't give you my consent, but neither will I ever criticize you if you agree." With that reluctant response, he agreed to come and he did show up the next morning.

Our Counter Intelligence Corps (CIC) had also come into Solingen with the troops on that first day, and they brought with them a list of prominent Nazis to be taken into custody immediately. Included on the list was the Oberburgermeister (mayor) as well as the heads of many of the city's agencies. We sought to replace them with senior civil servants who had not been active in the party. In this respect, our task in Solingen was different than any other city we entered, because a group of antifascist civilians, who produced convincing proof that they had for some time been carrying on underground activities and had helped in preventing serious fighting over control of the city, presented themselves. While we were grateful to them, they did present a problem. Some of them were openly Communist, and others were so bitter about what had happened to them that we doubted their ability to administer anything fairly. We were able to use some of them and thus escape a delicate situation, but we did have trouble with retribution some of our appointees visited on their enemies. That their hatred was justified was revealed when we heard that, in the suburb of Ohlig, seventy political prisoners had been shot just before the Americans arrived. We turned the case over to Counter Intelligence, and, when the information proved to be correct, we required the city to exhume all the bodies and place them on display in front of the City Hall. The labor force for this task was to be made up of prominent local Nazis, and the bodies were to be reinterned in a mass grave in front of the City Hall. When the bodies were displayed, they were in various stages of decomposition. Each person had his or her hands tied together behind the back and had then been shot in the head. It was a sickening scene, made worse by the stench of rotting bodies. There was no requirement that German citizens view the scene, but a large crowd came. More than anything else they seemed to be curious, and we saw no evidence of mass guilt.

The first days in Solingen were hectic for other reasons. Some fanatical Nazis were alleged to be holed-up in a house and were said to be ready to shoot it out with anyone who came to get them. That problem proved easy to solve. A squad of infantry came with bazookas and announced over a loudspeaker that, unless the men promptly came out, they would blow the house up. This was not an idle threat. Combat soldiers saw no reason to endanger their own lives by assaulting a house unnecessarily. Blowing it up would be much easier. The occupants decided to come out and there was no problem.

Interspersed with these activities were military court trials for the violation of military government laws. The largest number of cases involved curfew violations committed by displaced persons. They were Russians, Poles, French, Italians, and a mixture of Baltic peoples. Many of them thought of themselves as members of the Allied Forces and didn't know that they must obey the curfew. Our objective was to make it known to them through the trials that it was dangerous to be outside during curfew hours, but the trials themselves were often hilarious. I particularly remember one involving some Italians and another some Russians.

I had learned from earlier experience that there were great differences among the displaced nationalities as to the nature and purpose of trials. The Italians viewed them as theater, not to be confused with reality. When they were questioned they would tell a story full of heroism and compassion in explanation of why they were out during curfew. Even so, if they thought of a better story as they went along they would not hesitate to abandon the first version. If I had the audacity to question the veracity of some of the things they told me, I would get a look intended to suggest a petty interest in truth that would almost certainly be less interesting than what I was being told.

On one occasion when I was trying Italians I found eight people in line before me, but only seven of them were named on the charge sheet. I proceeded to identify the unknown eighth person and got his name. He wanted to say something, but I shut him off and said he could talk later. When I finally got to him he said, "I don't belong here, I just got in line when an official called for all Italians to come this way!" Suspecting that I might not be hearing all the truth of the matter, with all the dignity

I could summon I asked an official to remove him until later when I would consider his case. As it turned out he was in jail for robbery, not curfew violation. If he hadn't said anything, I would have given him a modest fine and let him go. Now he was still in jail on a much more serious charge, and he was heard bemoaning his lack of good fortune in speaking out. Many years later, when I was in Italy while working on a book, my American colleague, who was about to pick me up for a spin around Rome, called to say that he would be delayed by a minor auto accident caused when he was hit while backing his car out of the drive. He promptly reported the incident to the police, but when the Italian maid heard him talking she gestured wildly to him and said she would gladly appear in court and testify to the fact that she had seen the accident and it was all the other person's fault. In truth she had not seen the incident at all, but she was already preening herself for a magnificent court appearance! She assured my friend that no Italian would ever tell the police that an accident was his fault. I concluded that my wartime experience was not unique!

The Russians were a special case. Given the tension that existed between our two countries even then, there were some doubts about whether we should try Russians at all or whether they should simply be turned over to the Russian Army at a later date. Since it was a curfew case, and would result only in a minor penalty if they were convicted, we decided to proceed.

There were complications from the outset. The Russians were all peasant types, had haircuts trimmed as if a bowl had been put over their heads, and their faces showed pleasure at being there. They spoke no English except to say periodically, "Americanski good." Meanwhile the progress of the trial was delayed because we had no interpreter who could go from English to Russian, and the Russians could speak no significant German. We finally found two interpreters, one of whom could go from English to German and the other from German to Russian. There was, however, a further complication. The interpreter who could go from German to Russian had left his glasses home and could not read the charge sheet to the Russians. This was resolved when another German in the well-filled courtroom promptly came to the front, took off his glasses, and offered them to the interpreter. When the latter found he could see with them, the two shook hands, expressed great friendship for one another, and asked about their respective families.

In the course of the trial there would be long periods of interpretation, followed by one of the interpreters saying to me, "He said, 'No.'" Throughout this exchange the defendants would periodically announce, "Americanski good."

I tried with great courtesy to maintain the dignity of the court, and, when it was over, found the Russians guilty and ordered them to pay a modest fine. Their smiles remained fixed in place, and they asked to talk to me a minute as they left. What they said was, "We blew up the bank a few days ago so we have all the money. Wouldn't you like some more of it?" (The money was German marks that were useless anyway.) I believe this was the only time Russians were ever tried by an American tribunal, but it will remain in my memory forever.

During the time that we were in Solingen the war ground to an end. There were still enormous problems in dealing with the denazification of Germans, sustaining and returning displaced persons, supplying food to the population, protecting public health, and so forth, but when the war ended on May 8, 1945, the political situation changed. Germany was divided into zones. The British took the north, the French the center, and the Americans the south. We were therefore ordered to go down near the Austrian border. As we left, we took with us a truckload of wartime booty consisting of the fine-steel dress swords that the factories of Solingen had made for the German army, navy, and air officers. Many of them were quite handsome and were good trading material for other captured military items. I ended up bringing a number of them home and also supplying some of my army friends with them.

We also took with us a displaced Russian by the name of Mike. He couldn't speak English and we couldn't speak Russian, but each of us knew enough German to communicate. He had attached himself to us along the way and we used him to perform various duties. He proved to be very useful, he was a friendly man, and he wanted to go with us as we moved south. We recognized that we would ultimately want to turn him over to the Russian army, but we were not near them at the time. The British, who were replacing us, did not want Mike and we were reluctant to abandon him in such uncertain times.

Mike stayed with us until we were in Bavaria. At that point we were near a Russian liaison officer, so we took Mike to see him, not wanting to prejudice his return to Russia. We explained that we would be pleased to be able to keep him for awhile but that, of course, Mike wanted to go home eventually. Mike and the Russian officer then stepped aside and talked a bit, following which, with much mutual saluting, we departed with Mike. During the ride back Mike was chuckling to himself and when we asked what he was laughing about he said, "The officer asked me if I wanted to go home, and I told him I did, as soon as possible. If I hadn't said that I would have been on the next train!"

Regrettably, not long after our visit with the Russian officer, Mike got some pure alcohol, drank it, went berserk, attacked some officers, and was thrown in jail. The only way to get him out of jail was to send him to the Russians, which we did. We never heard from him again, but we do know that, after they returned to their homeland, the Russians executed many of their citizens who had served in Germany.

Most of our time in southern Germany was spent in the city of Landshut, but we had lots of time to visit the surrounding areas. There was not much destruction outside the big cities and the economy could adjust more easily to problems of food and housing.

We visited Oberammergau and found that the residents were planning to restrict the next production of their famed Passion Play to American Army personnel. The main problem, we were told, was that the director was in custody as a leading Nazi, and St. John and three of the apostles were in the United States as prisoners of war!

On June 10 we visited the infamous concentration camp at Dachau. Because there are individuals (some of whom purport to be scholars) and groups who today insist that the concentration camps were all a myth, let me quote from a letter I wrote to Sally immediately following our visit to Dachau.

> I spoke with a Lieutenant who came to the camp when it was taken and he showed me pictures that he took with his own camera at that time. They showed bodies, stacked like cordwood, waiting for the crematory. He said the pile included about three thousand bodies.
>
> The Camp is large, on the order of a huge prison. The buildings are largely barracks. Pillboxes (concrete machine gun nests) are situated around the area. There are two barbed wire fences, one of which is electrified. There is a moat running through the camp, and a rail line carrying armored cars. There is a large square where the inmates were gathered to hear the pronouncements of the camp

leader, and where they were made to stand for fifty-hour stretches for punishment. They got one meal a day, which consisted of 100 grams of bread and half a liter of soup. They had no clothes to protect them against the winter. Many, many of the inmates remain in the camp right now and are too sick to move. You see them around the camp and they look like just skin and bones.

Then there is the death house. In the middle is a large shower room without windows. There is a small glass peephole through which an SS man (fanatical Nazi member) could see. The hot shower which the occupants were to receive was to open their pores to the gas. The doors to the room are like huge refrigerator doors and they lock from the outside. This particular gas chamber was constructed but never used because the war ended before it was put to use.

Next door to the gas chamber is another building used for disinfecting the clothing of the victims so that it could be saved and used again. Also next to the gas chamber is a crematory. Large ovens, which are equipped with a big scoop, moved the bodies. Porcelain chips bearing numbers were then placed with the bodies to identify them after cremation. There are innumerable urns in the cellar right now, some of them still containing the ashes of some individual. On the right hand side of the crematory is a room for storing bodies ready for cremation. The day we were there five bodies of persons who had died the day before awaited burial in wooden coffins.

Nothing angers me more today than the bigoted scoundrels who would have a new generation, which has no firsthand experience with the war, believe that all of this never happened. Hitler knew that the big lie could convince those who are predisposed to believe it, and his modern successors rely on the same method. Those of us who know about the concentration camps because we were there have an obligation to speak out.

While we were in Bavaria we were under the impression that we were biding time before we were sent to the Pacific, where the war was still in progress. But on August 8, when we first learned about the atomic bomb that had been dropped on Japan, and then saw the Japanese surrender not long thereafter, we knew we would go home soon. Ironically, we were called upon for one other duty while I was still in

Landshut. After the Germans surrendered, there was a mad dash on the part of the Allies and the Russians to get control of the rocket scientists who had given Germany the expertise that permitted it to launch the original buzz bombs and the V-2's. On September 25 we received an order to find housing for something over 2,000 persons who were the families of the German scientists now being taken to the United States for research. We understood the logic of wanting the scientists, but, on the other hand, we were less than enthusiastic about rescuing them from a destroyed Germany when we had been the objects of their rockets for several months. Naturally, we followed our orders and the scientists did come to the United States. Later, some of them were important to our work with rockets and the space program.

The Army used a point system to decide the order in which we could go home. It was based on length of service, time overseas, presence in battle zones, etc. My hope was that I could get home by Christmas of 1945, and I made it by one week. While waiting I got a week in Switzerland for a rest period. It was the first time in more than two years in which I had been in a country where there was no destruction, the lights were on at night, and the people were well fed. While on that leave I met some incoming American civilians who were going to Germany to work with the occupation forces, but who had not seen any of the carnage. I couldn't help but notice that they were more tolerant of Germany than those of us who had been there for some time. Perhaps it was a good thing for those of us who saw the worst of Hitler's Germany to leave, but we worried a little about whether our successors would appreciate the horrors that had been perpetrated by that demonic man.

My orders home came on November 10, 1945. I was to report to Marseilles, France. The first part of that journey was via Army transport with one other officer. From Aschaffenburg, Germany, we took a small French box car—the famed 40 and 8—to Marseilles. In the box car were one officer (myself) and 30 enlisted men. We all had sleeping bags and K rations to sustain us. By lying with our heads next to the outside of the car and interlacing our legs toward the center of the car we could all stretch out. It wasn't the most comfortable accommodation one could imagine, but we were going home and our spirits were high.

The trip was slow. Tracks were still being repaired, priorities on the use of the tracks had to be observed, and it took us until November 20 to reach Marseilles. Once there, we were housed in a tent city until about 1,500 of us boarded a Victory ship. The sea was rough and it was not a pleasant trip. We arrived at Hampton Roads, Virginia, on Sunday, December 9, and were then sent to Camp Patrick Henry for processing. From there I called both Sally and Mother, and it slowly dawned on me that the war was really over and that I was home.

I was sent to Ft. Meade, Maryland, for discharge, though I could have gone to a point in the Middle West nearer home. The problem was that all my civilian clothes were in Washington and I had to pick them up. Being in Washington gave me a chance to see my old National War Labor Board friends and to talk a little with them about the future.

I was formally discharged on December 16, 1945, two days before my birthday. I took the train to Chicago that night. Most of the trains were full of soldiers, and even coach seats were at a premium. Sally came to Chicago and obtained a room for us at the old LaSalle Hotel. By midafternoon on December 17 we were together again. We had written to each other every day over all that time. The letters at both ends would come in batches—once I got a record fifty of them after hearing almost nothing for two months. Sally got one back marked "deceased," but fortunately she already had mail from me after that date so she knew it wasn't true.

I had accumulated leave time while in the Army, so I remained on the payroll as a captain until early March. That would give us time to figure out what we would do next, and for me to adjust to being a civilian again. By the time I was officially severed from the service I would have served just over three and a half years. I had been overseas for more than two years. I had not worn civilian clothes in all that time, and I was out of touch with changes in American life-styles. The cities I knew abroad were damaged or totally destroyed. Thousands of displaced persons had no homes to go to. Food was scarce and the scars of war would take a long time to heal.

I needed some time to become part of our family again. Sally made that easy. She was, as always, the center of my life. But memories of the war would linger with me always, and there is a camaraderie among men who have served together in dangerous circumstances that is different and special. I felt it most acutely then, and even now, when I hear "Taps" played. For me, there is in that hauntingly beautiful bugle call, which had signaled "lights out" during basic training and later "good-bye" to fallen soldiers, a sense of loneliness, a need for comradeship, a somber realization that death is an ever-brooding presence, and a recognition that love is forever. The words, too often neglected, flow with the music.

Day   is done . . .
Gone   the sun . . .
From-the-lake
From-the-hill
From-the-sky
Rest in peace
Sol dier brave
God   is   nigh . . .

Chapter 6

Starting Over

At Christmastime of 1945, I was a twenty-nine-year-old captain on terminal leave from the Army. We had an income for about three additional months before I was severed from the Army, and there was no driving necessity to find a job immediately. Accordingly, we spent our time in Rockford with Sally's family and in Paw Paw with my family. Using some of our savings, which had accumulated from Sally's earnings and my military allotment, we acquired the only new car available, which happened to be a four-door Hudson. We also made our contribution to the postwar baby boom, conceiving a child who would be born in September of that year.

By February we began to think seriously of where we wanted to live and what we wanted to do. We knew that Sally was pregnant, and we did not anticipate that she would continue to work. Practicing law somewhere was a possibility, but I was still enamored with the field of labor-management relations. If I stayed in that field, however, I wanted to be in the old familiar role of a professional neutral rather than a partisan. If that was the case, the government was the most likely employer, but I had doubts about whether I wanted to work for the government. My prewar experience with the Securities and Exchange Commission was still fresh in my memory, and I strongly suspected that it was more representative of government employment than my very stimulating experience with the National War Labor Board.

To test the water, I went to Washington to look around. I had the strong backing of my Wisconsin friends, plus many of the very well known figures from the NWLB. I shortly had two job offers, one from the Federal Mediation and Conciliation Service, which deals with labor disputes, and one from the Veterans Emergency Housing Program. I decided to take the VEHP job, partly because it paid a little better ($7,500) and partly because I knew the FMCS job would entail a lot of traveling that I didn't relish. Also, VEHP was a new agency that might be more dynamic than an old one, and I would be working on labor aspects of the housing problem.

We returned to Washington in April, even to our old apartment at 1630 Upshur Street NW, but not for long. We needed something bigger and we found it in one of the bedroom communities of Washington. Friends of ours from Wisconsin (Willard and Frances Hurst) had been in Washington during the war and were now returning to Madison. They were able to hold their rental house in Falls Church, Virginia, for us.

The Veterans Emergency Housing Program was headed up by Wilson Wyatt, one of the then-rising young stars in the Democratic Party. He had been a dynamic mayor, and I thought there might be some of the excitement that had accompanied the old NWLB. Unfortunately, it didn't take long to discover that the VEHP was not going anywhere. The people were fine, but the program never really got off the ground and the staff were underemployed. The whole agency would, in something over a year, largely disappear, but long before that I began prospecting for a new job outside the government. As a war veteran I had some priority rights to remain elsewhere in the government, but the idea of depending on employment rights to retain some kind of job had no appeal to me at all.

Meanwhile, and months before we had to make any decision on our future, a bundle of energy whom we named Nancy Jo Fleming, arrived on the scene. She came with a thatch of very dark hair, a loud cry, and enormous energy, which made naps largely unnecessary from the very outset. Given that combination of characteristics she could, and did, command a great deal of attention—but we loved it. Some of my old and now lifelong army friends joined us for Thanksgiving that year, partly to see the new arrival and partly to meet Sally, about whom they had heard a great deal.

As I pursued alternative job possibilities, my prewar friends gave me great support. Fred Bullen, who was then executive director of the New York State Mediation Board, invited me to come to New York to discuss becoming associate director of the board. While I admired Fred greatly, I did not want to live in New York and, though I paid a visit there, I declined to be considered.

While I was considering other possible alternatives, Jack Davis, who was a colleague at VEHP and had previously been a university professor, suggested thinking about joining a faculty somewhere. That was an entirely new and novel idea to me. I immediately asked what he thought I might do, and he replied, "Teach law, that is, after all, your basic discipline." I was dubious. I had done very well in law school, but I was now six years out, I had never practiced law, and I wondered why any faculty would want me.

Shortly thereafter, as if by magic, a letter arrived from Professor Nathan Feinsinger at Wisconsin. Would I be interested in becoming an assistant professor and the executive director of an Industrial Relations Center that the university proposed to create? Though the proposed salary, $6,000, would be less than I was already making, I knew that professorial salaries were not high, and if the job looked really interesting it would be far more attractive than a higher salary in an uninteresting position. It had the additional advantage that I could preserve my nonpartisan status in a volatile field. There was the further fact that the city of Madison was a wonderful place to live, and we would be back in the Middle West, where both Sally and I had our roots as well as our families. Surely, the proposal was worth pursuing.

After an initial exchange of correspondence, I went to Madison to be interviewed for the position. I knew before I went that in the immediate postwar climate (quite unlike the 1990s), labor-management relations were considered the most important domestic problem in the United States. The unions, finally freed from the wage restraints imposed on them during the war and feeling their oats, were striking for better working conditions and wages. Giant industrial unions had developed during the war and were now in a position to shut down major industries in support of their demands. Some of them, the coal miners under the leadership of the formidable John L. Lewis being the prime example, were willing to do so. Industry was uneasy and unsure about the postwar economy and the growing power of unions.

Some universities, Harvard and Wisconsin being prime examples, had long been interested in labor history and the field of labor-management relations. Professor Sumner Slichter, who had a Wisconsin background, was the key figure at Harvard, but he was also developing a new, young cadre of people at Harvard, including John Dunlop, who would later be secretary of labor.

Richard T. Ely published the first book on labor relations in the United States in 1886, and he had come to Wisconsin from Johns Hopkins in the 1890s. In 1904 he brought his former student, John R. Commons, to Wisconsin. Between them they built the country's premier labor program. By the time I came on the scene, Common's coterie featured such people as distinguished theoretist and historian Selig Perlman; Elizabeth Brandeis (the daughter of the Supreme Court Justice) and an authority in her own right on various types of social legislation; and Edwin Witte, an economist who was one of the principal authors of the Social Security Act. Commons, using his graduate students as research assistants, had pioneered a great deal of the social legislation that led to Wisconsin's reputation in that field. In addition, the Law School faculty featured Nathan Feinsinger, who, through his NWLB activities, possessed a national reputation as one of the best of the nation's mediator-arbitrators.

Aside from these outstanding individuals, there were some well-known labor and management programs for practictioners. The School for Workers was a noncredit entity that offered short courses to labor people throughout the year, with longer courses in the summer months. There was also a Management Institute that offered similar programs for business people under the aegis of the School of Commerce. Both were very successful.

In creating an Industrial Relations Center, which was largely the brainchild of Edwin Witte and Nate Feinsinger, the university sought to coordinate the work it was already doing and to cultivate teaching, interdisciplinary research, and extension programs that might contribute to industrial peace. My job, if I took it, would be to bring those things about. My assistant professorship, however, was a title without a real home, the hazards of which we did not fully realize at the time. I would manage the Collective Bargaining Seminar, which was offered jointly by the Economics Department and the Law School, and participate in it.

The more Sally and I thought about taking the Wisconsin position, the more we liked the idea. Though our experience with colleges and universities was confined to our student years, we knew that universities were full of interesting and very bright people, that one had a good deal of independence in one's own work, that there was a built-in cultural life, and that, though we would never get rich as a faculty member, it was a reasonably secure life if one did well. Some academics could, within limits, make additional money as consultants outside the university and, in my case, this might turn out to be so if someone wanted me to arbitrate or mediate labor disputes. And so we accepted the offer, and thereby began a lifetime career in academia, something we had never considered! We bought a three-bedroom house within walking distance of the university for $11,500 and prepared to settle down. Though our salary was only $6,000, we were aided in buying the home by the 2.5 percent mortgage money that was available to veterans.

We were to remain in Madison for five years, from 1947 until 1952. Those were happy years. Sally was at home, but we were able to free some of her time to participate in musical and other activities in the community. Nancy began going to a day-care center in the mornings, and she had good friends among other children in the neighborhood. She was always curious and inclined to wander, so when she went to her day-care center I used to say that she attended a school for wayward girls. She heard me say that and quite naturally repeated it to her friends or to other adults when she was asked about her "school." Since the term "wayward girls" did not at that time attach itself to girls of the most sterling character, it must have shocked some people to hear this term coming out of the mouth of a babe.

In April, 1949, Nancy was joined by a baby brother, to be known thereafter as James Edmund Fleming. We were delighted to have a boy this time, so that we now had "one of each." He proved to be a quieter baby than Nancy, and this somewhat eased Sally's problems as manager of the ranch.

The Industrial Relations Center was designed to function within the land grant college tradition, which meant that it had the tripartite functions of teaching, research, and service. I did no teaching at the outset, though later, when Professor Feinsinger was badly injured in an auto accident, I took over his Labor Law class in the Law School and, when Professor Lescohier retired from the Economics Department, I taught his course in Personnel Management.

In terms of fulfilling our service obligation, we arranged labor-management conferences on subjects of mutual interest. My favorite memory of those conferences involves Professor Walter Morton of the Economics Department. Morton was a cantankerous type who immensely enjoyed upsetting his colleagues. He came to one of our conferences in Milwaukee and, during the question and answer period, offered an observation about coal strikes. He first qualified himself as an expert by stating that he had been the private secretary of one of the mine owners before going into the academic world. He then said that strikes in the coal fields were not caused by the unions, they were caused by the mine owners who, when they found there was too much coal above ground, would instigate a strike to reduce the supply. He confirmed this out of his knowledge gleaned while privy to the work of the mine owner he had worked for. This became the big news of the conference and the *Milwaukee Journal* featured it in a front-page write-up.

The conference had been held on Saturday. On Monday morning my phone rang and I found myself talking to the irate top executive of the coal mine association. He was indignant about the remarks of Professor Morton and insisted on knowing what I was going to do about it. I explained that, during these conferences, people were invited to make their comments, we did not know in advance what they were going to say, and therefore the proper person for him to talk to was Professor Morton. He apparently did this, and I promptly received a call from Professor Morton who disguised his voice and did not initially reveal who he was. He too wanted to know what I was going to do about all this. I repeated my earlier suggestion to the coal mine executive, and Morton then revealed who was calling. A great and happy light then dawned on me. Our colleague who loved to distress others was now in some trouble. I compounded it for him by congratulating him on his forthright comments and told him we had the whole conference recorded and intended to publish the proceedings so that the world would know of his insightful remarks. He pleaded with me not to publish the comments, and I responded that this would be a great shame since this was the outstanding event of the meeting. He was very agitated about what action the mine association might take, and I did nothing to relieve him beyond congratulating him once again on his candor in revealing what was really behind coal strikes.

Eventually the whole matter dropped out of sight, though the coal mine association did issue a blast at Professor Morton in which it denied all of his allegations.

The coordination functions of the center worked much less well. The dean of the School of Commerce, Faye Elwell, was both opposed to and skeptical of the newly formed Industrial Relations Center. He viewed both Witte and Feinsinger as very prolabor, and he suspected that my role was to undermine his Management Institute. I was nevertheless helped by his associate dean (later to become dean), Erwin Gaumnitz, who was always constructive. The Manufacturers Association tended to share Dean Elwell's view and would have joyfully received news of the center's demise. We were never able to completely overcome this obstacle.

Developing interdisciplinary courses and research also proved difficult. I was probably not the right person to do it, since I had no expertise in such disciplines as sociology, psychology, or even economics. But there were other difficulties. Scholars in disparate fields do not easily work together, and they sometimes waste more time trying to do so than if they proceed on their own. We made only very modest progress on that front during my tenure.

Meanwhile, I was becoming increasingly conscious of the doctrine of "publish or perish." I had an LL.B. rather than a Ph.D., and had never written a thesis. That made me a little suspect. The prospect of having to write did not intimidate me, but the question of what I could possibly write about did. My seniors had, by and large, forgotten more about the labor-management field than I knew and I found it hard to think of a subject on which I could write. Yet I did understand that if I was to remain in the academic world, of which I was growing very fond, I could not gain respect as a faculty member without writing.

Two momentary solutions came along. The Committee for Economic Development, a national organization interested in progressive labor relations policies between labor and management, decided to do a series of case studies of companies and unions where there was a good relationship. With Ed Witte fronting for me, we got one of those grants and did a study of the Marathon Paper Company in Wisconsin. I did the work and wrote the study, and it was published under our joint names. Later on, when a congressional committee was studying the use of labor injunctions, we also did a study in that field for the committee. With that much background, I then wrote a lead article in the *Wisconsin Law Review* analyzing the recently passed and controversial Taft-Hartly Act, which modified the original Wagner Act.

Because there were always complaints from industry about what the School for Workers was doing, Edwin B. Fred, who was then president of the university, would periodically ask me to come and see him and he would then use me as an emissary to whomever was complaining. A significant part of the time the complaints came through Frank J. Sensenbrenner, who was both chairman of the Board of Regents (the university's governing board) and the chief executive officer of the Kimberly-Clark Paper Co. Mr. Sensenbrenner would receive complaints from friends in industry or the Manufacturing Association. My periodic visits with him were always good fun from my point of view. He was very conservative, but I liked him and he would periodically tell the president that, despite my unfortunate liberal views, he liked me. Our conversations were always the same. He would voice his latest complaint, which might be that students at the School for Workers were heard singing that revolutionary song, "Solidarity Forever." I would explain that this was, to labor people, like the loyalty song of a fraternity and it didn't mean that they were about to mount the barricades. He would then ask me to tell him about my life. This would all go all right until I came to the part about coming to the University of Wisconsin Law School. He would intervene and ask me who was the dean. I would say, "Lloyd Garrison," and add that I had great respect for the dean although he was no longer at Wisconsin. He would opine that this was my first mistake. Then he would ask what I thought of the LaFollettes and what they had done to Wisconsin. I would respond that I thought they had been enormously good for the people of Wisconsin. This would cause him to observe that this was my second mistake. That would bring him to Wayne Morse, who was by then a U.S. Senator, but who had received one of his degrees from Wisconsin. What did I think of Senator Morse? I would say that I knew him from the NWLB days and that he had been very good to me. To that he would respond by calling to his daughter to go and get the horsewhip—but all in good humor. He never got much satisfaction out of my answers but he was a strong man and, like many strong men, he could respect someone who was not intimidated by him. Since the routine was almost always the same when I saw him, I often wondered whether he asked me for my life history each time to see whether I would tell the same story. Perhaps he was only satisfying his own irritation by castigating my liberal friends. A side benefit of all this was that I got to know the hierarchy of the university quite well. It meant some added work, but it was good for the center and for me.

As an adjunct to the regular program, we accepted two or more groups of German students who came to the United States under the sponsorship of our State Department. The theory of the program was that it would expose the German students to democratic institutions as well as give them knowledge about how labor-management affairs were conducted in the United States. To manage this program, I hired Dan Krueger, who was then a doctoral student in economics. He was enthusiastic, and he worked well with the students. After he graduated, he went to Michigan State, where he became a very well known figure in the world of labor-management relations. Our programs worked well, and they gave the center some additional attention, both within the university and in the state with its large German population.

In many ways, the things that happened to me outside the framework of the university during 1947–52 were as important as the things that took place within the university. All of them came my way because of friends.

To begin with, Nate Feinsinger got me started in the world of arbitration. The two national agencies that maintain panels of available arbitrators are the Federal Mediation and Conciliation Service and the American Arbitration Association. The first is run by the Department of Labor, the second is a private organization. To get on their lists, which are sent to companies and unions desiring arbitrators, one must have experience and the endorsement of people who are known to be competent in the field. The truth was that I had relatively little experience, but I had gilt-edged endorsements from my NWLB friends. The result was that I was put on the list of both organizations, and I began to get some cases. I will write at more length about the field of arbitration; for the moment it is enough to say that this was how I got started.

When I arrived at Wisconsin in 1947, some of the economists who were active in the field organized the Industrial Relations Research Association, of which Ed Witte became the first president. The annual meetings were held in conjunction with the American Economics Association, and the membership soon included all the people across the country who were active in the field. I joined the group and later, from 1951–53, served as its secretary-treasurer. It was Ed Witte who was behind my appointment. It gave me the opportunity to know people all across the country and to become a recognizable name in the field.

In 1950, I was invited by the State Department to go to Germany to deliver a number of lectures in the field of labor-management relations. Also invited was Edwin Young, then a young assistant professor in the Economics Department whose field was labor economics. He was a canny, wise, and wonderfully humorous New Englander from Maine, and we had become and would forever remain good friends. He went on to be the dean of the Liberal Arts College, the chancellor of the Madison campus, and the president of the University of Wisconsin System before he retired.

I was very interested in going back to Germany to see what it looked like a few years after the war. We were to stay about three weeks, and that posed a problem for Sally and our two children. We resolved it by arranging for her to take them to California to visit her family, all of whom were out there by then. They flew out and back, went to Disneyland, saw the Rose Bowl parade, and had a generally good time.

Ed and I were immensely amused to find that we were, in the jargon of the State Department, VIPs (very important persons). No one at home had ever suggested any such thing, but our respect for the good judgment of the State Department went up immediately. Also, we found that this designation entitled us to stay in quarters while we were in Germany that were substantially above the ordinary.

The visit itself proved to be relatively unproductive. The arrangements in Germany had not been worked out in any detail and we were left largely on our own to do as we pleased. To some extent this was all right, because both of us had contacts in Germany and could satisfy some of our own interests. Perhaps more than anything else, we were uneasy about receiving a stipend and having all our expenses paid without doing anything that we thought of as very productive. Still, the fact that we had been invited to do this doubtless helped both of us in establishing ourselves on campus. It also helped in future years when the State Department once more asked me to give a series of lectures in the Scandinavian countries. This time I said I would go only if I could give them a series of topics about which I was willing to talk, and if they would then have their labor attachés in the countries I was to visit find out if anybody had any interest in hearing someone talk about those topics. They agreed, and I went to Norway and Sweden, had a very productive experience, and came home happy.

One event in Norway is worth recalling. Most of the business and academic people in Norway speak English, therefore there was no problem of translation when I spoke to them. But one evening I spoke to a trade union group and many of their members did not speak English; accordingly, I had an interpreter. There was always a question period afterward, and I was not surprised when the first question was: "Why do you Americans treat your black citizens so badly?" This was invariably, and quite justifiably, a question that European audiences asked. I responded that slavery was a sad chapter in our history, that we were making efforts to rectify the situation, but that it was very complicated and would doubtless take some time to make the necessary changes. The interpreter duly translated and we went on from there. Afterward our embassy representative, who was with me and who could understand Norwegian, told me what the interpreter said. Once he had translated what I said, he added: "Don't give this man a hard time, you know what we do to the Laplanders in this country!" Unhappily, we are not the only people in the world who discriminate against fellow citizens.

When the Korean War came along in 1950, President Truman found it necessary to once again try to impose a wage control system that would contain inflation. His initial efforts were not very successful and he therefore persuaded George Taylor, who had been vice chairman of the World War II National War Labor Board, to return as chairman of a new board. George was universally respected by both labor and management, and he had both an innovative mind and a very persuasive way of talking to people. He did not want to come to Washington because he was back in Philadelphia at the Wharton School, and he had no desire to leave. In a one-on-one conversation, the president appealed to George's patriotism, which was very strong. George then agreed to come for "about six months." He told me the story of his conversation with Truman in later years, and he was very moved by it. It demonstrated once again that when the president of the United States asks one of its citizens to take on an assignment in the interest of the country, there is a very strong likelihood that the answer is going to be in the affirmative.

This is relevant to me only because, to my total surprise, George called me and asked me to take a leave from the University of Wisconsin and come down and be the executive director of the board. The executive director was the one who would manage the board's activities and this was not an easy job. The board would be tripartite (labor-management-public), a strong staff had to be built (although some were already in place), and there was always the problem of resisting the pressures exerted by both labor and management to get certain cases in which they were interested on the agenda first. Part of my job was to manage that agenda. When the board members wanted to escape having to give an unpleasant answer to their constituents, they would tell them that they had to see me!

I was, of course, flattered by the call. George Taylor was probably the most respected man in the country in the field. He had always been friendly to me, but he was my senior and a mentor. I was relatively inexperienced in operating at such a high level in the hierarchy. Ultimately, we reached an agreement that I would come down and remain, but only as long as he was there. Putting a time limit on it was important to me, because it was hard to get a leave for a longer period and, anyway, I only wanted to do it for a man of the caliber of Taylor. Holding that position naturally enhanced my stature in the field. I dealt with leading labor and management people from a position of authority, and it was therefore important from their standpoint to know me.

I went down in April and remained until September. Sally and the children came down for the summer and we found a place in Falls Church that we could rent for that period. The work was hard and the hours were long, but it was exciting and I learned a great deal from it. I remember an occasion when a major union president came into my office, beat on the table, and demanded that I pull his case from well down in the pile and put it at the top. When I pointed out that I was under orders not to do this, he only pounded harder. After this went on for about fifteen minutes and neither of us changed position, he looked at his watch and said, "I have to catch a train to New York." We then shook hands, and he said he had enjoyed talking to me. I had reaffirmed an old lesson: disputatious situations are sometimes pure theater.

By the end of the summer, Dr. Taylor had the board functioning smoothly and he wanted to leave. The president reluctantly agreed. His successor would be Professor Feinsinger, who was already one of the public members. Nate and I agreed that I should carry out the original understanding that I would stay only as long as Taylor did. We thought it unwise for two of us from Wisconsin to be in sensitive positions, and, anyway, it was time for me to get back to the center. I was also anxious to be with the family back in Madison.

When the time came to leave Washington, the board members sponsored a farewell dinner for Dr. Taylor. Quietly, arrangements were made for President Truman to attend. This was sensitive because though the president wanted to come in order to return the favor Dr. Taylor had done for him, it was soon after an attempt on his life by dissatisfied Puerto Ricans, and the Secret Service was reluctant to have him go out. An agreement was finally made that he would come, but only if no one except the two or three of us who were in on it knew about it. This raised an interesting question. The board members discussed whether they should bring their wives to the dinner and were inclined not to because most of them were not in the city. I knew they would regret not bringing their wives if the president was coming, but I couldn't tell them that. Taylor himself did not know, but I knew that he always liked to have his wife at such affairs, so I told the other board members that George would want his wife to come and I was sure he would be pleased if they brought theirs. This they agreed to do.

The dinner was held in the Statler Hotel. The arrangement was that the president would not come for dinner, but would come right after dinner. The liaison man at the White House was Harold Enarson, who later became president of Cleveland State University and then Ohio State University. Our friendship began at that time and has continued ever since. I was to slip out at the appropriate time, signal the approach of the president, and the Secret Service would get him through the lobby and up to the second floor.

It all went like clockwork. As I watched the lobby I saw the Secret Service clear everyone out while they brought the president through. He came to the second floor, was announced, and found a seat next to George. Dr. Taylor was immensely pleased, as were the board members and their wives. So were Sally and I. The president spoke briefly, praising and thanking George, expressing his gratitude to the other board members, and saying how much he hated all the fuss that had to be made to get him from the White House to the hotel and then upstairs. His speech was easy, warm, and humble. Even those in the room who would not have agreed with any of his policies were impressed. Looking back on that evening, it is not hard to understand why Truman's stature has grown so since he left the White House. Despite a rocky start, he remained a man of the people, and this has finally been appreciated.

We returned to the campus in the fall of 1951 and resumed our usual pattern of life. I was now considerably better known in the world of labor-management relations and had the added confidence of having successfully managed a large and contentious organization. Still, there were problems with the concept of the Industrial Relations Center. Fostering a series of labor-management conferences was not really a very successful way of promoting industrial peace. There was no real way to coordinate the work of the School for Workers and the Management Institutes because each preferred a separate course. Interdisciplinary teaching could be encouraged, and there were examples, like the joint seminar between the Law School and the Economics Department that were highly successful, but much of this would probably happen without the existence of the center. There were teaching opportunities for me, but the Law School did not need another professor of law, and I was not an economist likely to find a home in that department. The university was ready to make me an associate professor and give me a higher salary, but I knew that a professor without a home base occupied an uneasy post. I had become a useful citizen of the university in the sense that the president found it handy to have me explain to some of his irate constituents why things weren't as bad as they thought and I rather enjoyed this, but it was not the stuff of a long career. I was becoming a utility player on the university team, but not one with professorial prospects.

Despite these reservations, we loved Madison and the university. It was, and is, a great place to be. We had good friends whose children were the same age as ours, the many activities on the campus were endlessly interesting, and my mother was living in nearby Beloit by then. Besides all this, we had learned a great deal about universities and it was a life that we wished to continue. The real question was whether we should look for a different job within the University of Wisconsin or look for a law school professorship elsewhere. While we were still thinking about that problem, the answer came along in an unexpected fashion.

The University of Illinois had a separate school called the Institute of Labor and Industrial Relations. It possessed a very substantial budget, a well-established research program, and an interdisciplinary faculty composed of economists, sociologists, psychologists, political scientists, and extension personnel equipped to operate separately with labor and management people. Shortly after the first of the year in 1952, I received a letter from a search committee at the institute asking if I would be interested in the directorship. Without knowing how seriously to take the invitation, or even whether I would be interested when I knew more about it, I accepted the invitation.

The initial visit went well, partly because I already knew a number of the members of their faculty. George Stoddard, who was then the president of the University of Illinois, invited me to have lunch with him in Chicago. Our meeting went well, and he offered me the job. I would be promoted to full professor (Wisconsin had just approved an associate professorship for me), and a salary of $12,000 on a twelve-month basis. I would have tenure in the school.

For all of the reasons I have already cited, it was very hard for us to consider leaving Wisconsin. Had the Law School been able to offer me a professorship, we might never have gone, but it had no need for another person in labor law, and it was increasingly clear to me that the Industrial Relations Center, as constituted, was not viable in the long run. This was confirmed when, not too long after we left, it was converted into a research center, in which role it has done very well.

There were, of course, some attractions in going to Illinois aside from the higher salary and the tenured professorship. Both Sally and I were natives of Illinois and we would, in a sense, be going home. Our children were still preschool, therefore their schooling would not be disrupted by the move and they were too young to make much of it one way or the other. Illinois was a bigger, wealthier, and more populous state than Wisconsin, and had a far larger industrial base. And so, in the end, we accepted the position effective September 1, 1952.

Chapter 7

The Land of Lincoln

We spent much of the summer of 1952 painting and refurbishing our house in Madison in order to sell it. The real estate market wasn't particularly good (it never seemed to be when we were wanting to sell a house!), and we finally sold it at only a little more than we had paid for it.

By the end of August we were in Urbana, living in a university-owned home on Vermont Street. It was walking distance from the university, which I liked, and in a fine neighborhood. The Bernt Larsons (he was in Engineering) lived across the street, and they were raising five boys, two of whom closely paralleled the ages of our children. Our cocker spaniel (Taffy), who was with us all our years in Illinois, was a pup from a brood their dog produced. We often picnicked with the Larsons and others, particularly on the Fourth of July—occasions when the day wound up with 72,000 people in the Illinois Stadium for a fireworks display. Our families became close friends and remain so to this day.

The Institute of Labor and Industrial Relations was, in many ways, a much more comfortable post than the one I left in Wisconsin. It had far better funding, and it had its own faculty, drawn from such disciplines as economics, political science, psychology, sociology, and I was, of course, a lawyer. Its students at that time were all at the master's level, there was a substantial and well-funded research program, and there was also a large noncredit extension program that was separately offered for management and labor people. For purely historical reasons, there was no conflict in the extension field between the institute and the Business School, and I spent little or no time defending what we did. Because it was relatively new, there was, nevertheless, a problem of establishing the institute's standing in the university's scheme of things, and it was to that end that I spent a good deal of time thinking of ways to give it a favorable image.

President Stoddard was very friendly from the outset. Soon after we arrived, he invited us, along with some other new faculty members, to a barbecue at the president's house and that helped. The provost, Coleman Griffith, was the man to whom I reported and he too was very friendly. Unfortunately, though it did not affect either the institute or me, both Stoddard and Griffith left office at the end of that academic year.

Stoddard was an outspoken and courageous man who clashed with the Board of Governors over their earlier firing of the dean of the Business School, and later over the drug, Krebiozen. It was an alleged cancer cure and was sponsored by a distinguished member of the Illinois medical faculty who was simply mistaken. The evidence had become increasingly clear that the drug had no usefulness, and Stoddard had the courage to say so and to stop the participation of the university in it. Given the nature of cancer, public reaction to the discontinuation of any drug that is alleged to have value tends to be adverse. The board, already uneasy with Stoddard, fired him and the provost then resigned. It was something I thought of later when I was asked to become a university president—not a very secure position!

Quite fortuitously, something happened that first year that greatly enhanced the institute's standing in the community. I read in the paper that Frances Perkins, Franklin Roosevelt's secretary of labor, and later, under Truman, a member of the Civil Service Commission in Washington, was about to retire from the CSC. I had known her very casually, the way a quite junior member of an establishment knows one of the top officials, when I was with the National War Labor Board. I knew that she was a very effective speaker and that her political experience spanned the years of Theodore Roosevelt, Al Smith, and Franklin Roosevelt. She had known the great and the near great from around the world, and she was clearly the highest ranking woman in office.

It occurred to me that Madam Perkins might be induced to come to the University of Illinois for a lecture series after she retired. I suspected that the chances of getting her to do this would be far greater if I gave her some detail as to the nature of the lectures, so I listed about a dozen potential talks on the great people she had worked with. Finally, I suggested that I would be in Washington shortly and that if she was interested perhaps we could get together and talk about it. All of this went to her in a letter, to which she promptly responded by inviting me to come and have dinner with her at her home. Her daughter was also at dinner, the only time I ever met her. In any event, she liked the idea and she agreed to come. The provost sealed the appointment and gave us some additional support for the lectures.

Madam Perkins spent six weeks on campus and took the university by storm. It is difficult for anyone to lecture over a period of six weeks and still draw large crowds, but hers only kept getting larger. More important, from the institute's standpoint, she put us very prominently on the local map. Top people from around the university came and her talks were fascinating. A special benefit, from the standpoint of our family, was that we got to know her very well by having her at the house a number of times while she was on campus. She was a great and fascinating woman. Though people thought of her as quite liberal, perhaps even radical, and for her time perhaps she was, she had a firmly fixed set of values that would be considered quite conservative now. I remember, for instance, that when I tried to get her to lecture on Harold Ickes, the highly combative secretary of interior during the Roosevelt years, she wouldn't do it. Mr. Ickes had by then said some unkind things about her in his memoirs, and she would not respond in kind. She said to me, "No, I am not going to talk about Harold. You have to understand that what he said depended largely on what he had for breakfast!" I found that while she would not hesitate to differ with a position that someone took, she would not engage in mudslinging. Would that there were more like her in the world.

Her lectures were such a success at Illinois that Cornell University then invited her to come to Ithaca. She was so successful at Cornell that they kept her there the rest of her life. When I found that I was going to be in New York, I would frequently inquire whether she might be in the city, where she maintained an apartment. When she was, we would have lunch. Late in her life I teased her a little about the fact that she resided in a home Cornell maintained for top-notch male students. The students could ask any faculty member to come and live with them, and they repeatedly chose her. She responded to my teasing by saying, "You know, I think the real reason they choose to have me is that my eyesight is no longer very good!"

Madam Perkins came back to Illinois to lecture a time or two in the next five or six years, and when she did she would always come to the house to see the family. By then our youngest child, Betsy, had been born in 1954 and was about three years old. Betsy would go with me to pick up Madam Perkins, and invariably Madam Perkins would have a little gift for her. One night when she first got in the car, Betsy said to her, "What did you bring me tonight?" Later I gave Betsy a little lecture about not asking people what they had brought as a gift. The next time we went, Betsy changed the theme. She said, "I'm not going to ask you tonight what you brought to me!" One can never quite conquer children.

Madam Perkins had some wonderful stories about the political figures she had known and worked with. Somewhat to my surprise, she seemed more attached to Al Smith, when she worked with him during his gubernatorial years in New York, than to FDR. But she had fascinating stories about Roosevelt, including one about the time he made his famous speech to the Daughters of the American Revolution. Before he made the speech, she said, he called her over and read its famous opening line—which was, "Fellow Immigrants"—to her and asked what she thought about it. She said his eyes were dancing and she knew he had not the slightest intention of changing it, no matter what she said. Nevertheless, she went through the ritual of saying that it would almost certainly offend the members of the DAR and that this might not be either necessary or politically wise. To this he only laughed and went on to another subject. And he did, of course, use that now famous salutation.

There were a number of other famous guests of the university whom it was my good luck to meet and to know during those years. Part of that time I was the chairman of the University Lectures Committee and it was my duty to meet and entertain some of the visitors. When William O. Douglas, then one of the leading justices of the Supreme Court, arrived, it turned out that he needed a clean shirt, there was no time to go to the store, and mine were too big for him. Fortunately, one of our neighbors was the right size and loaned the justice his shirt for the night.

Joseph Welch, famous for his rebuke of Senator Joseph McCarthy in the hearings that the Senate held in connection with the Army, came and told me a wonderful story about Senator Dirksen, who was one of the senators conducting the hearing. Prior to the hearings, the committee had held a private meeting to discuss procedures and timing. The press made such a fuss about the privacy of the meeting that the committee decided to make a transcript of the private session publicly available. Before doing so, however, it took the precaution of sending a copy to each of the senators *to insure accuracy*. It transpired that, in the original transcript, Senator Dirksen had said that he "wanted just a few minutes to *praise* Senator McCarthy." When he returned the laundered version, his statement read that he "wanted just a few minutes to *appraise* Senator McCarthy."

John Kennedy came to the campus the year after he lost his bid to become the running mate of Adlai Stevenson in the 1956 presidential race. We used a university plane to fly him down from Chicago, and he came in midafternoon, thus giving me a few hours with him before his speech that evening. I found him entirely engaging, but I was amazed at how quickly he turned to politics. We did not know each other prior to that meeting, yet he almost immediately turned to the question of whether I thought people in Illinois would support a Catholic for the presidency. Though I knew that university cities are never a good weathervane for what the general population will do, I told him I thought Catholicism would not be a bar. He talked about his loss of the vice presidency but was by then inclined to think that it was a good thing because Stevenson's candidacy was doomed to defeat and Kennedy had not been on the ticket. I saw him on one or two occasions after that day, while he was president, but never with such an opportunity for leisurely talk.

The mid-1950s were, of course, the years of the McCarthy terrorism. While there were certainly Communists in our society (I knew some of them in the labor movement), the senator seemed to find them under every bed. His own excesses ultimately brought him down, though in the beginning thousands of good, solid, honest conservatives thought he was performing a great service for the country. The denouement came with the Senate hearings. I remember that I had been telling my beloved family members in Paw Paw, practically all of whom were solid Republicans, that he was a very dangerous man. They tolerated my views but did not accept them. Then came the televised hearings. I saw and watched a part of one day of it with my mother's sister, Addie. At the end of the day of viewing a dark, scowling, rude Senator McCarthy, she said, "I don't like that man any more. He is not a nice man." My aunt might have been conservative, but she was also a person who valued decency and good manners, and she suddenly saw the crudity and cruelty of the senator.

Despite the fact that my attention during those years had to be focused on the university, I think back on them now as essentially family years in which our children were growing up. Nancy entered school there and finished high school in Champaign-Urbana. Jim went through his sophomore year in high school there, and Betsy was to be in the eighth grade when we left. We had, after our first two years in Champaign-Urbana, built a house in Champaign on LaSell Drive where we lived the balance of the time we were in Illinois.

It was in Illinois that all of the children learned to ride their bicycles, stayed overnight with friends (reluctantly at first!), learned to swim and dive under Sally's tutelage, joined the boy and girl scouts, took part in school events, and explored their musical talents. Nancy was born with perfect pitch, and once she heard something could go to the piano and play it. To get her to learn to read notes, her teacher had to give her pieces she had never heard because she would otherwise play the music by ear. Jim experimented with several instruments before finally settling on the guitar. In his adult career as a radio performer, his program has always been a combination of talk and music. Betsy inherited some of her father's genes (which were not very strong on the side of music), but she too plays the guitar. Sally had played the violin since she was a child and was an accomplished musician. She also sang in the Presbyterian church choir a part of the time, played with various musical groups, and was active in civic affairs, including being one of the founding members of the Urban League in Urbana. When we would all sing in the car, the children would occasionally say to me, "Daddy, watch our hands, and when they go up, you go up, and when they go down, you go down!" They knew who had the musical talent in the family.

During our Illinois years, we always took vacations in different parts of the country, partly to give the children some idea of the size and diversity of our nation. For several years we went to the YMCA camp in Estes Park, Colorado. As born-and-bred midwesterners, the Rocky Mountains always gave us a thrill and we had wonderful times exploring the trails. At other times we vacationed in Vermont, Kitty Hawk (where we all first experienced the surf), Florida, in the Indian Rocks Beach area, the Mobile, Alabama area, and Wisconsin, near Tomahawk, several times. We seldom took our dog, Taffy, with us, which meant that we had to take him to a kennel. Betsy worried about this, so I made up an elaborate story about how Taffy, too, was going to a camp where they had dog races, swimming, and other entertainment that he would greatly enjoy. When we returned she and I would go to the kennel to get Taffy and he would, of course, greet her with enormous enthusiasm, which served to convince her that he had, indeed, had a good time at his camp.

Whenever we were traveling the children would tire of being in the car and we would have to devise ways of distracting them. Sally, with the patience of Job, would let Betsy comb her hair for more time than I could believe. We could distract the other children by playing games in which we would sight something outside and ahead of the car and then the others had to guess what it was. As a hint, the first letter of the object had to be given. This worked quite well, except that Betsy, who was too young to spell, wanted to play. She would give us a letter, but it had nothing to do with what she was thinking of. That complicated the game a little, but she usually picked something quite obvious, and we could avoid guessing it long enough to satisfy her turn. Our driving was further complicated by the fact that Nancy was prone to car sickness (as I had been when I was young), and she had to ride in the front seat. Sally and I would trade off driving, but, in order to keep Jim and Betsy at relative peace in the back seat, whichever one of us wasn't driving had to sit between them. Ah, the joys of parenthood!

One summer I was asked to join some other professional colleagues in conducting minimum wage hearings in Puerto Rico, so the whole family went. Betsy was only about two and had all the restless energy of a normal two-year-old. There had been a recent hurricane not long before we arrived, and the day we landed the newspaper headline read, "Hurricane Betsy does $2,000,000 Damage." We should have kept that headline to remind us of the ways of our small daughter.

Near the end of our time at the University of Illinois, I had a sabbatical coming, and we wanted to take the family to Europe. At the same time I was working on a book on arbitration. The children, having been brought up in an academic community, were quite familiar with the idea of sabbaticals, and they knew it often meant a trip abroad. The trouble was, I was writing a book that required the resources of our own Law Library, but this was not compatible with being in Europe. This disappointed the children, but we all reached an agreement that I would take a semester off, finish my book, and then we would all spend two months in Europe during the summer. Nancy was just then finishing high school and would be going to college the following year, Jim was two years behind her, and Betsy was another five years younger than Jim, which meant that she was about seven years old at the time. We wondered how she would fare in Europe, but our fears never materialized. She was the life of the party; perhaps she didn't quite understand about foreign languages and readily assumed everyone spoke English—at least at her level.

We started in London, flew to Paris, drove down into Switzerland and then back up through Germany into Belgium and Holland, and then flew back to England and visited Scotland. It was a wonderful trip. Nancy, and Jim to a lesser extent, knew French quite well and could carry us in the French-speaking countries. I knew enough German to get us around in Germany and parts of Switzerland, and for the rest, English would do. We made few reservations, except in the big cities, and simply found places to stay overnight, usually outside cities. At lunchtime, we would go to a market and get wonderful bread, cheese, fruit, some meat for sandwiches, and some soda pop of one variety or another. It was then easy to find a small park or roadside stop where we could eat. Sally and I somewhat wistfully realized that it was probably the last time all our children would be free at the same time to take such a vacation, what with Nancy going away to school in the fall. We hoped the trip would give the children the desire to travel around the world and see different cultures and different ways of living.

Things went well at the institute and I was also doing a good bit of arbitrating labor disputes, including sitting on various kinds of federal boards. One of those was the Atomic Energy Labor-Management Advisory Committee. This was a small group of experienced arbitrator-mediators who usually worked in groups of three. Strikes were not permitted in atomic installations, for reasons of safety, and it was the task of our little group to go to the installation, hear the contentions of the parties, and either achieve a settlement or recommend one the government would then pressure the parties to accept. It was a presidential appointment, and I was first asked to serve by Cy Ching, the grand old man of the field, who was then serving as chairman. When he called he wanted to know whether I would accept an appointment to the committee *if invited*. I asked about the time it would require, which was only periodic, and then said I would serve if asked, but I also said that it seemed to me unlikely that President Eisenhower would appoint me since I had held similar appointments under President Truman. Cy assured me that the president had told him there would be no political qualifications. Thereafter, a few months passed, which was not unusual because the appointment required a rigid Q security clearance. One day when I was out of town, Sally received a telephone call from a friend at the university saying that Senator Dirksen was inquiring about my political party affiliation with respect to some federal appointment. I had told her that if this ever happened to state the truth, which was that I always thought of myself as an independent but that this was usually spelled Democrat. Not long thereafter I got an embarrassed call from Cy saying that Senator Dirksen had vetoed me and that the appointment could not be made. This didn't bother me, since I always suspected it would happen, and I had enough to do without one more thing. About a year later I got another call from Cy. His inquiry was essentially the same as it had been earlier. Cy was aging by this time, and, as I listened, I thought he had simply forgotten the earlier episode. While I puzzled over how to respond, Cy's much younger wife came on the telephone and tactfully let me know that this was a new inquiry. I asked about Senator Dirksen's objections and was told that Ike had told Cy that this time he wouldn't ask the senator. So I became a member of the panel. I served for several years, during which time we visited installations all over the country. The best part of it was making friends with some of the many fine arbitrator-mediators from all over the country. One of them was Father Leo Brown, a Jesuit out of St. Louis, who was loved and respected by all of us.

Meanwhile, sometime in early 1957, I met the incoming dean of the Law School at Illinois, Russel Sullivan, in President Henry's office, where both of us had come for appointments. Sullivan was a long-time member of the Illinois faculty, he taught labor law and constitutional law, and he was succeeding the retiring dean. As we chatted, he told me he was going to drop labor law and teach only constitutional law after becoming dean, and he asked who I knew around the country who might be interested in becoming a member of the faculty to teach labor law. I mentioned a couple of names, and he then said, "What we would really like is for you to come over to the Law School full time. Would you consider it, and if so, would you come over and talk to the current dean and myself about it?" I said I always made it a practice to talk to anyone about anything interesting, and I would come and see them. Shortly thereafter we got together and they made me a very attractive offer. I would become a full professor of law, would have summers off, could retain my present salary (which was for twelve months), would teach labor law, torts, and a couple of seminars in collective bargaining and arbitration, and could continue my arbitration work.

The package was very attractive to me. The law was always my first love, I could have summers off to write and arbitrate, I could teach the courses I knew best, and I would have no more administrative duties. I had never had time to write while I was an administrator, and while I had once wondered what I could possibly write about, it suddenly dawned on me that I was both an academic with the desire to write and an experienced practictioner in the labor field who knew the problems of the real world. I could write about those problems. It was also a good time for me to leave the institute. I had just gotten enough private commitments of money for a new building to cause the administration to make a commitment to it once we raised a little more, and I thought that was perhaps the the last contribution I could make to the institute. I was then forty years old, about to be forty-one at the end of the year. One of Russ Sullivan's arguments in favor of my coming over to the Law School was that it would probably be the last move I would make. I didn't think much about that one way or the other. We were leading a very happy life in Champaign-Urbana, we had many friends, and we had no real desire to leave.

I remained director of the institute through 1958, while they searched for a new director, and at the same time took over the Law School appointment with a somewhat reduced schedule for that year.

The Law School years were very happy ones for me. I liked my colleagues, the environment, the teaching, the freedom from administrative chores (which was not total since I continued to serve on a number of universitywide committees), and I started to write. Between 1958 and 1964, I wrote a series of articles that appeared in the Stanford, Michigan, Virginia, and other law journals. I also wrote a book on labor arbitration and coauthored another with Murray Edelman, of the institute faculty, both of which were published by the University of Illinois Press. Having summers off made possible the sabbatical trip we took to Europe.

Toward the end of 1959 David Henry, who was then president of the University of Illinois, asked me to go to India for six weeks on a university assignment. At the end of World War II, India was indebted to the United States and was unable to pay except in rupees. The upshot was that our government agreed to forgive the debt, or portions thereof, if the Indian government would use the rupees to develop several land grant–type agricultural colleges in India. When such an agreement was reached, several of the midwestern colleges of agriculture were asked to help supervise their development. Illinois was one of the schools involved, and its project was the Agricultural University of Uttar Pradesh. The problem I was to address was that two of the terms of the original agreement had not been carried out. One had to do with the autonomy of the university from the government, and the other was that the main support for the college was to come from the deeding of a 15,000-acre state-owned sugar beet farm to the university so that it could largely support itself. The university would continue my salary while I was gone, the U.S. State Department would pay all my expenses, and, as an incentive to go, I could go round-the-world by traveling one direction going and the other direction coming back. This would be no more expensive since Illinois was halfway from India no matter which way one went.

When Sally and I talked about it we decided that if she could go too it would probably be the one time in our lives (little did we know) when we would have a chance to go around the world. Except for our trip to Europe with the family, she had not had the same opportunities I had had to travel, and we viewed this as a golden opportunity. Our children were then old enough to stay with a young graduate couple who agreed to come and live at the house. We would pay all of Sally's expenses. If we went the day after Christmas, we would be back early in February and colleagues would fill in for me at the Law School in the meantime.

We flew to Paris immediately after Christmas, then, after a day in Paris, on to Rome where we had New Year's dinner with an old friend at the American embassy. Knowing that I would be out in the countryside in India much of the time, and that this would not be as interesting to Sally as some of the other things she might do, we had arranged that she would pick up a tour of the Holy Land by flying to Istanbul and then going roundabout into Turkey, Greece, Jordan, Syria, Egypt, and Israel. It was, of course, all complicated by the fact that one could not go directly into Israel from the Arab countries. Part of the time, including the last leg of the trip to India, she would be on her own and she had never traveled abroad alone. Perhaps she will sometime write of her experiences during that time. A very attractive American female, traveling alone, is not without adventures.

When Sally and I parted in Rome, our understanding was that she would rejoin me in Delhi, India, and that we would then start the return home. During the time we were apart, which must have been two or three weeks, we knew little about each other because we had no advance addresses that were very reliable.

My recollection is that when I arrived in Delhi, I was met by someone from the American embassy and was then taken to a hotel. The next day or two were taken up in talks with the embassy people and in meeting Ellsworth Bunker, who was then the American ambassador to India. The problems I was to address were well known to the embassy people, and I was asssured that there was no doubt about the nature of the agreement and that it had not been fully carried out.

There was an American advisor, employed by the University of Illinois, at the site of the University of Uttar Pradesh, and I was to stay with him. He and his wife proved to be delightful people, and I thoroughly enjoyed being with them. Officially, I was there to advise the vice chancellor (under the British system, which the Indians had adopted, the vice chancellor is the equivalent of an American university president). He was an Anglo-Indian, married to a British woman, and they had two children.

The vice chancellor welcomed me and in turn offered advice as to things I might do. I immediately set about doing them, sometimes in his presence and sometimes on my own. After watching the rather lethargic civil service operatives for a day or two, I concluded that the reason the autonomy bill hadn't been signed by the governor might be that it had never reached his office. Accordingly, I began a search for it and, to my astonishment, found it within a day. Sure enough, it had never been transmitted to the governor. To my further astonishment, I persuaded them to give it to me and I then took it to the governor. Since I was not entirely sure of his willingness to have the state of Uttar Pradesh give the university autonomy, I opened our conversation by asking about the bill. He assured me that the state had indeed agreed to such an arrangement, and that the bill had been passed by the legislature but never given to him. I thereupon produced the bill, and he was in the very awkward position of either signing it or betraying that he had no intention of doing so. He signed.

That left me with the other problem, how to get the 15,000-acre sugar beet farm deeded over to the university. That one baffled me for most of the time I was there. Everyone agreed that the transfer had been promised and no one purported to be opposed to it. But it didn't happen. I had never been in a negotiation where everyone agreed, but no one seemed to know why the agreement could not be consummated. I kept prowling around and was at one point told that the secretary of agriculture had the power to make the conveyance. I went to his office, was told that he wasn't in, and they were not sure when he would be. Having anticipated this, I brought along a large book, announced that I had nothing else to do for the next few days, and I would therefore be glad to wait. After an hour or two of this, the secretary suddenly appeared and agreed to see me. He, too, was full of assurances about the matter but said he had no one to draw a deed. I promptly assured him that I was a lawyer and that I would be glad to draw a deed. I was comfortable in making this offer, despite my lack of knowledge of Indian law, because I was confident he would never call my bluff. He agreed to look into the matter. Still, nothing happened.

Finally, I went to see the civil service counterpart of the governor (another copy of the English system). He had been helpful to me and I didn't know where else to go. It was obvious that someone, somewhere, didn't want the land transferred, but I could not find out who it was. He made what I thought was a very helpful suggestion. Consummation of the deal required approval by both the university regents and then the state government, in that order. As we looked at the calendar of my remaining time, the problem was that the regents met the day after the governor and his cabinet met and this would throw the procedure out of order. Thereafter, I would be out of the country, a result I had begun to suspect was the devout hope of someone who remained nameless. My friend, the civil servant, then made his suggestion. He would put on the agenda approval of the land transfer when the cabinet met, but they would not announce that they had approved it until the regents acted. Confident that I had solved the problem, I then attended the meeting of the regents shortly thereafter, in fact the day before I was to leave. When called upon by the vice chancellor, I proudly related that the problem was solved and that all that was required was a vote of the regents, which I assumed would take place immediately. I was stunned when the vice chancellor thanked me profusely and said he would appoint a committee to study the matter! The meeting was then adjourned.

More in sorrow than in anger, I promptly sought out the vice chancellor. It was clear to me that he was the culprit. All the time that I was supposed to be helping him, he had no intention of letting anything happen. So I simply told him that it was clear he was blocking the transfer and that he at least owed me an explanation of why he had done this. His explanation called for compassion if not admiration. He was a professional civil servant of the Indian government, and he had simply been posted to the position of vice chancellor. He knew nothing whatsoever about agriculture and he feared that if the farm was transferred he would have to run it efficiently. As long as it remained with the state government, the government would have to run the farm and take the responsibility for it. If he failed, it would ruin his career. What he really wanted was an assignment in Switzerland on behalf of his government. He could then send his children to Swiss schools.

There was nothing further I could do before departure. I reported to the University of Illinois that we at least now knew why the farm had never been transferred, and that to make this happen would almost certainly require the appointment of a new vice chancellor. It took another year to solve the problem, but I had no further contact with it.

Sally was to join me in Delhi on what turned out to be the very day that Queen Elizabeth was to arrive for a state visit. Such an occasion calls for several *million* people to line the roads leading to the city. I thought I would tell Sally that I hadn't had much time to arrange a greeting party, but the few million that were there would have to do.

When I got to the airport, I found out that her plane was down somewhere with mechanical problems and would not arrive that day. Nor did anyone know when it might arrive. I then searched out all the other incoming flights and found there were no others that day. The further problem was that Sally did not know where I was staying in Delhi, and now I did not know when to come and meet her. I went to all the other airlines on which she might arrive, told them my plight, gave them an address and a telephone number, and asked that they page incoming flights with a call for her. Then I stayed near the phone in my room. Sure enough, the next day I got a call from her saying that she was at the airport and would come to the hotel along with an Australian journalist she had met. When she arrived, she said we must leave immediately to see the Queen because her journalist friend, who apparently carried all sorts of different identifications, knew where we could see her up close. I thought that for a novice traveler she had matured with amazing speed. Anyway, we did go to the proper spot, there was almost no one else there, and the Queen and Prince Philip passed within ten feet of us.

Sally had only a day or two in India, but we did manage to visit the Taj Mahal and to see some of the beauties of Delhi. Going home we flew to Bangkok for a couple of days, then on to Hong Kong, Japan, Hawaii, and finally home. It had been a marvelous experience for us. Aside from a few travails, Sally had greatly enjoyed her time in the Middle East, and the children were in fine shape when we reached home.

Sometime in the early fall of 1963, I received a letter from Fred Harrington, who was then the president of the University of Wisconsin. Would I be interested in coming to talk to him about becoming the chancellor of the University in Madison? This was a new position, resulting from the fact that the university was expanding into several campuses over which the president would preside, while chancellors would head the individual campuses.

Wisconsin had always been dear to our hearts. Many of our old friends were there. The city of Madison is beautiful and, with its lakes, is enormously attractive. I was always more attuned to the liberal political climate of Wisconsin than the more conservative atmosphere in Illinois. Nancy had just started at Beloit College, which was only fifty miles away, and my mother, who had remarried, was also living in Beloit. And I was, of course, flattered that I would be considered for the position.

The other side of the coin was that we had always been happy in Champaign-Urbana, we had many close friends there, I liked being a professor with summers off, our children, Jim and Betsy, were happy and would be reluctant to leave, and we would diminish our income because I could probably no longer arbitrate. It would also mean largely abandoning my law school interests.

Still, there was never any doubt about going to Madison to talk with people there. I strongly suspected that my old friend Ed Young, who was then dean of the Liberal Arts and Science College at Madison, was behind all this, and I am sure he was.

There were a number of conversations over the next few weeks. Though Fred Harrington and I did not know each other at that time, we proved immediately compatible, and that was a major consideration to me.

Eventually the deed was done. We would go to Madison on September 1, 1964. Jim was greatly depressed by the move because it would deprive him of his last two years in University High School, where he was very happy. Betsy was younger and was less entrenched, but Sally and I realized we were doing something both the children probably would prefer us not to do. We thought we knew that they would nevertheless adjust to the new situation and not be hurt by it.

We had left Madison in 1952 for Illinois with regret. Now we would leave Illinois with regret to return to Madison. I was forty-five years old at the time and would be forty-six at the end of the year. Surely, I thought, this would be our last career move.

Chapter 8

Moonlighting

Because university professors acquire expertise in their various fields, they are frequently asked to make speeches, join in community ventures, serve on peer panels, or participate in a variety of other things. Within stated limits, they may also enhance their incomes by paid consulting or some other application of their knowledge. The slang term for this is *moonlighting,* and in the twenty-year period between the time I joined the faculty at the University of Wisconsin in 1947 and 1967, when I became president of the University of Michigan, I moonlighted as a professional arbitrator and mediator of labor disputes. In my last active year as an arbitrator, 1966, I was president of the National Academy of Arbitrators, which is the association of professionals in the field. In the period after 1967, I had time to engage in this activity on only a very limited basis.

I got into the field initially because of my experience with the National War Labor Board just before I went into the Army. I was, nevertheless, a relative neophyte because my experience had been so limited. After the war, my friends for that period gave me their endorsement and, since a number of them were well established in the field, their help was indispensable.

Despite the somewhat accidental way I stumbled into the field, it represented an area of public policy in which I had long been interested. While I was in law school I always liked best the public law courses. Franklin Roosevelt was in the White House, a changing Supreme Court was expanding the constitutional reach of the federal government, and labor unions had, since the passage of the Wagner Act in 1935, been busy trying to organize more American workers. The great mass-production industries, such as autos, farm implements, steel, rubber, chemicals, oil, the mines, and the electrical industry, were particular objects of attention because of the integrated nature of their operations and the large number of employees involved. John L. Lewis, who was quite willing to defy even the president of the United States, was the absolute master of the union in the coal industry and he was a colorful presence on the scene.

Professionals who arbitrate labor disputes are, for the most part, chosen jointly by the parties to the dispute; therefore, they must be regarded by both labor and management as fair-minded neutrals. Quite obviously unions do not want arbitrators who are thought to be hostile to unions. On the other hand, companies do not want arbitrators who are thought to be biased in favor of unions or hostile to management. Philosophically, I could easily fit into the neutral mold. I had grown up in a small town where there was neither any industry nor any form of organized labor. When I studied labor law in law school, it seemed fair to me to say that only by organizing could workers hope to match the bargaining power of the corporations. The idea that there would be collective bargaining contracts between companies and unions in which the rights of each would be spelled out appealed to me as a way of creating a private industrial jurisprudence akin to the public law that governed our rights as citizens. That workers could be arbitrarily fired or disciplined without any recourse in the absence of a labor contract offended my sense of fairness. The courts had been quite hostile to organized labor in the early years, and submitting disputes to the courts therefore had little appeal to unions. One solution, dating back as far as 1865, when the iron puddlers of Pittsburgh submitted wages to a different kind of tribunal, was arbitration. From that time on, it was an accepted device for dealing with labor disputes, but it was not until after World War II that a contractual arbitration clause became almost universal. The reason was simple. During the war, the NWLB was charged with keeping labor disputes from interfering with the nation's productivity. One way to do this was for the board to heartily endorse the inclusion of arbitration clauses in collective bargaining agreements and, in fact, to order recalcitrant parties to include such a provision in a contract on some occasions. By the time the war was over, both labor and management recognized the merit of including grievance arbitration in their contracts, and they continued to do so. This, in turn, generated the market for professional arbitrators. The obvious candidates for such a position were the many employees of the NWLB who were by then seasoned veterans, known widely to both labor and management. Many of those individuals are now retired, but, in the period between the end of World War II and at least the 1980s, that group constituted the core of the arbitration fraternity.

My own approach to arbitration was the product of exposure to Professor Feinsinger, at Wisconsin, and to the public members of the NWLB. Their orientation was toward finding a solution both parties could live with, even if it was not their first choice. Since a mediator has no power to order the parties to do anything, such a solution requires consensus. Arbitration is different in the sense that the arbitrator is given the power by the parties to make a final and binding decision. Even so, it was the view of my mentors that abstract justice from an arbitrator was unproductive if it resulted in a decision that the parties, rightly or wrongly, felt they could not live with. Accordingly, I tried, in my own practice, to find answers the parties could accept. Perhaps this is best illustrated by some examples.

In Chicago, I was asked to hear a case in which a worker had had a heart attack on the job and had undergone a period of recovery. When he eventually felt able to return to work he was, quite naturally, first examined by the company doctor who declared him unfit to work. The union doctor, on the other hand, said he could work. A grievance was filed and the company and the union then referred him to a third doctor, who was a general practitioner. That doctor simply said that the patient had "symptoms consistent with a heart attack." That finding was not very helpful since everyone agreed he had had a heart attack. It was at that point that the parties decided to go to arbitration in accordance with their contract.

When I met with the parties and heard the evidence, I said to them, "I am a lawyer, not a doctor, and I have no more idea than you do whether he is fit to work. Why don't you let me refer him to a heart specialist and we will all agree to accept that doctor's decision?" They did not want to do this. They were tired of doctors and they wanted me to decide. This made no sense to me because if he really wasn't fit to work I might be sending him to his death. Still, the parties wanted nothing to do with another doctor. At that point I reached in my pocket and took out a coin, which I poised on my thumb nail. I looked at the parties and said, "Who wants to call it?" They were dumbfounded. They said, "We can't do that, it would be a totally capricious way to decide!" I said, "No more capricious than asking a lawyer about the condition of a man's heart. I've already told you that I don't know whether he can work again. Why should you pay me to think about something about which I cannot possibly know the answer without consulting a heart specialist?" After a pause, they then agreed that I could pick a heart specialist and that we would all take the answer he gave.

The upshot of the case was that I picked a heart specialist who was then provided with a copy of the man's job description so that he would know what the job required. Upon examining the man he advised us that the individual had a very serious heart condition and could not work again. That ended the case. From my point of view, the method was far more rational than my making a decision. The company could easily accept the result because it vindicated their own doctor's view, and the union could accept it because it had fulfilled the union's obligation to fairly serve its member.

On another occasion, once again in Chicago, I was asked to hear a major electric utility case involving the handling of high tension wires that were stretched across poles. The practice had been to have two men on each pole so that if one of them contacted a live wire the other could save him by methods with which they were all familiar. The company now proposed to put only one man on each pole. It argued that the poles were close enough together to permit the man from the next pole to come to the rescue within the allowable time.

A case of that kind is worrisome for an arbitrator because it may involve life or death for an employee. If the company is right, and there is no danger, it can be said to be entitled to a more efficient method of operation. If it is wrong, and a man dies because he could not be reached in time, a fatal mistake would have been made.

Because I had arbitrated for these parties before, I knew that they had a testing ground where they tried out new methods. There was a good relationship between the company and the union, and the company made it a practice to hire supervisors from the ranks of the workers. Some of those supervisors had been linemen. I therefore suggested that we all go out to the testing ground and that the company use supervisors who had been linemen to run some tests. There was already agreement on the time within which a rescue must be made, and we could then see whether a lineman on the adjacent pole could reach the man in trouble within the time allotted. Both parties agreed to this, and they further agreed that I would abide by the tests in making my ruling.

We went to the testing ground, several tests were run, and in each case the rescue was made. I adopted that demonstration as my award. I never supposed that everyone would be happy about it because, among other things, it might eliminate some jobs. The virtue of the approach was that the parties themselves agreed upon a way of deciding the case, and they knew a great deal more about their business than I did.

A third example illustrates a different kind of problem, one where the parties find themselves bound by an agreed practice that is important to them but may lead to an inequitable result in a given case.

The case involved one of the major bus companies. One of their best drivers, with a fine record over a twenty-year period, found himself caught in a pocket of dense fog on one of the turnpikes. He debated pulling off to the side and stopping but decided that this might simply result in being hit by another, oncoming car. Instead, he chose to creep along, hoping to clear the fog and emerge without damage. Unfortunately, ahead of him there was a flatback truck carrying some steel beams that extended several feet beyond the back of the truck. Before the bus driver could see the beams, they crashed through the front of his bus and killed a passenger.

The bus company had a flat rule that anytime a bus rear-ended a vehicle, the driver would be discharged. Rear-end collisions were intolerable, and the union did not disagree with this rule. Nevertheless, when this particular driver was discharged, a grievance was filed. At the hearing, the union argued that while the rear-end rule existed and was desirable, there were special circumstances in this case that justified a different result. The company conceded that the man was one of their very best drivers, that he had an admirable record, and that they would regret losing him. They nevertheless felt that the rule was so important to them that they could not fail to follow it.

In good conscience, I could not see the fairness in discharging a man under these circumstances no matter how firm the rule was. What would any of us have done had we been driving the bus? Stop and perhaps allow someone to run into the bus? Continue as the driver did? Anticipate a protruding steel beam that might come through the bus? If everyone could agree that this was one of the very best drivers the company had, did that not, in and of itself, say something about the judgment he had made to continue driving rather than stopping?

The arbitration tribunal consisted of three people, one from the union, one from the company, and myself as the chairman. In our posthearings discussions, I said I would find it very difficult to sustain the discharge even though I recognized the validity of the rule and its importance to the company. I argued that there were times and circumstances under which even the most acceptable rule should not be applied. The company member asked for time to discuss the matter with his superiors. The result was that the company agreed that if I would simply make a reinstatement award with neither any recitation of the facts nor any analysis to justify the decision, they would abide by the result and at the same time maintain the validity of the rule. The union agreed, and that's how the case came out. I thought then, and I think now, that it was a fair result and that it in fact helped the parties get out of a situation that left them all very uncomfortable.

Still another type of case illustrates how blinded we can all be by prevailing attitudes and past practices. It involved a major manufacturing company and one of the large industrial unions, and it took place in the early 1950s. The company employed both male and female janitors, but the women were paid ten cents less per hour than were the men. There was a clause in the contract that called for "equal pay for equal work." The women filed a grievance contending that they did the same work as the men and they were entitled to equal pay.

The company argued that men did the heavier work and women did lighter work, but the evidence suggested that this was not entirely accurate. Some of the male janitors had suffered industrial injuries and were given janitorial jobs because they could not cope with more exacting jobs. On the other hand, some of the women appeared to be very strong.

There was in existence at the plant a job evaluation system that called for examining the elements of each job. Jobs were then classified into groups and rates set accordingly. The analysis of jobs for male and female janitors came out in the same classification although some elements within the analysis varied. Theoretically they were therefore entitled to the same rate, but women got ten cents less. The company explained the scientific nature of job evaluation to me, including the fact that it had the virtue of looking at jobs, not individuals, and therefore avoided any personal bias. When they had finished, I asked them to explain it to me once more, thinking that in doing so they would see the obvious inconsistency between this alleged scientific system, which did not look at individuals, and the fact that if the job was held by a woman, she got ten cents less. It mattered not, I got the same explanation. I tried one more tack. Saying that I would like to be sure I understood the system, I would like to tell them how I understood it. When I finished, they agreed that I had accurately described the system. I then said, as diplomatically as I could, "Then I don't understand why women get ten cents less than men. They are in the same classification, the system of analysis is supposed to avoid looking at who holds the job, and yet women get less. How can that be?" They looked at me in astonishment and said, "But women always get less than men, therefore there is a differential."

I ruled in favor of the women, but later on I used the case in my labor law class. After stating the facts of the case as clearly as I could without giving any indication of how it had come out, I asked the class to tell me what they thought the ruling should be. Almost all of the class members were men, but there were two or three women in the group. They unhesitatingly and overwhelmingly said that the company was right. The main reason seemed to be that "everyone knew women were paid less than men!"

At the risk of extending case recitations too far, two others may be worth including, solely because they represent aberrations in rational human behavior.

The first involved a little company in a small town in Illinois. It was wholly owned by the man who ran it, and, though the company had a union contract, it had almost certainly never arbitrated. There were several issues, of which the discharge of an employee was one. The arbitration board was tripartite, one from the company, one from the union, and myself.

When we came to the discharge case, the owner held up a big briefcase, patted it, and said, "I could tell you a lot of things about this man, but I'm not going to!" I tried to explain that I knew nothing about the case, that the grievant insisted he had been fired without just cause, and that, unless the owner told me what the cause was, I would never know and that the man would have to be reinstated. It didn't phase the owner. I called a recess and took the company member out in the hall where I asked him what was going on, and whether he knew why the man was fired. He said he had asked the owner the same question I had and he wouldn't tell him either. When I said that would mean we would have to reinstate the employee, he said, "I can't help you." The union was befuddled about how to present its case, or even whether it needed to say anything. In reality, it needed no rebuttal since no case had been made, but I asked them to go ahead anyway, thinking that it might be a good experience for the owner. Unfortunately, the union didn't start to put in its case until after lunch. By that time the owner was yawning. He immediately stated that he always took a nap right after lunch and that he was leaving, but that it was all right for us to go ahead anyway. We did, the case was finished, the employee was reinstated, and I do not know why he was fired to this day. Why didn't the owner, who did not seem unduly agitated about the case, simply reinstate the employee? Maybe he regretted the decision but didn't want to admit it. Maybe a supervisor did the firing and the owner simply wanted to appear to be supportive, while at the same time letting an arbitrator reverse the firing. Maybe his wife told him the man had six children and it was a shame to fire him. The important lesson of such a case is that there is often more to a dispute than a strict examination of the facts may suggest.

A final example illustrates the same situation, but with the union this time asking the arbitrator to decide. A worker had been denied a promotion to which he thought he was entitled. When the grievance could not be settled, the union brought the matter to arbitration. Since an arbitrator's authority traces back to the contract, at the outset of the hearing I inquired as to what provision of the contract the union claimed had been violated. Having looked through the contract in advance without finding any such provision, I suspected there was none and that the union was bringing the case because a member felt very strongly about the matter and refused to accept the union's explanation that he had no case. Sure enough, when the union representative responded, he looked me squarely in the eyes and said: " I'd like the grievant to explain that to you." The worker welcomed the opportunity. He launched into an explanation of the injustice he had suffered, but never said a word about any clause in the contract. It was a classic case of an inequity in a worker's mind that was, nevertheless, not a violation of the contract. Having been unable to persuade the member that an inequity did not always end up being a violation of the contract, the union simply wanted me to tell him that so they could not be accused of failing to represent him fairly. "Passing the buck" in this fashion can be viewed as bad practice, which it certainly is if engaged in regularly, or it can be accepted as a part of the political aspect of human relationships. Every arbitrator is familiar with such cases.

Some Variations on the Theme

Most of the disputes that are arbitrated in the labor-management arena arise under the contract between the parties. Neither side is normally willing to arbitrate what are called "interest" disputes involving the terms of the contract, though there are exceptions. Nevertheless, there are variations on the theme and the more experienced an arbitrator becomes the more likely it is that he or she will be asked to take on some different assignments. I think of three categories of cases that illustrate the point. One is the kind of case where the government intervenes whether or not the parties desire such intervention. Another is the case where the company and the union have an operational problem and they think the advice of neutrals might help to resolve it. And, finally, there is what lawyers would call the sui generis case, that is, one that has no particular category because it is unique.

As to the government intervention type of case, I have already discussed the Labor-Management Committee of the Atomic Energy Commission and how it worked (see chap. 7). The government's objective was to interfere with normal collective bargaining as little as possible, therefore no cases were referred to our panel unless the parties found themselves unable to agree. In that event, the Atomic Energy Commission (which was at that time an independent agency) would order the parties to submit their case to the panel. We would convene the meeting in a hotel near the site, and would spend a day or two trying to resolve whatever differences existed. Any issues that remained unresolved would then draw from us a written advisory as to what would, in our judgment, constitute a fair settlement. If the parties accepted the recommendations, that would end the case. If they did not, the government would then pressure them to accept our recommendations or some variation thereof. Since public funds were supporting the installations, the private operators had little option but to accept. Most of the time they did this without too much grumbling.

I served on the AEC panel for several years in the late 1950s and early 1960s. My favorite memory is of a night in Las Vegas following an all-day hearing. Father Leo Brown and I were there, and he was an avid and superb poker player. It was the time of the Democratic National Convention at which John Kennedy was nominated and he was to make his acceptance speech that night. We had another day to go on the hearing, but we had the evening free. Father Brown never thought it quite appropriate for him to stay at the glitzy motels, so he always stayed at a local parish house. Nevertheless, we agreed to have dinner that night and to watch the convention. Father Brown allowed that since it was such a hot night he thought he would return to the parish house, abandon his clerical collar, and join me wearing a sports shirt. I knew what this meant, but I accepted it at face value. He returned, we had dinner and then strolled along the streets, stopping occasionally to enter one of the motels to view the gambling tables. We then watched the convention until there was a break, during which he suggested that we go out to the lobby where we could "watch" the poker tables. Lacking his poker skills, I shortly thereafter made a discreet exit in order to hear Kennedy's speech and Father Brown said he would join me shortly. To my total lack of surprise, he never did. The following morning he admitted, with some obvious satisfaction, that he had not only played for some time but that he had emerged a winner! He was a dear friend, and I miss him.

My other primary effort on a national scale was serving as chairman of the Emergency Panel in the dispute between the New York Shipping Association and the International Longshoreman's Association in 1962. Their strike tied up all the ports from New York to New Orleans. Federal legislation permitted the president to intervene on such occasions and to appoint a board that could then make recommendations as to a settlement.

The late Bill Simken was then director of the Federal Mediation and Conciliation Service, which actually handled the mechanics of such an arrangement. He was another old friend from NWLB days and he called and asked me to chair the panel. I was not anxious to do it because disputes in that industry were notoriously hard to settle, partly because containerization (a method of packaging cargo in huge containers that could then be loaded by cranes directly on to the vessels) was coming into increasing use and was eliminating jobs for longshoremen. When I demurred, noting the unlikelihood of success, he said, "Yes, I know, but it's your turn" (to fail!).

Big strikes are always hard to settle because, by definition, they almost always involve fundamental issues. They will, of course, ultimately be settled but the timing is often a problem. Sometimes the union cannot control its own members, particularly where jobs or reduced benefits are at stake, and sometimes management cannot make a settlement without demonstrating that the losses a strike will entail are worse. Thus, timing becomes critical. To make a long story short, in the longshoremen's case, the first time I met with the union president he said to me, "We are not yet ready to settle this strike. If you call separate meetings of the parties, I will say publicly that any fool knows you can't get an agreement without a meeting of both sides. If you call a meeting of both sides, I will say publicly that any fool knows that you cannot settle a dispute like this without meeting privately with each side." Having said that, he smiled, and added, "Nothing personal about this, you understand, it is just that we are not yet ready to settle." (That was a statement I heard later from students just after they had finished defaming my character. They wanted me to understand they were just speaking for television!).

In those days, the various New York piers were ethnic preserves. One would be Irish, another Italian, a third Afro-American, and so forth. Our panel spent two or three days going through conversations with the parties. Once during that time, the head of the union took me to a big luncheon at a New York hotel in which were gathered the black members of the union. After he had talked to them for a few minutes, he announced, without telling me in advance, that I wanted to speak to them. Why he did this, I do not know. Perhaps he wanted to make me out to be a dummy in whom they should have no confidence, or perhaps he assumed that anyone in this kind of game could always talk without preparation. In any event, I managed to do so, but it did not help. Shortly thereafter I talked further to Bill Simken, we asked for a hiatus in our efforts, and the strike was eventually settled when the time was ripe. So much for strikes in the shipping industry!

My last effort for the federal government came during the Carter presidency in 1980, when he made an effort to contain wage increases by appointing a Wage Control Board. It was tripartite, and I was one of the public members, the others coming from labor and management. The powers of the board were largely hortatory, and we scored no great triumphs, though it is possible to argue that the publicity the board got and its constant admonitions may have had some effect on the rise in wages.

Along the way, I participated in some quite different tripartite negotiations in which job displacement was the principal focus of attention. These are some examples.

In the late 1950s, the Armour Packing Company, the Meatcutters Union, and the Packinghouse Workers set up a joint commission to deal with job elimination caused by automation. Clark Kerr, then president of the University of California and an old friend from the days when both of us directed industrial relations centers at universities, and I were the public members. Clark was chairman and I was the executive director. The other members came from the company and the two unions. The idea for the commission came from Fred Livingston, a forward-looking New York lawyer who had also had some NWLB experience. Competition in the meatpacking industry was increasing, the companies were under pressure to find new ways of reducing labor costs, and the unions were under pressure to preserve jobs.

Our discussions continued for well over a year, at which time Clark and I wrote a monograph on the subject with our ideas of what could be done. We had succeeded in facilitating the discussions of the company and the unions, the company had from the outset imposed an internal "tax" on its own products to finance the effort and to provide alternatives for displaced workers, and the unions had participated in good faith. Our proposals were an early version of retraining efforts for workers, though this was not a very satisfactory solution for those who were going to be displaced.

Once our report was out the workers were dissatisfied. It could hardly have been otherwise. Still, both sides wanted to continue their efforts, if for no other reason than to reduce some of the tensions that would accompany the negotiation of a new contract. That meant that something had to change to make the process look different. Clark and I talked about it, and I suggested that I resign, thereby making room for a new public member. Clark was the more prestigious of the two of us, and though we held the same views and had written the report together, the process would best be preserved if he remained and I resigned.

George Shultz, who was then a professor at the University of Chicago and was later, among many other things, secretary of state, succeeded me. The project continued for another year or two and was generally helpful to the parties although it could not, of course, resolve all the problems inherent in the job displacement arena.

One of the beauties of the mediator-arbitrator profession is that the parties are always able to change their neutral members because those members are, by definition, subject to the continued approval of both sides. All arbitrators and mediators know that they will, sooner or later, be sacrificed to the exigencies of the occasion. There is generally neither any ill will nor disruption in friendships involved. The "politics" of the assignment are such that there will always be casualties among the public members. Displaced neutrals understand that their demise for the purposes of a particular case may nevertheless be the catalyst that makes it possible for the process to continue and perhaps to succeed.

As the result of my participation in the Armour study, I got a certain amount of national publicity that suggested that I was well informed on the problems of automation. My telephone rang one day with a call from New York Governor Nelson Rockefeller's office saying that the governor wanted to convene a meeting of a few national experts on the subject, and would I come for a private discussion? Aghast at the idea that I had become an "expert" in a field in which I really knew relatively little, I demurred, saying that I was not really an expert and that I could suggest the names of many others who knew a good deal more than I did about it. At that point, I learned another lesson. If someone is convinced you are an expert in something, it is hard to convince them otherwise. The response to your disclaimers will be either, "What becoming modesty," or "We don't really need experts, we just need to talk to people with good sense who are knowledgeable in the area." I got both replies, and I ultimately went to the meeting. It turned out to be a very pleasant conversation in which none of us had any brand new solutions to the job displacement problem. I never knew whether the governor felt better about the problem or not.

About this same time, U.S. Industries started a foundation designed to address the displacement problem. It was directed by Ted Kheel, a New York lawyer and another old NWLB friend. Ted asked me to serve as a consultant to the foundation, which I did for a year or two. The company had international holdings, and some of our meetings were held in England, including a meeting with some British academics that both George Shultz and I attended.

In some ways, the most interesting of my tripartite advisory roles came in a matter involving the Pittsburgh Plate Glass Co. and the Glass-workers Union. During World War II, when it was hard to get and retain skilled workers, the incentive wages at the company's plants had gotten out of line and needed to be revised. Since "out of line" meant that they were too high, the company and the union had the problem of how revisions could be made acceptable to workers.

Once again, I was one of two public members in a group otherwise composed of company and union people. The discussions had hardly begun when we neutrals discovered an underlying fact that neither of us knew about. It involved a whole new industrial process, which was

quite fascinating and would totally displace skilled grinders and polishers, who were among the best-paid workers. An Englishman by the
name of Pilkington had noted that when his wife placed hot lard in a
tin of cold water the lard would congeal for disposal and the sides
would be perfectly smooth. Pilkington knew of the grinding and pol-
ishing process in the making of glass and he reasoned that, if lard
would congeal in water, perhaps molten glass would if placed in an
appropriate solution. He therefore tried to find such a solution and was
ultimately successful. The result was that his process was licensed
around the world and had the potential for displacing grinders and
polishers.

The hard reality was that the company, having licensed the new
process, needed to use it. It could accomplish this in either of two ways.
One would be to install it in the old plants by agreement with the union,
and the other was by going South (into largely nonunion areas) and
building new plants. Thus the option for the workers was to either
accept a revision of the incentive rates or face the fact that the plants
would move and their jobs would be lost. Workers in different plants
chose different options, depending on how they assessed the company's assertion that it would have to move South. Once they found
that the company was serious, they tended toward the revision solution. Our panel probably made a contribution to a peaceful change in
production methods.

The experience in these displacement negotiations was a good one
for me, though I never was sure how much I contributed to any solution. The progress of the new technology was inexorable, and the bargaining power of the workers steadily diminished. In a competitive
world, new technology means cost savings and companies find such
savings necessary to their ability to compete. I learned a good deal
about the realities of the business world and the difficulties involved in
trying to soften the adjustment for workers. I took satisfaction from the
fact that the many union leaders with whom I worked remained my
friends, and that the company people were usually sympathetic even
when we could not resolve all their problems. It also left me with a
feeling of deep compassion for workers who found that their liveli-
hoods were being lost and their futures made uncertain.

Finally, there were, in my bag of experiences, what I have called the
sui generis cases. The most interesting of these was the UAW's (United
Auto Workers) Public Review Board. I served on it for about six years,

from 1966–72. Walter Reuther was the head of the union when I first joined the board and he did what only a very few unions have ever been willing to do, that is, allow members to grieve against the union and let outsiders decide the merits of the grievance.

On the board at the time I served were one rabbi, one Catholic priest, one Protestant minister, and two of us who were professional neutrals in the labor field. The chairman, Monsignor George Higgins, was the priest, and he was an expert in labor-management matters. We would hear grievances from anywhere in the country. Most commonly the cases at that time involved questioned political behavior in the election of officers, or alleged discrimination against one union employee in favor of another. We would render a decision, which the union had agreed to accept in advance. Occasionally, Walter would think that we were egregiously wrong. We would then be invited to have dinner with him, at which time he would explain how wrong we were. Monsignor Higgins would gently remind him that all of us would be glad to resign and he could find a new board, or he could accept the fact that we might occasionally make decisions Walter thought were wrong. At that point Walter would say, "No, no, no, I don't want you to resign, I just want you to use a little better judgment!" We would go away friends, though Walter would have other occasions when our decision would trouble him and we would have dinner again.

Though I did not always agree with him, Walter Reuther was a great man. He was filled with enormous energy, novel ideas, the rhetoric of a born leader (even when his rhetoric was endless), a very quick mind, and a dynamic charm. At my request, he came out to the University of Michigan a time or two to talk to student groups who wanted to hear him. This was during the time of student radicals, for whom Walter was much too tame. They would go after him without realizing that they were confronting one of the country's most nimble experts in the art of confrontation. After all, it was Walter who had triumphed over Communist elements in the union at an earlier time. He loved jousting with students, perhaps because he was much too skilled for them to handle.

In 1972, when I was invited to become a member of the Chrysler Corporation Board of Directors, I thought I ought to resign from the UAW's Public Review Board. There was no direct conflict of interest, because the UAW board dealt only with internal grievances, but I thought the confidence of UAW members in the work of the Public

Review Board might be eroded if they knew a member of that panel was on an auto company board. Walter was gone from the scene by then, due to a tragic plane crash, but I wrote to the union and said that I thought I ought to resign. They were kind enough to reply that they saw no conflict and would like me to remain on their board. I finally resigned because I admired the courage of the union in setting up such a board and did not want to do anything to hurt it. The union finally concurred, and I left the board with regret.

There were other ventures of a similar kind. In 1980, along with Ben Aaron (another old NWLB friend and long a professor at UCLA), I was the cochairman of the Big Steel–Steelworkers Union nationwide arbitration panel in the event they were unable to agree on the terms of a new contract. This was a novel agreement since few companies or unions would ever agree to arbitrate the terms of a new contract. Fortunately, they never had to resort to the panel and we were never used.

In the early 1980s I served as a member on the UAW-Chrysler Legal Services Board. The company and the union had agreed that the company would finance certain routine legal services employees might require. An office was set up for this purpose, and on the board were people from the Union, Chrysler, and the public. Gabriel Alexander, long the umpire under the Chrysler-UAW agreement, was the chairman. After Chrysler pioneered the legal services benefit for employees, the other auto companies adopted similar programs and they were all ultimately managed out of one office (although as separate entities).

Finally, I arbitrated a case or two in 1983 that raised the question of whether unions could, over the objection of other union members, use dues paid by members for nonunion purposes. The Right to Work Movement, which always opposed unions, raised the question, but it was a legitimate issue that ultimately went to the Supreme Court and has now been pretty well resolved in the sense of defining what are, and what are not, legitimate expenses payable out of dues.

As I look back now on my experiences in the field of labor-management affairs, I realize how much I benefited in my later career from the lessons I learned about human behavior, the politics of confrontation, human conduct as theater, decision making, and the art of negotiation. It isn't always the merits of a dispute that determine whether and how it can be settled. Sometimes old solutions have to be repackaged with new labels in order to make them acceptable to parties who resent the old labels. Timing is often critical, and what is impossible to settle today may be settled with relative ease tomorrow. Patience is essential. Anger is best used when it is a planned display and is, therefore, controlled. It is unwise to assume that your opponent's views are held less honestly or sincerely than your own. Saving face can be critical to success. And, finally, always remember that one's greatest successes are likely to be achieved when others think they are solely responsible for what happened.

Chapter 9

Back to the Badger State

The chancellorship was a newly created position when we came back to Wisconsin in 1964. The need for the position came about, as it had in other states, because, in the baby-boom post–World War II years, many of the large state universities opened branch campuses in order to accommodate enrollment demands. The president presided over all of them. This made it necessary to delegate more of the individual campus duties to another executive officer. In the process, the titles *president* and *chancellor* became somewhat confusing because some universities called the top executive of the system president and the top executive on a given campus chancellor, while others did exactly the opposite. The result was, and is, that one has to know the local terminology in order to know which is which. In any event, I was to be the chief executive officer of the university in Madison.

While I had never held a position in the university world comparable to that of chancellor before coming back to Wisconsin, I had been a professor for seventeen years at two Big Ten universities, I had headed a small school at Illinois, I had served on a great many committees associated with the larger university, and I was therefore familiar with the work of practically all of the schools and colleges that make up a big university, with the exception of the Medical School at Illinois, which was located in Chicago.

The governance of a public university is quite different from that of its private counterparts, though with the increased intervention by one or another level of government in all universities this has become less so over the years. With respect to Wisconsin, Professors Curti and Carstensen put it this way in their preface to the two-volume history of the University of Wisconsin, published in 1949.

The American state university is many things, and its history has many faces. It shares with privately supported and controlled institutions of higher learning many common characteristics and problems; and both owe a great debt to the European university. But the American state university is a public institution and—like a state prison, a state hospital, or a highway system—its success or failure in winning appropriate authority or procuring adequate funds from the legislature has seldom rested exclusively on its merits. A host of politically pertinent but often educationally irrelevant elements have usually helped to determine the success or failure of the university with the legislature and the state. Moreover, as a new type of educational enterprise, subject to direct and indirect pressures from without and within its walls, its courses of study have come to reflect not so much a clearly defined educational philosophy as a vast repository of often conflicting and contradictory functions imposed upon it by individuals and groups who at one time or another have stood in a position of power.

Put more succinctly, the message is that trying to effectively manage a public university requires not only an understanding of the academic objectives, but also a good deal of finesse in dealing with external political forces. To better understand the problem, let me spell it out in a little more detail.

The state legislature is composed of a great variety of individuals. They will vary in their political philosophies from the far right to the far left. They will come from different educational backgrounds, as will their constituents. They know that higher education is popular with the electorate, therefore they are generally well disposed toward it. But some of them will deem it wise to attack the university, very often for its alleged elitism or its "radical" faculty members. Others will simply want a favor, perhaps involving admission for a poorly qualified student. Another may want a course in the foreign language of a substantial number of voters in their district even though there is no demand among students for such a course. Still others will want ready, and preferably free, access to athletic events. The list could go on indefinitely, but the point is that there will always be pressure to make decisions for reasons other than merit.

Interest groups can be as important as individual legislators in terms of their wishes, and this can be exploited by alert deans whose wishes happen to coincide with those of the interest group. I think of an example involving the School of Agriculture. It wanted a new Ag Science building, and while this would be desirable it was not high enough on the university's list of priorities to be funded. Coincidentally, the state had about run its course in sustaining a high tax on margarine, which had been designed to protect dairy farmers. The dean worked with the powerful Ag lobby to pressure the legislature to phase out the tax over a period and identify a part of the revenue during those years for the building of a new Ag Science building, the occupants of which would research new uses for agricultural products. The ploy worked like a charm. We suddenly had a new building for which we had not asked! It wasn't a bad thing, the building was both useful and needed, but our priority system had been circumvented.

For the most part, there is nothing venal about what legislators do in the course of supporting their public universities, it is simply that their priorities do not always accord with those of the institution. This may make effective governance more difficult for the president, but it is the price we pay in a democracy for public support of education.

Clashes between the university and the state legislature are not the only governmental hazard. There are frequent conflicts of interest between the cities in which the universities are located and the university. If the city happens to be the state capital, the problem is exacerbated because there are then politicians from two governmental bodies present in the locality and their priorities do not always mesh with one another.

Municipal clashes can take place over such things as the condemnation of property for university use, who will police the campus, who will supply fire services, or whether the university or the city will attempt to curb unruly conduct on the part of students. A further perennial complaint of the city is that the university, being a state institution immune from local taxation, takes too much of the city's land off the tax rolls, thereby diminishing the city's tax revenue. Appeals to the state legislature to right this alleged wrong usually draw a reply that the legislature will be glad to move the university to another city. For its part, the university points to the great economic benefits it brings to the city and suggests the city ought to thank it rather than complain. Eventually such disputes are settled, or at least temporarily laid to rest, but they occupy a good deal of the time of top executives on both sides.

In more recent years, the federal government has, through its programs, also directly impacted universities. Examples include environmental regulations, affirmative action with respect to personnel, gender equity in sports, and rules governing the disposition of student financial aid.

If politics affect the operation of the university from federal, state, and municipal authorities, the same can be said about internal problems, and in this respect there is little difference between public and private institutions. Wherever people are working together, problems will inevitably arise and universities are not an exception to this rule. Tension arises out of the fact that research tends to have more prestige than teaching, and teaching more than service (extension), though the alleged mission of the land grant or state university is tripartite and therefore emphasizes all three. There is merit in the claim that research weighs more heavily in rewarding professors than teaching, but the complexity of the matter is widely misunderstood. A professor who is simply a fine teacher but does not publish will remain largely unknown beyond the confines of his or her university. If he or she aspires to scholarly recognition, or perhaps a better position elsewhere, publication is a sine qua non, because it is through their publications that professors get their national and international reputations. The ideal is obviously a person who is superb in both teaching and research, but this is not always the case. Some marvelous teachers do not publish, and if this is so their teaching talent should be fully recognized and maximized without being penalized for the failure to publish. Some fine teachers who do publish do not produce a meaningful product, and their time would be better spent concentrating on teaching. Some professors with great talent in research do not teach well, yet they continue to find it required of them. In toto, all this spells out a constant problem for the university administration, because it runs headlong into long-established practices. Rationalizing the system so that great teaching, great research, or a combination of the two, so that talent can be employed at the optimum level, is an internal political problem as long as the university culture remains as it is. There are at least two potential solutions to this problem, neither of which is popular in academia. One is to separate research and teaching, as the Europeans do, into discrete institutions (though presumably they could be kept separate even within a university). The other is to give equal credit to teaching and research, but to adjust the loads of those who wish to, or are best at one or the other, so that the duty is concentrated in only one area. There is a downside to either of these approaches, but it is not impossible that such a change will eventually take place.

Since university people possess all the frailties of the rest of the human population, there are also prejudices galore. Scientists frequently believe that their counterparts in the social sciences and the humanities are engaged in very "soft" research, by which they mean that the quantitative documentation for what their colleagues do is lacking. While rebutting this claim, the social scientists and humanists take note of the greater availability of money for "hard" research and sometimes move in the direction of quantitative methods that end up making their publications less interesting or understandable than they were before. Professional school faculties sometimes label those in the liberal arts as "unfocused." Meanwhile, those in the liberal arts quietly suggest that engineers believe everything can be solved by use of the computer, whereas human problems do not lend themselves to such treatment. In the medical school there is a perennial battle between the clinicians and the research scientists. The latter may label a surgeon a "talented plumber," who would nevertheless fail without the work of the researcher in supplying the know-how to cause the body to accept the invasion of surgery. Since the clinician is able to augment his salary by virtue of a clinical practice, the researcher naturally feels entitled to share in some of that income in support of research. To this, the clinician replies that he or she works enormously long hours under great pressure and deserves every cent. Since clinicians need to stay in practice to maintain and increase their skills, forbidding them to practice would be both unworkable and unthinkable. Nor could they work without charge, even if they were disposed to do so, because their extraordinary skills should not be denied to the public. The result is that some kind of "practice plan" has to be worked out that will accommodate both interests. The administration must then help design a system that it can approve. I once remarked that there were, as far as I could see, three possible systems, each of which would last for about ten years. By that time, alleged deficiencies would demand a different solution, in which case one of the two now forgotten plans could be resurrected and applied for another decade. Like the grass on the other side of the street, the old, abandoned system might look greener to those who never served under it!

And then there are the students, about a third of whom turn over every year. That means that there is little collective memory of what has happened in the past. What appear to them to be new and exciting ideas for reforming the university come to their attention, and they have no way of knowing that most of the ideas are old hat and have already been thoroughly discussed. If this routine were not more than offset by the perennial sense of enthusiasm and renewal that new students bring with them, it would be unbearable.

In order to cope with all these problems, Sally and I were giving up a happy home in Urbana, a nine-month school year in favor of a twelve-month year, and a salary that, while higher than my Law School salary at Illinois, was considerably less than our augmented income from my mediation and arbitration activities, which I would no longer have time to do. In addition, we would have to sell our house in Champaign and buy a new one in Madison, since the university had not yet acquired a home for the chancellor. True, we would have a car and an entertainment allowance, but there was no economic incentive to take the job. It was the excitement of a new challenge and our love and respect for the University of Wisconsin that brought us back. For me, a large part of that respect derived from a statement made by the Wisconsin Board of Regents way back in 1894.

> We cannot . . . believe that knowledge has reached its final goal, or that the present condition of society is perfect. . . . In all lines of academic investigation it is of the utmost importance that the investigator should be absolutely free to follow the indications of truth wherever they may lead . . . we believe the great state University of Wisconsin should ever encourage that continual and fearless sifting and winnowing by which alone the truth can be found.

What better incentive could one who cared for the academic world have than that statement?

Before moving to Madison in the fall, we had a brief vacation in Denmark, Norway, and Sweden, partly for pleasure (Sally had not been there) and partly because I was finishing an article on the Swedish Labor Courts for publication that year and I needed some additional information.

During the ensuing year at Wisconsin I made the deliberate decision to have almost no staff. This was possible because I had available the staff that served the president, and because the relationship with President Fred Harrington and Vice President Robert Clodius was always so cordial. They, too, were having to adjust to the new system. Our offices were close together, and we proved to be very compatible. Since I had not known either of them before coming back to Wisconsin, this was a real bonus. On many campuses there was, and still is, tension between the president and the chancellor arising out of the division of duties between them, particularly on the number one campus in the system. We never had serious problems. We fell into a pattern of duties that seemed to satisfy both of us, and I shall always be grateful for the guidance and kindness shown to us by all the people at Wisconsin. Prominent among them were Edwin and Phyllis Young, who had been our friends since we first came to the university in 1947. By 1964, Ed was dean of the Liberal Arts and Science College, and was later both chancellor at Madison and then president of the university.

In retrospect, perhaps the most interesting thing about our move was that it was made without any inkling of the student turmoil that would soon overtake universities and take up so much time and effort in the years that followed. Indeed, our first year at Madison was a quite normal university year. I used to write a newsletter to the faculty and staff each month and, on looking at some of that material, I find that the things I talked about were, and are, typical of the academic world. What should we do about a possible second campus in Madison? How large should we let the university become? What should we do about the reward system for teaching vs. research? What should we do about making increased computer facilities available? To what extent should we consolidate our libraries? To what extent should instructional television be used? What could we do to improve inadequate recreational facilities for students? Of the many demands for building monies, which were the most important? How could we help students in this large university identify with smaller groups so that the size of the university would be less apparent? Looking at all those questions more than a quarter century later, I am reminded of their durability, for many of the same problems trouble us today.

The Board of Regents, which governed the university, met monthly. The relationship between the board and the top administrators is critical, so perhaps this is the proper point to examine the problems inherent in that relationship.

Public university boards are usually either elected or appointed or some combination thereof. The numbers vary, there is some degree of geographic distribution from around the state, and their political views are mixed. In recent years there has been a special effort to include women and minorities on such boards.

Members of governing boards are, like the rest of us, of varying quality and disposition. An argument over whether they would be better if appointed, rather than elected, takes place perpetually. My own conclusion is that it is not the method of choice that makes the difference, it is the caliber of the people who are willing to run or to be appointed. If they are appointed, this leads back to the governor and his or her willingness to avoid political rewards and choose the best people possible. If they are to be elected, political parties need to act responsibly in making their choices. Unfortunately, the system does not always work well. The most frequent complaints about governing boards are that they try to micromanage the university or that they abuse it for political reasons or to advance certain favored programs, like athletics. When this happens, it is very detrimental to the university. My own experience with the Wisconsin board during the days of my chancellorship was limited because the president handled most of the problems. There were occasional difficulties, but they were surmountable, and I found the experience enjoyable. The members were my friends, they were devoted to the university though they did not always agree on things, and they reminded the academic community that there was a real world outside academia.

On the academic side, clearly the most difficult problem facing the Madison campus during my first year was the appointment of a new dean for the Medical School. For three years or more there had been only an interim dean because a schism within the school made any appointment impossible. I had been in the academic world long enough to know that fights of this kind occur occasionally and that, when they do, reason falls by the wayside. I had, in fact, invited the chairmen of the various departments to dinner at our house on one occasion to discuss Medical School affairs. While there was no open hostility displayed among them at dinner, I was told later that it was the first time some of them had spoken to each other in years.

We did not at that time have a search committee, perhaps largely because there was so much divisiveness within the school. Enough work had been done, however, to identify a number of candidates from around the country who would make fine deans, and I set about seeing them. To my dismay, they were uniformly aware of the turbulence at Wisconsin, they knew several of the people who made up the contending forces, and they were wary of coming to Madison. Usually I had to go elsewhere to see them, and, while they always treated me with courtesy and interest, nothing could persuade them to come to Wisconsin. I finally came to the conclusion that the only solution was to avoid further interim appointments and name someone from our own school as dean. This might not be popular, but it would break the log jam and it would demonstrate that cliques within the school could not make progress impossible. My candidate was Peter Eichman, who was then associate dean. He was not attached to any of the groups, he was well liked by all, and while he did not have a big name nationally he was a calm, solid, and responsible man who had been doing a good job as associate dean. Nevertheless, it was probable that his appointment would be blocked by opposition from within the school if it became known that his appointment was imminent.

I had, of course, kept both President Harrington and Vice President Clodius aware of my efforts to find a new dean. We were in agreement that the best thing to do was to back Peter Eichman. We nevertheless concluded that the only way to bring this about was to keep it a tight secret among the three of us until the Regents met and were asked to confirm the appointment. We could not put the item on the agenda in advance because this would trigger furious activity to find out who was being proposed. No on-campus group has better or closer ties with individual Regents than the doctors because so many of the Regents are their patients. The minute a Regent knew a name, he would call his doctor friend and inquire. This would likely kill the appointment because the question would not be whether Peter was an appropriate nominee, but why someone from one of the contending constituencies was not being named.

The day before the Regents met, the president told the chairman of the board of the proposed appointment. The chairman was Arthur DeBardeleben. He was a lawyer from upstate Wisconsin, a passionate protector of freedom of speech, and a very strong man. He would keep the secret. He also agreed that when the proposal came before the board, he would not grant a motion for a few minutes break, during which various of the Regents would call their doctor friends. The day of the meeting came, the appropriate moment for the chancellor's items arose, and I proposed the appointment of Peter Eichman as dean. Immediately, one or more Regents asked for a momentary adjournment. The request was denied by the chairman. Both the president and I strongly backed the appointment. Everyone knew what the problem was, Peter was a perfectly respectable candidate, and he had already told me he would accept if it was offered to him. After a somewhat wary discussion, the appointment was made. There was a mild fuss about the way it was done, but there was probably more relief than criticism afterward. Fortunately, Peter brought peace and relative quiet to the school and people got down to other business. And I had survived my first real test!

Little more need be said of the Medical School except that, during my time as chancellor, the long dormant question of what to do about expanding hospital and Medical School space came up. The existing area was landlocked and our available space would be further to the west. Separating the old and new facilities would be undesirable, but building an entirely new medical center on the new site would be very expensive. A. W. Peterson, who was the long-time vice president for finance at the university, came to talk to me about it. He thought that we should take the bull by the horns and move to the new site. His argument so impressed me that I asked him why, if this was so clearly the right thing to do, we didn't do it? He said it would be very difficult to accomplish and we might fail. Perhaps because I was relatively unsophisticated about these things, I said I thought we ought to go for it. We later cleared this with the central administration, made the decision to move, and embarked on the long road to building the center. About ten years later, long after I had left, the new medical center came into being.

By the second year of my tenure as chancellor, I had acquired a staff. James Cleary, a faculty member in speech, became the vice chancellor for academic affairs; Robert Atwell, who was then working in budget analysis in Washington, became the vice chancellor for administration; and Barbara Newell, who was on the economics faculty at Purdue, but who I had known earlier at Wisconsin and Illinois, came on to be my assistant. All three of them went on to become university presidents. Jim went to the State University of California at Northridge, Bob to Pitzer College in the Claremont group and later to the presidency of the American Council on Education, and Barbara to Wellesley and later Florida. They were, because of their individual talents, a first-rate group, as their subsequent success demonstrated.

In 1964, fund-raising, or, as it is now called, development, was not a major activity in most public universities. This was in large part because tax dollars supported the institutions, and private support was the province of the private colleges and universities. This did not mean that there were not occasional gifts of buildings, endowed professorships, or scholarships, but it did mean that little concerted effort was put into fund-raising. It was also true that corporations were reluctant to give to public universities because they were state supported. Nevertheless, I did find myself engaged in some efforts to raise special funds. I remember two of them because they were unique.

The first involved the construction of a tennis-squash facility. Arthur Nielsen, of TV ratings fame, was a Wisconsin alum, as were his children. All of them were very good tennis players and regularly played in father-son tournaments in the Chicago area. At one point we received word that he was interested in giving the money for a first-rate indoor facility to be constructed out near the dormitories along Lake Mendota. This would be a great asset to the campus because of the Wisconsin climate, and it was the type of facility the state would be unlikely ever to fund because it was already hard-pressed to take care of the need for academic buildings. I was invited to Chicago to see Mr. Nielsen. Once I got there I found that not only was he interested but he had, in fact, already planned the whole facility. His devotion to tennis was such that he had built two similar projects in the Chicago area and had the benefit of that experience. The planning was complete, right down to the size of the light bulbs and the differential air conditioning that would be needed in various parts of the building. The building would obviously be named for the Nielsen family, but we did have a few clearances to obtain from our own planning and construction people and the state. This proved to be manageable, and the building was constructed. It now provides one of the finest indoor tennis and squash facilities in the country. The eye-opener to me about the whole negotiation was the fact that the donor not only had a clear project in mind, he had a detailed plan for it. I would not have expected this to be the case and, in my later experience, it did not happen often, but it does happen on occasion. The reason, I suspect, is that the donor is so infatuated with the project (which is in the nature of a memorial) that he or she derives an enormous satisfaction out of designing it. The result can be disastrous if the proposed building is a monstrosity. The university then has the job of either rejecting the offer (and thereby totally alienating a helpful future donor) or living with a bad building. Fortunately, there was no problem on the Nielsen building and it fitted into its location beautifully.

At about the same time, I had the opposite experience with another project. Because the traffic at the foot of Bascom Hill and the Student Union was very heavy, we thought it might be wise to construct a simple overpass. The plans were made, it was constructed, and we had absolutely no success in getting anyone to use it. It became known as "Fleming's Folly," and rightly so. I did learn from it, though. Students will not climb up steps and then climb down some other steps in order to avoid the hazard of being hit by a car. They regard the streets as their territory. The fact that accidents occur, even to the point of a student being killed, only seems to mean to them that drivers must exercise more care.

My other fund-raising venture involved a renowned biochemist, Professor Harry Steenbock, then retired. In the early 1920s he discovered a way to recover vitamin A in its pure form. This proved not to be patentable for reasons of delay, but a little later he discovered how to create vitamin D in foods by irradiation with ultraviolet light. Steenbock knew that it would be questionable for him to apply for a patent since he was a paid staff member of a state institution, but he resented the idea that he was bound to turn over the product of his research to the university. It was also true that patenting his process would protect the public against unscrupulous use of it. The resolution of this dilemma was the establishment of a trust, under which the patent would be assigned to the university and placed under the auspices of a newly created corporation called the Wisconsin Alumni Research Foundation (WARF). Receipts from the patent were to be divided between the trust and Professor Steenbock, with the latter receiving 15 percent. WARF used its share of the money to fund research, grants, scholarships and fellowships, and other, similar ventures.

As it turned out, the vitamin D process made a great deal of money, and through WARF's investments, made a great deal more to the immense benefit of the university. Steenbock also made a large amount of money, but he was frequently at odds with WARF and was always suspicious of it. I got into the picture because the College of Agriculture wanted to build a new library, and it hoped that Professor Steenbock would put up much of the needed money. Biochemistry was in the Ag College, hence he had a long-standing tie to it. I was asked to go see him, but I was carefully briefed on how to approach him. He was, first of all, very conservative in his political views and took no pleasure in any of the social reforms for which Wisconsin was famous. Since I favored all those things, I was an unlikely visitor for him; nobody could think of a better solution, so I went. Before going, the chairman of WARF called me over for a chat, in the course of which he told me that Professor Steenbock was hostile to the foundation and was always convinced that he was being deceived by it. He predicted, therefore, that Professor Steenbock would work the conversation around to suggest that the money really ought to come from the foundation, or that if he did promise to contribute he would then spend his time plotting how to pass the obligation on to the foundation. The chairman simply wanted me to know in advance that this was likely to happen and that, while I wasn't to say so, WARF would certainly contribute to the building and make sure that it got built. Armed with that assurance, I could hardly fail in my mission. I then visited the professor.

Dr. Steenbock was not a hail-fellow-well-met type. He looked and acted like the serious scientist that he was. His visage was stern, although he was friendly enough, perhaps because by then Sally had gotten to know his wife and they were good friends. He was friendly to the idea of a library, and, I think, liked the thought that it might be named for him. Predictably, he also thought that WARF ought to make a contribution of unspecified proportions. We managed to avoid all social subjects on which our views might differ, and we parted amicably with the understanding that he was interested and would consider the matter. The upshot was that, after a certain amount of further bargaining, the library was built although I have forgotten exactly how the funding was shared.

Another of the duties that fell to the chancellor, and sometimes to his wife, were visits to foreign locations where the University of Wisconsin had projects. This was, of course, a pleasant item on our agenda. There would always be a certain amount of suspicion as to the necessity of such visits and whether it was an appropriate use of university resources. The latter point could be answered because the expenses were generally borne by some foundation or were included in the contract under which the university was working. In the aftermath of World War II and the realignment of much of the world that resulted therefrom, it was the policy of the United States to engage in a great many foreign aid projects, often in the fields of agriculture and/or education. Since the great state universities of the Middle West were very knowledgeable in agriculture, they were obvious resources for our government in carrying out American foreign policy. Under those circumstances, it was important for the top executives in such universities to know and understand the work their schools were doing abroad. The fact that such trips provided for those who were privileged to make them an opportunity to see the far places of the world and to broaden their own understanding of the world was a plus in every sense of the word.

In the fall of 1965, and regularly a time or two annually thereafter, I traveled to foreign countries in connection with university projects. First, it was to Nigeria, where our Schools of Agriculture and Education, along with some other universities, had projects involving collaboration with newly built Nigerian universities. We visited several of them and were greatly impressed. Unfortunately, it was right at that time that civil war broke out in Nigeria. On one plane trip we were not permitted to land at a given airport because there was fighting around it. The war subsequently damaged some of the universities and wiped out some of the gains that had been made. Education can make little progress in the presence of political turmoil, of which Nigeria has subsequently had more than its share.

In the fall of 1966 I visited Aix-en-Provence in France, where we had a student exchange program. While in that part of the world, I also went to the University of Freiburg, in Germany.

In January of 1967, Sally and I both went to the Philippines, where there was an agricultural project involving, among other things, the new, "miracle" rice that was to enormously increase production of that product all over Asia; and to Indonesia, where the United States was supporting a leadership training program run by the University of Wisconsin. There was great tension in that country because Sukarno was just being ousted by Suharto, and it was not clear who was really in power. We then moved on to Singapore, where we were pleased to stay at the fabled Raffles Hotel, and to Bangkok, where there were also UW programs with the government of Thailand. In Japan we stayed at the famous Imperial Hotel built by Frank Lloyd Wright, and visited universities in Tokyo and Kyoto with which we had ties. I remember that when we went to Tokyo University, it was also having student problems and there were activist signs all over the campus. We ate at the student cafeteria before our appointment. There were three fixed meals one could buy. Each was shown at the start of the line, and beside it was a colored poker chip that identified that plate. To order, you simply took the appropriately colored chip and showed it to the attendant, who then produced that meal. There were, quite naturally, chopsticks but no silverware. I wondered how to eat the soup until I watched others hold the bowl up to their mouth and then push the noodles into their mouth with the chopsticks.

We ended the tour in Hawaii at the East-West Center. At all of these places, Wisconsin had programs, and over the years many of the government officials had taken degrees at Wisconsin. This gave us ready access to top officials in all countries, and made the trips very worthwhile in terms of better understanding the various cultures and in assessing the value of what we were doing abroad. The high regard all of these governments had for the University of Wisconsin and for the joint enterprises was apparent.

Back at home, a problem with serious, long-term implications was becoming a topic of discussion. The University of Wisconsin had two major campuses, one in Madison and the other in Milwaukee. In addition, it had a number of two-year centers around the state that performed some of the same functions as community colleges in other states, and it was also about to open two new four-year campuses in Green Bay and in the Racine-Kenosha area.

In a separately governed system, there were a number of teachers colleges around the state. In the course of the postwar baby boom they had expanded, and were clamoring to become universities with an extended array of offerings. This idea had strong support from their respective faculties, partly because it would offer more prestige. It also had community and political support because it promised an expanded economy for the various localities. It was not long before the legislature gave the necessary approvals and several new universities, having their base in the former teachers colleges, were launched. The problem this posed in Wisconsin, and in other states that followed the same pattern, was that faculties then wanted graduate programs. To some extent this could be justified, particularly at the master's level, because accessibility is improved by having such programs offered nearer home and at hours that working people can manage. If it moves on to the doctoral level it becomes far more dubious, for a variety of reasons. Most important, there is the question of quality. Many of the faculties had not been recruited with graduate studies in mind. Then there is the question of demand, because there is a limit to the opportunities for people trained at the Ph.D. level. And, finally, there is the question of cost because graduate training is far more costly than undergraduate education and requires more in facilities and faculty time.

From a strictly financial point of view, higher education was becoming one of the great commitments of state government and it therefore needed to maximize the use of the appropriations the state provided. In expanding the teachers colleges, the emphasis had been on providing a broader education for undergraduate students. The financial implications of adding graduate work received little consideration, and by the time they were considered the cat was out of the bag! Meeting the demand for expanded undergraduate studies was politically popular. The accompanying and inevitable demand of the faculties for graduate work was hardly considered. When graduate work came into the picture, the legislature began to hear demands that it take a closer look at whether all the expenditures that had been authorized were necessary. The most logical answer was thought to be better coordination of all the institutions. Thus, instead of separate governing boards, there would be a single board for all institutions, thereby "coordinating" their offerings and running a more "efficient" system. In theory this sounds fine, but efficiency and coordination are not the hallmarks of a democracy. In order to protect the interests of all the institutions in the constellation, the sole governing board must be fairly constituted. In practical terms, this means that the various interests must be accommodated. By the time those interests are taken care of, the door is then open for bargaining and the trade-offs that are so dear to the political world. The upshot is that there is an inevitable leveling pressure that is likely to be particularly hard on the premier university in the system.

Ultimately, Wisconsin went the route of a great many states in consolidating its system of public universities. Whether this has resulted in significant savings, I do not know, and it may be unknowable because no one can say what the alternative cost would have been. Whether it hurt the University of Wisconsin in Madison in terms of its national stature is debatable. If it has, there will be those who will argue that the move was nevertheless justified because it distributed the resources of the state more evenly and made higher education more accessible everywhere. Those who believe the move has been a mistake will argue that the most prestigious institution in the system, the University of Wisconsin in Madison, has been diminished.

Into this already complex set of problems, student turbulence suddenly made its appearance at the University of California in Berkeley in 1964, and it had become a fact of life in Madison by 1965. How we dealt with that is a different story.

Chapter 10

The Advent of Student Turbulence

When the student problems began at Berkeley in 1964 it seemed to the rest of us, as we watched from afar, that it was a local dispute. We soon learned to the contrary, and the last two years of my tenure as chancellor at Wisconsin were greatly affected by student problems. This did not mean that all other activities ceased, because all the usual problems and planning continued. But it did mean that much of my own time was to be taken up with students.

One has to recall the setting in order to get the flavor and intensity of the student upheaval. Our country was involved in a very unpopular war in Vietnam in which, as time passed, we found that we were being deceived by our own leadership about the progress of the war. The military draft deferred college students as long as they remained undergraduates, but it left men uneasy knowing that their less fortunate peers were going into the service. Reserve Officer Training Corps (ROTC) programs existed on a great many college campuses. At Wisconsin, the program had always been somewhat suspect on the ground that it was an inappropriate activity in an educational institution. The unpopularity of the Vietnam War exacerbated that suspicion. Scientific research in support of the military, which was considered not only proper but essential during World War II, was now anathema to some students and faculty. Companies that made particularly gruesome war products, such as napalm, were made unwelcome when they came to recruit students as prospective employees.

Separate, but of equal intensity, was the feeling about racial injustice. The battle to force some of the southern universities that had always been closed to blacks was on, Martin Luther King was pushing his peaceful resistance campaign, and the issue had a strong appeal to the idealism of students. In the spring of 1965, our own daughter Nancy had, with other Beloit College students, walked the fifty miles from Beloit to Madison to show their solidarity with those who were marching at Selma, Alabama. We held a reception for them at our house when they arrived.

To top it all off, John F. Kennedy, who was still regarded as the shining white knight at that time, had been assassinated. Within the next five years, both Martin Luther King, Jr., and Bobby Kennedy were to meet the same fate. By nature, students are disposed to challenge their elders, and their respect for authority in any form was being undermined by what they saw happening in the society around them.

In the presence of all this ferment, various student protest organizations came into being. Probably the most prominent was Students for a Democratic Society (SDS). Its founders had met, produced a charter, and organized chapters across the country. SDS was viewed as a radical organization, but it was not violent in its inception. It was confrontational, and this could make things a bit messy as well as angry. It seems always to be true, however, that such activist groups as SDS find it impossible to maintain discipline in their own ranks. They cannot control what all their members or hangers-on will do. Once a confrontation gets underway, it can easily get out of control. Television had made obvious to all those who were watching civil rights disputes that even peaceful activities, carried on by large numbers of people, are difficult to manage without incident.

I came to dispute-resolution problems with a substantial amount of experience. For twenty years, I had been involved in labor disputes and mediation. I was accustomed to angry exchanges, even threats. I knew that there was a certain amount of theater about all such activities, and that attempting to bait the adversary and cause an intemperate response was an age-old tactic. Though some of the rhetoric sounded revolutionary, my own estimate of the student situation was that there was only a tiny core (twenty-five people) who were genuine, would-be revolutionaries. The public tended, because of the continuing cold war with Russia, to label them all as communists. Some undoubtedly were since they were the sons and daughters of well-known communists, but others were more nearly anarchists, nihilists, or simply idealists who had grown cynical with the world around them. Beyond that group, there were then concentric circles of student groups that could be mobilized around a given issue. A number might hold somewhat radical political views but were not violent or destructive, a still larger group would be sympathetic over certain issues and would swell the crowd, and a still larger number were simply curious. If one watched the crowds that were assembled for any occasion, the number would generally vary from one hundred to perhaps five hundred. The problem could be compounded by the presence of juvenile or community dissidents who were not a part of the university. Only on a relatively few occasions were there more than that, and those occasions tended to be limited to when the police or the National Guard came on the scene.

Leaders of campus protests were always very shrewd about picking a spot to protest where classes were being released on the hour and thousands of students would be milling around. While this could make a momentary difference, and certainly placed a premium on how the protest was handled, it did not change the fact that, on a campus of thirty-five or forty thousand students, not more than 1 to 2 percent of the students regularly took part in most of the protests, and some of that number were merely curious. To put it another way, 98 percent of the students were not participating in a destructive manner. Nevertheless, even one hundred people pose a problem if they are determined to cause trouble. From a tactical point of view, this meant to me that, in coping with demonstrations, we should do everything possible to avoid actions that would be seen by other students as unfair, repressive, or unwarranted because this would only swell the ranks of those who were disposed to trouble.

There was, for me, still another problem in dealing with the issues that troubled students. I, too, thought that our engagement in Vietnam was wrong. I, too, was shocked at racial violence and our societal unwillingness to face and try to resolve racial problems. I, too, thought that universities had to revise some of their policies with respect to the kinds of research that would be accepted.

In short, I and a great many others within the university could sympathize with some of the objectives the student groups were trying to achieve. Where we parted ways was when some students tried to coerce others to their point of view by making it impossible for a dissenting point of view to be heard or in resorting to violence. It was then that they demonstrated the totalitarian ways that characterize both the far right and the far left.

In the face of this dilemma, I tried to think in tactical terms. How could we encourage orderly change to take place without bowing to tactics that could destroy a university that, as much or more than any other, had for so long encouraged "that continual and fearless sifting and winnowing by which alone the truth can be found"? I knew from the long and sometimes bloody history of labor-management disputes in the United States that force in the resolution of our civil problems should only be used as a last resort. It more often than not only makes the problem worse. If this was true, then we ought to continually signal our willingness to make changes, to consult with both faculty and students, to initiate proposals, and to refuse to react to verbal insults or attacks or even minor disruptions. The use of police or the National Guard ought to be resisted as long as possible, and then they should be used only sparingly. To behave in this manner would, I knew, bring vigorous criticism from those who were understandably outraged at what was happening on campuses. They would want to strike back by expelling such students or at least prosecuting them to the hilt. On the other hand, if we avoided severe retribution, we might be able to hold the great bulk of the students with us and demonstrate that the bitterness, hatred, divisiveness, and truly violent behavior could be contained. To do so would also bring about some much-needed change.

It is, of course, one thing to say that force should be avoided, that one's temper should be restrained in the face of great provocation, that the gross personal insults and obscenities must be ignored, and that the sadness of a total lack of civility would have to be largely endured. It is another thing to pursue that course of action! All of my personal instincts were offended by such conduct, but I was convinced that if I showed this I would be doing exactly what the violent protesters wanted me to do.

There were to be many troublesome incidents while I was at Wisconsin, but two or three of them are perhaps worth recounting. The most famous one, I now suspect largely distorted by myth, arose in February, 1967. A vigorous, but not violent, group had taken over one of our administrative offices in Bascom Hall. It was not my office, but one nearby, and I went to the other office and talked to them a bit. They even suggested that they would restrain me within that office unless I agreed to their demands, but I made it clear that I would leave when I was ready and they did not attempt to stop me from doing so. They were protesting allowing Dow Chemical, which produced napalm, to recruit on campus. Later, after I was back in my own office, the students were arrested for trespassing when they refused to leave the building. The SDS group promptly called for a mass meeting that night to condemn the arrests. When I became aware of what had happened, I met with Joseph Kauffman, who was our dean of students and whom I had

Left: Robben and Teddy,
    circa 1921
*Below left: From left to
    right:* Teddy, Mother,
    and Robben, 1921
*Below right: From left to
    right:* Teddy, Father,
    and Robben, 1922

From left to right: Robben, Teddy, and Jack, circa 1926

Left: Beloit College
        basketball practice,
        1937
Below: Robben in Paw
        Paw High School
        baseball uniform, 1934

Robben and Jack in uniform, World War II

Left to right: Sol Barsy, Ed Amyot, and Robben Fleming at Tizo Ouzo, Algeria, 1943

During leave in Scotland, 1944

Left: Preinvasion
posting in
England, 1944
Below: Military
Government
Detachment at
Landshut,
Germany, 1945.
Robben: *front
row, far left*

Right: At home in Urbana with Sally, Nancy, and James, 1952

Below left: Hosting Frances Perkins at the University of Illinois, 1952

Below right: At home in Urbana with James, Sally, Nancy, Betsy, and Taffy, 1960

Left: Robben and Sally, taken when the appointment as Michigan's president was announced, 1967. (AP Wirephoto.)
Below: Bascom Hall at the University of Wisconsin, Madison, site of the Chancellor's Office

At home in Madison with Betsy, James, and Sally, 1967

Delivering the presidential inaugural address at Hill Auditorium, 1967

Addressing the Michigan Legislature, 1967

Leaving a student demonstration on the Diag, 1968

Anti-ROTC demonstrators at North Hall entrance, 1969

Anti–Vietnam War demonstration on the Diag, 1969

A student demonstration in front of Hill Auditorium, 1970

Tenting on the Diag, 1970

BAM strikers at the west entrance to Hill Auditorium, 1970

Appearing on *Meet the Press,* April 26, 1970

The ACE delegation to China with Deng Xiaoping at the Great Hall, 1974

Local Michigan alumni form an impromptu welcoming committee in Hong Kong, 1974

Right: With President Ephraim Katzir of Israel at Rackham Auditorium honorary degree ceremony, 1975

Below: With President Gerald R. Ford at Michigan, 1976

Speaking at a dinner given in honor of my retirement from Michigan, 1979

Left to right: Newton Minow, Robben Fleming, and Walter Annenberg at the Corporation for Public Broadcasting, 1980

recruited from a high position in the Peace Corps. He and I sat in my office chatting about what to do about the students who were in jail. I was concerned about having them in jail when the evening meeting took place because I knew that this might make them martyrs in the eyes of other students. Joe suddenly said, "Why don't we bail them out?" I thought this was a great idea, and, since I had just received a substantial check for writing a chapter in a book, I said I would put up the money. The necessary arrangements were quickly made. Eleven students were involved: three were freshmen, four were sophomores, two were juniors, and two were seniors. The bail was something in the neighborhood of $105 each. I paid with a check, and the students were released. Both Joe and I then went to the rally that night in the Bascom Hall auditorium that held several hundred people. Some of the SDS people talked, and both Joe and I then talked. The SDS people were puzzled as to just what to do. It was hard to castigate the university, or us, in view of the fact that we had bailed out the students. Both Joe and I explained why we could not permit one set of students to dictate to other students whether or not they could interview for employment with a given company. Among other things, such a stand was inconsistent with their view that students were adults who were competent to make their own decisions. After perhaps an hour, all the steam went out of the meeting and it adjourned with no further plans being proposed for student action. Among other things, that experience taught me how important it was to not allow a dissenting group to capitalize on an incident without listeners hearing the other side of the dispute. Thereafter I was always insistent on showing up to defend our positions.

Madison had two newspapers, one of which was the *Capital Times*, which was owned by William Evjue, and had the editorial view of liberal Democrats, while the other was the *State Journal*, which was conservative and was generally Republican in its views. Both played up the bail out. The *Capital Times* glorified me as a battler against oppression. The *State Journal* was critical, but not without some degree of understanding. The state's conservative press and conservative legislators were critical, but the incident gained a great deal of national attention, much of which was favorable.

Most people were probably simply puzzled by the incident, and therefore it was a subject of great discussion. Almost no one, as far as I could see, understood why I had put up the bail. Bail only meant that the students would get out of jail, which was what I wanted lest they become martyrs in the eyes of students and thereby greatly magnify what was essentially a relatively minor incident. Having been arrested, the students would still have to be tried. All the bail did was to asssure their presence at the trials. Months later the trials were held. Several of the students were found guilty and either fined or required to do some type of community service. Through a glitch at the court, some of the bail money was returned to some students. Later I recovered the bail for five students, two had no money, and four simply skipped away from any repayment. In this they were abetted by their lawyer, who persisted in saying that the money properly belonged to the students because they had paid it. There was total local knowledge that this was not so, but the lawyer never recanted, probably because that was how he got his fee! In any event, I lost some money, but it was worth it and I never sought to be recompensed. The lawyer's conduct I found reprehensible. Activist attorneys who allege that they are fighting for social justice are not always as pure in their motivations as they would like us to believe.

Later, several of the parents of the arrested students wrote to me thanking me for providing bail. One had this to say, and I suspect it represented the views of many bewildered parents of the time.

> Some how it seems to me that times have gotten more and more trying, although our own antics must have given our parents and mentors some anxious moments back when. But youth, nowadays, it seems to me, must needs struggle with increased competition, a more disturbing culture and the prospect of what looks like perpetual war.
>
> So our job as parents takes on a little more drive as we try to impart strength, wisdom, and patience to our children. The first easily apparent result is that *we* are aging a little faster. The rest remains to be seen.

There were, of course, other incidents. At the Business School, the place set aside for job interviews was in a basement room with a narrow hallway approaching it. Students who were determined to prevent companies that made products related to the war effort from coming to campus threatened to disrupt the interviews. In any event, we felt that whether a student chose to interview or not was his or her own business and that we could not permit other students to make this impossible.

As the standoff approached, our campus police came to me to ask what they should do. I thought it essential that the interviews proceed, but I also thought allowing them to take place at the usual site would be a disaster, largely because disruption would be so easy at that location. In addition to everything else, the Business School was located right at the top of Bascom Hill on which thousands of other students would be coming and going from classes. This meant that if we had to use the police it would be easy to create an incident and get otherwise noninvolved students to participate. So I insisted that we hold the interviews at the Field House, which was several blocks off the main campus and where there would be no additional students. Despite protests from some of the business faculty, who considered my action "gutless" and said so, we followed that plan and avoided any problem. There were those who said I had no principles. I thought the problem was not one of principle but of tactics. I had been taught in the military that if you are going to have a skirmish it is better if you pick the terrain! I argued that we were preserving the principle that one group of students could not dictate to another whether they could interview a given employer, but doing it at a site we could protect. That answer did not satisfy my critics.

There was another occasion on which students occupied a section of the business office building where there was a large lobby in which they chose to make their stand. I do not recall what the issue was. By closing time they were not disposed to leave the building, so the question came up of whether we should force them out. Because of the nature of the building, there was no problem as long as they simply remained in the lobby portion and did not try to roam around and disrupt any of the offices. Accordingly, we told them they could remain in the building and hold meetings all night if they wanted to, just as long as they did not go elsewhere in the building and did not interfere with business when the building opened the next morning. Naturally, we would keep security people in the building to see that these conditions were met. Having thought that we would evict them, they had no counterplans and their occupancy of the building for a couple of nights proceeded on the terms agreed upon. Then they left peacefully. There was little criticism of that incident since no one seemed to find a principle that was being violated.

There were other, less publicized incidents that were, in their own way, even more troubling. Some of the most activist students decided it would advance their cause of educational reform if they informed their professors at the outset of a new course that the first day would be spent in deciding what role, if any, the professor would play in teaching the course. This was not something that had great appeal to the professoriate. The more conservative faculty members promptly responded that they would manage the course and that if the students preferred another method they could change courses. Others, who genuinely thought that there might indeed be some merit in changing the way a course was taught, were willing to listen. Still others, whose sympathies were with the students, welcomed the approach until they discovered that it was meant to apply to their own courses! When some of the activist students came to see me to talk about this tactic, I said: "Let me see if I understand what you are proposing. Let us assume we are talking about a course in surgery in the Medical School, and the subject is the performance of an appendectomy. Now we all know that we have an appendix, but most of us are not entirely sure exactly where it is. Since we know it is in the midsection somewhere, one way to go at removing it would be to simply open up the midsection and look around. We might find some other interesting things in the process and even wonder which was the appendix. The process might be very exciting, but if any of us were the patient wouldn't we feel a little better about it if the professor who already knew where the appendix was made the incision? And if that is so, might it not be true in most cases that the professor knows more about the course than the do students?" They didn't think I was very funny. I wasn't sure I was either, but sometimes the temptation to goad them a little was too overwhelming to pass up.

Equally disturbing to all of us who believe that the university is a place where all kinds of views can be expressed was the fact that the radical left mobilized to disrupt any speaker whose views they did not approve. Meanwhile, they insisted that their own views, and those of people whom they approved, must be heard. What this affirmed for those who were thoughtful about the subject was, of course, that this was basically a totalitarian approach. Hitler and Mussolini accepted no deviation from their views. Neither did Stalin and the communists at the other end of the political spectrum.

Protecting a speaker whom the radical left did not want to have speak was not a problem of physical attack. The difficulty was that noise and insulting behavior made hearing difficult and unpleasant. Some speakers could handle this, others could not. Henry Kissinger came to speak once during Lyndon Johnson's presidency, while the

Vietnam controversy was heating up. He was still at Harvard and also an advisor to Governor Rockefeller of New York. He maintained his calm, overpowered the critics with his superior knowledge, and even made them listen. But he was an exception.

Even more exasperating, from my point of view, were graduate students who were teaching assistants. Some of them were so sympathetic to the radical students that they would use class time to discuss current controversies that were unrelated to the subject matter with which they were supposed to deal. They were entitled to their personal views on any of the matters in question, but they were not entitled to use class time to discuss them when such things were irrelevant to their courses. We would hear about this because students who did not like it would complain, and we would, in turn, ask the deans and the department heads to take appropriate action. As a general proposition, they did so, but it was not always as effective as one might wish.

Inevitably, those of us who held high academic office during the period of unrest got a good deal of publicity. Some of it was favorable, some was not, largely depending on the views of the TV or print reporters who were talking or writing about us. Many presidents of universities lost their positions as a result of the turmoil and others simply retired. Governing boards were therefore obliged to look for successors, and chancellors or deans at other universities were, quite naturally, logical candidates. Thus I began to hear shortly after the new year in 1967 that my name had been submitted at a number of places. One usually first gets this information from friends who write to say that they have submitted your name. The first call came, I think, from the University of Michigan, to be followed shortly thereafter by a call from the University of Minnesota. In both cases their presidents were retiring, Met Wilson at Minneosta in July and Harlan Hatcher at Michigan at the end of the year.

I had very mixed feelings about taking a presidency anywhere. It was evident that the current student unrest was going to continue because the problems that lay behind it were unresolved. While I had had some success up to that time in dealing with student problems, it was a very iffy business and there was certainly no guarantee that in so volatile an area this could continue. We loved the University of Wisconsin and living in Madison. Many of our old friends were there, and we had already asked our children to make a move three years earlier.

There is, of course, one's own ego that is salved by having two major universities pursue one for the presidency. My peril of survival was probably as great at Wisconsin as anywhere if student unrest got out of hand. Our oldest daughter, Nancy, was already away at college, and our son, Jim, had graduated from high school and was enrolled at Wisconsin. He was living away from home. Our youngest daughter, Betsy, would go with us if we moved, but she was a very resilient child who adapted easily to new circumstances. Sally had established herself firmly at Wisconsin, but she was, and is, a "people" person who endears herself to everyone wherever she goes.

One other thought went through my mind. How would we feel if I got fired from a very visible position? I could make a living all right, and I wouldn't go anywhere without also being made a full professor of law with tenure. I could also return to the world of arbitration and make a good living. But would I even want to remain at a university where I had just been fired as president? I wasn't deceived by the fact that so far things had gone well at Wisconsin. There was a small but hard-core group of students at major universities who were genuinely intent on total disruption. One might outwit them for awhile and hold the bulk of the students to a rational course, but the chances of total success were not high. The activist students at Wisconsin were by then calling me "The Silver Fox"—"silver" because of my gray hair and "fox" because they felt I was outwitting them and this was somehow unfair. They had by then decided that allowing themselves to be bailed out of jail was a mistake and that they should have refused in order to become martyrs. (But I had in my files, from one of the girls who was arrested, a letter of thanks on the ground that she did not want to be in jail!)

The other side of the case was that, because of my personal background, I was better prepared to deal with disruption than were most presidents. The academic world had been good to me and to our family. Perhaps I owed it to that world to try to pay it back in its time of trouble.

Anyway, those were my thoughts as presidential feelers came. Minnesota had the more urgent problem, since Met Wilson would leave in July of 1967. Michigan had a little more time since no replacement was needed until January of 1968. Nevertheless, it was the Michigan delegation that I saw first. One of its Regents, Robert Briggs, called to say that he was the chairman of a "nameless" committee and could he and another Regent come and see us? Neither of us wanted any publicity about this, therefore we asked him to come to the house for dinner. With him came William Cudlip, who was another of the Regents. We dispensed with any help at the dinner; Sally cooked, and Betsy helped with the service. They took a cab to the house and I returned them to the airport. We talked for about two hours, it was a very pleasant occasion, and they left, saying that they were still in the search process and would be in touch with me again. I didn't take the Michigan probe too seriously for a reason that academic people will easily understand. I knew that in the top hierarchy at Michigan were two lawyers. The executive vice president, Marvin Niehuss, was a lawyer, as was Allan Smith, who was the vice president for academic affairs. No university is likely to want three men from the same discipline at the top of the administrative team. Much later, after I was at Michigan, I mentioned this to Bill Haber, an old friend on the Michigan faculty. He had a wonderful sense of humor and he said to me, "That was never a problem, I told them you weren't a very good lawyer!"

The Minnesota pursuit began almost immediately after the visit by the Michigan Regents. They, too, wanted to send a delegation down. This time there was a half dozen of them, and we had them at the house for lunch, once again in total secrecy. Because of their need for speed, they wanted us to come to Minneapolis soon for a visit. It happened that we were due for a trip or two out of town and I couldn't make the visit immediately.

I was uneasy about dealing with two universities at once. If I was going anywhere, I didn't want to bargain one against the other. To avoid this, I called Robert Briggs at Michigan, told him that I had talked to Minnesota and that they were having to proceed more rapidly than Michigan. He urged me not to make any decision without first talking again to Michigan.

Not too long thereafter we did visit Minneapolis. They sent a private plane down, Sally and I flew up and visited Met Wilson at the president's house, and then I had lunch with the Board of Regents at a downtown club. I had a feeling they were going to offer me the presidency, and I really didn't want this to happen until I knew the outcome of the Michigan visit. Sally and I still hadn't forced ourselves to think seriously about leaving Wisconsin or, if we did, where we would like to go. Accordingly, before any offer could be made, I told them that I had promised Michigan not to make a decision until I had talked further with them. Unfortunately, this did not deter the Minnesota offer. The chairman of the board pulled from his pocket a firm contract that he hoped I would sign. It is now in the archives at Michigan. I said I must honor my pledge to Michigan, and that I would have to reserve an answer for at least another week. There was then talk about how to keep the news out of the press. We agreed that if the press learned about our visit, we would both say that there was a visit, that we had talked, and that we would talk again. With that, their plane flew us back to Madison. Sally and I had no sooner reached our house than the phone rang and a Minneapolis reporter told me that he was informed that the presidency had been offered to me and would I comment. I stuck to our agreed line, saying that we had talked and agreed to discuss it further later. But I also called my principal contact in Minneapolis, told him of the call, and he responded that someone at the luncheon had obviously leaked the story. The story then broke in the Minneapolis papers, and one of the papers insisted on coming down for a family picture that they subsequently printed.

The following week Sally and I went to Detroit to have dinner at the Ponchartrain Hotel with the Michigan Regents and a representative or two of their faculty, alumni, and student committees. We talked for about two hours, most of it consisting of my response to questions from the group. The bulk of the conversation centered on how to deal with student problems. I outlined my philosophy, told them that I thought force must be avoided insofar as humanly possible, that indignities and insults could be endured if they averted violence, and that I thought these problems would last for some unspecified time, but that they would eventually end. Everyone was very kind to us during the course of the dinner.

The next morning we were invited to visit Ann Arbor, where Sally had never been. I knew the city a little because I had lectured at the Law School. We ended up having a very gracious lunch with President and Mrs. Hatcher at the president's house. All of this was done quietly in order to avoid publicity. Following the luncheon, Bob Briggs drove us back to the airport and, in the course of the drive, offered me the presidency of Michigan, a move that had apparently been agreed upon by the Regents at a meeting earlier that morning. I told him I had promised to talk once again to Minnesota, and that Sally and I would have to think about the matter over the weekend before replying. Then we flew home.

Finally, we were up against a decision. Up to then it had all been rather heady fun and games. We talked about it on the way home and over the course of the weekend. I also talked to Fred Harrington, whom

I had kept informed. On Monday I called both Michigan and Minnesota saying that we had decided to go to Michigan. It was a very hard decision to make, but some of the factors that went into the decision were the fact that we preferred a small city (Ann Arbor) over a big city (Minneapolis–St. Paul), we shivered a little at the thought of going still further north, and we knew that Michigan was one of the two or three best public universities in the country.

We knew a few people at Michigan, but not many. We were leaving many old friends in Madison, and we would face a future fraught with problems. Meanwhile, a *Minneapolis Star* sports reporter wrote the following in his paper.

> Who knows to what lengths Michigan went to land Fleming? A no-cut contract? Three draft choices to be named at next year's Commencement? A trade in which Wisconsin gets two political science professors plus a blond laboratory technician in exchange for Fleming? . . . Michigan, I think, is capable of these manipulations. . . . I think you have the answer in the disclosure that Fleming visited in Minneapolis a few weeks ago and . . . was required to park a car at the University. Having undergone this shattering experience, Fleming was happy to return to his job . . . on (the) Madison campus.

The Madison City Council passed a very generous resolution saying that: "Upon his assumption of the duties of Chancellor, Dr. Fleming showed great abilities as a skillful negotiator, a distinguished leader and a brilliant administrator."

The governor, Warren Knowles, very kindly invited us to come to dinner at the governor's home along with some guests of our own choosing. We invited the Harringtons and my brother Jack and his wife. It was a lovely evening, but as we stood on the terrace before dinner and looked out over the sunset on Lake Mendota there was also a degree of sadness about it all.

The following year the University of Wisconsin invited us back for me to receive an honorary degree. It was immensely pleasing to receive a great ovation from the crowd in the stadium.

So ended our official affiliation with the University of Wisconsin. All three of our children have degrees from that institution, and we have nothing but affection for it.

Today, because of a recent Michigan law, we would have had to be publicly announced as a potential candidate for the position at Michigan, we would have had to be interviewed by countless people, we would have had to say to a university at which we were very happy that we were interested in going elsewhere, and we would run the public risk that we would not be chosen, whereupon Wisconsin would sense that we were not totally devoted to its interests and wonder whether we were right for that university. Would we have been willing to submit to the present procedure? Certainly not! What possible incentive to consider another position is there for one who knows that other universities are searching for a president but who has not applied for or given any indication of interest in the position, if he or she must be put on public display and then possibly turned down? It is no answer to say that many states now have such laws and that they manage to hire presidents. Of course they do, there is no other way to get it done. But is it either the way to get the best people, or is there any evidence that it produces better results than the previous process? And how is it that the public is better served? Those questions remain unanswered.

I have never understood the argument of the press that it is vital to the welfare of the state of Michigan that its university presidents be chosen by full public exposure to the process. The *Ann Arbor News*, which might have been expected to understand the problem more than many other newspapers, has been among the strongest proponents of the law. Why? Does it not trust the publicly elected Regents and the alumni, faculty, and student search committees to make good judgments? Does it contend that the University of Michigan has made bad choices for presidents in the past and that all this be cured by public disclosure? If that is the argument, the local paper has never said so. Or are the newspapers in their perpetual battle with the television and cable stations for primacy in the news field just hoping for a way to publish additional news whether or not it has undesirable side effects?

I did not apply to be a candidate for the Michigan presidency. My name was, as I have already said, submitted by friends without my knowledge. The contact with me was initiated by the Regents. Neither of us knew at that point whether we were interested in the other. Because the meetings were conducted in private, we had a chance to explore our mutual interests without my being labeled a candidate or without the university having to feel any sense of commitment.

The present law is, in my view, bad public policy. If the old system has to be changed, I would suggest that, after the position has been announced, the names of all those who are either applicants or have been *recommended without application* be disclosed with care taken to distinguish between the two categories. Let the press then investigate *all* of the people as much as they want to, but let the rest of the process proceed privately. That way people who are not candidates in any sense of the word, but who might consider it if this could be done privately, would be protected. In the meantime, if those who have not applied are asked about it, they can fend off inquiries by simply pointing out that they have not applied and that they are happy where they are. Of course, the press will say this approach imposes more work on them. There is an easy answer to that. Do they want a process that gives the greatest likelihood of getting the best choices or do they simply want a process that minimizes both their reporting difficulties and the chances of getting many potentially good people to consider the position?

The Michigan legislature currently has before it a bill that would change the present law. I hope for the sake of the University of Michigan that it will do so. The iniquity of the present law has now been further demonstrated by a recent judicial decision to require publication of *all* materials related to the most recent presidential search, *including the letters of those who were promised confidentiality.* For all practical purposes, that ends the possibility of getting candid recommendations from colleagues who know the candidates best. Would you write a letter assessing the strengths and weaknesses of a given candidate whom you know well if you knew in advance that the letter could be published in the newspapers? I think the answer is self-evident. Is it good public policy, then, to have the law in its present form on this matter? I think that, under pressure from the press and the media, a great disservice to the state has been done.

Chapter 11

Becoming a Wolverine

Once the decision was made to go to Michigan, we paid two visits to Ann Arbor prior to moving there. One was in connection with a press conference to announce my appointment and the other was later in the summer for me to make a speech there in the course of the university's celebration of its sesquicentennial. The latter fitted in nicely with a trip we had already planned to the World's Fair, which was taking place in Canada that summer.

Secrecy about the appointment had been pretty well maintained, though the newspapers did get word of it the day before it was announced. I was introduced at a small press conference where a dissident student promptly assailed me and made it clear that, in his view, I was neither wanted nor needed at Michigan. The next morning I nevertheless had a lengthy and quiet conversation with a large number of students and it went very well. The dissident student was to become well known to me in the next few years. He was in a perpetually troubled state and he always had difficulty maintaining his composure. Fortunately, he had no influence with others, even those who shared some of his views, and he later got in trouble with other students because of his threatening ways.

By sheer accident I had long since agreed with Professor Russell Smith, a member of the Michigan law faculty and an old friend of mine, to be a guest in his labor arbitration seminar that same day. We had exchanged visits before, and I could not very well cancel the seminar date without revealing the announcement that was to be made that day, so I fitted the seminar into a period right after the press conference.

Before actually moving to Michigan, a number of questions remained to be answered in both Madison and Ann Arbor. Wisconsin would need to name a new chancellor and that might take time. That problem was solved when, after consultation with President Harrington, we jointly decided that I would leave the chancellor's position on September 1. I would be a lame duck if I remained in office, a tentative decision was made that my successor would be someone already at Wisconsin, and Michigan was willing to have us come to Ann Arbor in September so that we would have an opportunity to get acquainted with the university before taking office. To assist us, Michigan rented a faculty home for us on Morton Avenue within walking distance of the university, and we lived there for most of the fall semester. I wanted to remain out of the way of the current administration until I took office, so I asked for and got an office in the Law School during that time.

Our other complication was that our daughter Nancy, who had just graduated from Beloit College, wanted to be married in our home in Madison on September 1. That would momentarily delay our move to Ann Arbor, but since we would not need our own furniture until later, our Madison home could remain intact for Nancy's wedding. She and Josh Reckord, a fellow Beloit graduate, were married by an Episcopal minister in our backyard with just a few family friends on both sides in attendance. We had a small reception and luncheon afterward, and the day was a warm and friendly family occasion. After a brief honeymoon, Nancy and Josh were slated to teach in the inner city in Milwaukee.

The day after the wedding we set out for Ann Arbor. We hitched a small trailer to our car to carry odds and ends and strapped our canoe to the top of the car. It didn't occur to us that perhaps we ought to arrive in a little more style, and we afterward suspected that there was a good deal of amusement on Morton Avenue when the new president drove up with a wife, two children, a reddish brown Dachshund named E.B., and a rental trailer that the family began to unload.

Our son, Jim, promptly returned to Madison where he would be a sophomore at the University of Wisconsin, and Betsy enrolled in Tappan Junior High School in Ann Arbor.

Having four months to get to know the University of Michigan before assuming any responsibilities was a very good idea. It gave us a chance to get to know the Regents, many of the alumni and alumnae clubs, many faculty members, and a number of students. We accepted a great many invitations, particularly to student residences, attended all kinds of cultural events, and participated in the fun of the fall football season. I visited all the deans in their various schools and colleges and tried to get a picture of their problems. In the process, I was very impressed with the depth and quality of the university. John Hannah was still president of Michigan State University, and he very kindly invited us to come and visit their impressive campus. Later in the fall, Michigan State awarded me an honorary degree and I spoke at their commencement. I knew the rivalry between the two universities was strong, but I wanted good relations between us, and John Hannah felt likewise. We became good friends.

Harlan and Anne Hatcher were also very kind and helpful to us in getting to know the city and the university. During the monthly Regents' meetings in the fall, Harlan insisted that I sit with him at the head of the table, although he conducted the meetings and I was largely, and properly, simply an observer.

In terms of where we could live, the Regents offered either the President's House, built in 1840 and expanded periodically thereafter, or Inglis House, which was adjacent to the Arboretum, and was built in 1928 and given to the university in 1950 through a bequest of a Detroit businessman, James Inglis. The President's House was one of the original university buildings in the middle of the campus, and Inglis House was about a mile away, off campus. Because of the student unrest on most campuses, some presidents did not want to live in the middle of the campus where they could be continually exposed to protests.

Sally and I thought about the two options and decided on the President's House. It was better suited to large-scale entertaining, it had a certain mystique growing out of its history, it would resolve a lot of parking problems in attending events on campus, and besides Inglis House was being used for many other purposes that were important to the university. As to the students, I wanted to establish at the outset that I could not be intimidated by harassment or calls to appear and defend myself from one or another alleged defect in the character of the university or myself. On the contrary, I viewed such appearances as opportunities to tell the other side of the story to those who were uncommitted. We never regretted our decision to to live in the President's House. It is a wonderful and gracious old home, and we were very happy there. It was well staffed with a cook, a gardener, and a housekeeper who kept us in a style to which we were unaccustomed!

Whenever a new president of a university is named, there will eventually be some kind of inaugural ceremony. I had taken office on January 1, 1968, and the inaugural was planned for March 12, 1968. We were given an opportunity to provide input as to the occasion, but aside from expressing the view that it be modest in scale and economical in cost, all the work was done by others.

The nicest part of the inaugural from our point of view was that it provided a glorious opportunity to have old friends and family come to Ann Arbor to be with us. Sally's parents were both gone by this time, but one sister and her husband came from California. Unfortunately, my mother, to whom I owed so much, was too ill to come, but all our children (plus Josh), a half dozen of our family from Paw Paw, Illinois, my brother and his wife from Wisconsin, old friends from our Wisconsin and Illinois days, and assorted comrades from my Army days, did come. I was especially moved by the fact that some of those I knew in the Army simply read about the event in the national press and called to say they were coming. There is a special bond that somehow seems to tie together those who have shared a wartime experience, and their presence twenty-two years after we were discharged meant a great deal to me.

The ceremonies attendant on the inaugural extended, as I recall, over a two-day period, starting with a dinner on Friday night and ending with a purely friends-and-family dinner at the President's House on Saturday night. The weather turned out to be beautiful. March days in Michigan are not noted for warmth and sunshine, but that day was so nice no coats were necessary. By Sunday, incidentally, there was a blizzard! The committee that planned the event did a beautiful job and Hill Auditorium, where the ceremony was held, was ideal.

In the course of the inaugural there would be a colorful academic parade, and then an assortment of speakers before I would be installed and then invited to speak. Among the speakers would be someone from the student government. They chose a graduate student who promptly composed a speech strongly asserting student rights and suggesting that I was on trial and might not fit the bill. He had provided a copy of the speech to the university in advance, as had the others, and I was promptly advised that his remarks were not going to be very palatable. Any thought of either censoring what he said or refusing to let him speak would nevertheless be a major mistake, because to do so would generate more controversy than would his remarks. The essence of what he said is captured in the following quote.

> The University has long been, but it cannot remain, an aristocracy.
> The time is near when students will demand equality and justice here, as they have demanded them elsewhere, and the faculty will have to learn humility as many administrators have already learned humility.

That our new president has the courage to serve, I have no doubt. That he also has the knowledge and wisdom to lead us well through the profound transformation that has already begun, we can only hope, and wait, and see.

The audience, which was largely composed of academics and alumni, thought the remarks presumptuous and accorded the student only a little polite applause.

In preparing what I wanted to say, I did, of course, want to be serious, but I also wanted to lighten the occasion with some humor. I knew there were going to be student problems ahead and that they would be unpopular with the public, but I wanted to keep them in perspective and not leave the impression that I thought this was a time of great crisis. Accordingly, I tried to mix humor and substance. Here are some excerpts from what I said.

. . . in preparing for this occasion I turned to Professor Howard Peckham's recent history of the University of Michigan. . . . The book is organized around the various presidents . . . , and it is not long before the gigantic figure of President Tappan strolls across its pages. Let me read a brief passage about Tappan.

> Henry Philip Tappan arrived in Ann Arbor . . . in the summer of 1852, fresh from Europe. He was forty-seven years old, six feet tall and handsome, with side and under-chin whiskers. In the semirural town of Ann Arbor, he was unmistakable . . . Outdoors, he carried a cane and was invariably accompanied by one of his huge St. Bernards, Buff or Leo. In a day of stovepipe hats, he wore a felt hat tipped to one side. He walked briskly to stores not unlike the lord of the manor in the marketplace of the peasants.
>
> He looked like a university president. The students were not merely impressed, they were almost overwhelmed. Some of them more than fifty years later remembered him with awe. Their comments paint him best: "It was a liberal education even for the stupid to be slightly acquainted with him."

After reading that far (about my illustrious predecessor), I stopped for contemplation, and to wonder about my own qualifications.

Aside from being six feet tall, my image seemed inappropriate. In place of the two huge St. Bernards, I possessed only a small daschshund who had never learned to walk with a leash and who therefore protested every step of the way, making choking sounds designed to attract the Humane Society. I did not own a cane nor a top hat, and the whiskers were all on the students. Instead of walking through the marketplace like the lord of the manor, I found myself dodging both pedestrian and vehicular traffic, just to stay alive. And if the students were awed by me, they had most extraordinary ways of showing it. As a matter of fact, in persuading our own children to attend this ceremony, I thought it best to describe it as my "thing"!

This part of my address was well received, probably because it lightened the tension resulting from the student's remarks. I then turned to the more serious part of what I had to say, from which I shall only quote briefly.

Having said along the way that "a university is also a place for the dreaming of great dreams," I went on to say of these dreams:

The first of these is that we can preserve at Michigan the kind of climate in which controversy can flourish, and do so in an atmosphere of dignity and respect for others. The university is, by definition and by tradition, a marketplace of ideas, and as such, controversy neither can nor should be avoided. Yet the halls of academe are populated by human beings, with all the normal human frailties. Students, and even faculty, can sometimes so lose their perspective that they seek to stifle views which differ from their own, or they impute to others motives less worthy than their own. When this happens, historic public-student animosities are renewed, legislators hear from their constituents, and alumni submerge memories (of the antics) of their own days on campus. Perhaps most serious of all, the fabric of the university community itself is threatened.

This is a time when a great international issue—the war in Vietnam—and a great domestic issue—race relations—divide our people. The realist would have to say that both issues are likely to get worse before they get better. The campus cannot be isolated from the mainstream of national life. It is predictable that strong differences of opinion will divide us. Is it too much to hope that in this home of the intellect we can conduct ourselves with dignity and respect? Or will we have to concede that the humanizing influences and values which we believe abound in the university are always betrayed in a time of stress? My dream, my belief, my commitment is that on this campus we can and will preserve our community in its time-honored values.

As an aside to this point, however, I am impelled to add that those of us who urge dignity and restraint must not put these qualities ahead of human welfare. It is often easier for critics of the present generation of students to fulminate against their bad manners, which are frequently displayed, than to accept the fact that underlying the bad manners may be a dedication to human well-being not found in their critics.

That part of what I had to say was, of course, directed both at the students and at their critics. The *Michigan Daily,* largely the captive of the activists in those days, talked in its report about allowing controversy to flourish, but said nothing about doing it in an atmosphere of dignity and respect for others. Nor did I expect what I said to have much impact on the critics of the students. What I was trying to accomplish was to state what the ground rules were by which I intended to be guided.

The years 1968 through 1970, and to a lesser extent thereafter, were to be accompanied by a great many student confrontations that I will deal with in another chapter. For the moment, I would prefer to talk about some of the other aspects of managing a university.

The faculty of a college or university is its most precious asset, thus a premium is placed upon good relations between the faculty and the administration. There is, by history and tradition, an expectation that the faculty will participate in the management of the enterprise. Though this is in accord with good management theory, it is not easy to apply in a big university because the many schools and colleges have their own traditions, and they are not always entirely compatible. Nevertheless, there is always some kind of centralized faculty entity that attempts to speak for all of the faculties. At Michigan there is an elected Senate Assembly that has a smaller executive committee called the Senate Assembly Committee on University Affairs (SACUA). At the time I came to Michigan, faculty representation on the central body was undergoing some change, and one of the things they wished to do was to have one of their own members chair faculty meetings instead of having the president do so. They were thoughtful enough to ask my view of this, and I told them that I had no substantive objection to this, but I did have one reservation about it. In a big university, it is impossible for the president to know most of the faculty personally and, if they do not even see him in faculty meetings, he may become a rather remote figure to most of them. This might in turn promote estrangement between the faculty and the president and this would be bad for everyone. They agreed that this was a legitimate concern, but they still wanted to chair their own meetings. The compromise they offered was that the president would be invited to all faculty meetings (I was, in fact, also a member of the Law faculty), and he could speak any time he wanted. This settled the matter, and over the years it turned out to be a very good arrangement.

Apart from the matter of who would chair faculty meetings, there was also a question of how some formal pattern of meetings between the president and SACUA could be arranged. I was entirely favorable to that idea and I proposed regular meetings at which there would be an advance agenda so that each of us could be adequately prepared. That was satisfactory to them, and we followed this practice throughout my term. Our contacts were not limited to the formal occasions, since there was also an understanding that there could be special meetings as needed. There was a further understanding that they could present directly to the Regents some of their concerns, one of which was their analysis of the salary-benefits picture at the university. The Regents also invited SACUA members to have dinner with them once a year so that they could get to know one another better, and the chairman of SACUA always played a prominent role in the conduct of commencement ceremonies.

There were other ways in which we tried to promote faculty-administration relations. I tried to visit a school or college faculty meeting periodically, and they would invite me to to talk about anything I wanted to. This was especially useful during the days of student turmoil, because it gave me an opportunity to help them understand our reasons for restraint in dealing with students.

We used other tactics in trying to promote good faculty-administration relations throughout our years. One of the most useful was an annual series of faculty-spouse dinners at the President's

House. We would deliberately mix faculty members from the different schools and colleges. They always seemed delighted to come to the big, old house. We could entertain about thirty people at a time, and after dinner we would place chairs in a huge circle in the living room and then have a seminar. The subject of the seminar was always some current university problem that was of general concern. I would start it off by posing the problem and then ask them how they thought we ought to deal with it. Because those attending were from very different schools and colleges within the university, they often did not know each other, and I knew that they would be bound to have differences of opinion. This was exactly what I hoped to demonstrate, because this would make it clear that any decision those of us in the administration made would be wrong from the standpoint of some people. Perhaps this would give them a little more sympathy with decision makers. Sally and I always felt that the dinners did more than anything else to maintain good relations with the faculty.

There were many other ways in which we tried to promote harmonious relations. Each vice president had an advisory committee with which he or she met regularly. Students wanted representation on committees of this kind, and we agreed. The vice president for academic affairs met regularly with the deans, and the president was always invited to those meetings (but not as chairman). From very early in my tenure, I had on my staff William Cash, whose function was to handle minority relations within our office. He was a Michigan graduate who was with the Department of Education in Washington when he joined us, and he performed very useful and dedicated service for us.

SACUA members were extraordinarily helpful during the days of student turbulence in rendering advice, in counseling their members on events, and in supporting the actions we took. The Senate Assembly also annually hosted a speech by the president in the fall term on the state of the university. We did not always agree on matters, but there was never any rancor about our disagreements and they were always understanding about our inability to please all of the faculty all of the time.

Quite apart from faculty relationships, there are also always public policy problems that a state-supported educational institution must face. One of them is the perennial dispute that arises about how many out-of-state students should be admitted, particularly if this means a limitation on in-state students. Historically, Michigan and Wisconsin had always had a large number of out-of-state students. In Michigan,

this was no problem in the very early days because there was no enrollment pressure, but as both Michigan and Wisconsin became very well
known and respected universities they drew heavy out-of-state enrollments, particularly from the East where there was a dearth of public
institutions. Once enrollment limitations had to be imposed, the inevitable result was that some in-state students were denied admission in
favor of some out-of-state students who were able to demonstrate better academic records. This quite naturally annoys in-state families who
put pressure on their politicians to restrict out-of-state enrollment. In-
state taxpayers are convinced that they are subsidizing out-of-state students while their own children are being denied entrance. This is not
literally true, because the taxpayer subsidy provides only part of the
cost of educating students. Out-of-state students pay higher tuition,
student financial aid (which now comes heavily from federal sources)
takes into account tuition differentials, and endowments, which come
from both in- and out-of-state sources, underwrite some of the cost.
Furthermore, national and world recognition is promoted by the presence of out-of-state and international students and this in turn greatly
benefits the state.

In Michigan, not even the legislature has ever insisted that no out-
of-state students be admitted so long as there are in-state applicants.
The question is what limits, if any, should be place on such enrollment.
Eventually an unwritten agreement is reached, which hovers around
25–30 percent of the undergraduate population. The graduate school is
not a problem because, by that time, students are old enough to be able
in many cases to claim residence anyway, and the pressures are not the
same. For the president of the university, the issue nevertheless continues to be sensitive, and one that periodically takes up a good deal of
time. It happened that my arrival coincided with one of those times, and
I made a good many speeches and held a number of conferences with
legislators in temporarily settling the matter.

Another of the pending items when I came was the fate of the
Residential College. During the sesquicentennial year, donors had been
solicited to support the project. It was to be a unit within the larger
College of Literature, Science, and the Arts and was expected to be
experimental. Its creation was somewhat controversial within LSA, but
it did have the endorsement of the college and the enthusiastic support
of its sponsors. There were, however, some problems. Attractive as the
idea was to a great many people, it got no support from donors. This

meant that if there was to be a Residential College, it would have to be funded by such money as the university could generate internally, and the scale of the project would have to be cut back. There was one further matter to be considered. The per-student cost of the Residential College would be higher than in LSA. In a time when students were skeptical of everything in the university, this fact would probably generate criticism and it did.

I well remember going to a dormitory for a discussion with students and being accosted by the charge that we were putting more money per student into the Residential College than in LSA, and that this was unfair. Happily, student research on such matters is frequently incomplete and I appeased them by asking a question. The cost of teaching different subjects, e.g., English versus chemistry, is quite different. One requires a very good library, the other requires both a library and expensive equipment. When you come to college, do you want free reign to study in whatever field most appeals to you? If so, aren't you better served by a tuition that is the same regardless of what you study? They seemed relatively satisfied with the idea of choice, and we moved on to some of our other alleged injustices.

We did make the decision to remodel the East Quad dormitory as a home for the Residential College, and it has been in existence since that time. For the many students who like the program, it has generated undying support. Those who don't like it can move back into LSA.

There was another problem with respect to the two branch campuses in the cities of Flint and Dearborn. They had been started because enrollment pressures on the Ann Arbor campus could not be accommodated, and the initial financial resources to support them came, in Flint, from the Mott Foundation and, in Dearborn, from the Ford family, which gave Henry Ford's home and its grounds as a campus. The idea was to put the schools immediately adjacent to a two-year community college that could give students the first two years of a liberal arts course. The branches would then offer the third and fourth years, and the students would receive a University of Michigan degree. Unfortunately, all of this sound and rational thinking was not working out as planned. Not enough of the students who went to the community colleges took the liberal arts curriculum, and without it they were not eligible for admission. Thus, the two branch campuses were not growing as expected. The alternatives were to close them down, which would have deeply offended the sponsors in both cities, or to make them four-year colleges and assume they could prosper in that mode. While we preferred the latter route, it would be hard to take that position if the community colleges to which they were joined were to oppose such a move. My own position was that I would support giving the branches four-year status if the heads of our campuses could assure us that the community colleges would not oppose us. To my surprise, they did not and we made the decision to proceed. The state Board of Education, which had certain coordinating functions in the field of higher education, would not be pleased because it was opposed to branch campuses, but it did not have the power to prevent such a move since our Regents were, by constitutional mandate, given the power to govern the university. The upshot of all this was that we did make both schools four-year institutions and, fortunately, they prospered. Both are now solid, stable institutions with enrollments in the six- to seven-thousand range.

And then there was the matter of appointing a new athletic director to succeed the highly respected Fritz Crisler. Fritz, incidentally, was someone I had first met while I was in high school, though no one knew that. He came from the little Illinois town of Earlville, which is only a few miles from my home town of Paw Paw. One year they had a basketball banquet at which Fritz, who was then athletic director at Princeton, spoke. My team was invited to attend. When we came to Michigan, I reminded Fritz of this occasion, and we always had a very cordial relationship. Johnny Orr, while he was the basketball coach at Michigan, used my relationship with Crisler to tell one of his funny stories. He said that when he was applying for the position he saw Crisler and got only scant attention, but right about that time my appointment was made and Fritz learned that both John and I were graduates of Beloit College. John always insisted that Fritz then called him back, suddenly showed enormous interest in him, and made him the basketball coach. There wasn't a word of truth in the story, but it made good telling.

The appointment of an athletic director at any school that has a strong athletic tradition is always one of a president's worst headaches. Countless almuni, plus myriad sports fans, not only take an interest in it, but assume expert status in giving advice. They are affronted if their advice is not followed and often vituperative in expressing their opinions of anyone who dares to ignore them. Many of them have candidates who are usually well-known coaches. In vigorous opposition to all the publicity that attaches to the appointment are many academics and those members of the public who regard athletics as peripheral to the university in the first place and overemphasized in the second.

Since the search for a successor to Fritz was well underway when I came, I did not have anything to do with its initial phases, but the actual appointment would not be made until I was in office. Three names emerged from the search committee: Don Canham, who was the track coach at Michigan; Bump Elliot, who was the football coach; and Davey Nelson, a former Michigan great but then athletic director at the University of Delaware. I knew Bump, and was one of his great admirers, but I did not know either Don or Davey.

Allan Smith, then our academic vice president, and I made an appointment and talked with Davey. He was devoted to Michigan, but thought he would not like to be considered since he enjoyed his position at Delaware. That left Don and Bump. Bump was perhaps the most-loved football coach Michigan ever had, but he had not had recent success with his team. Among his supporters were clearly people who wanted him to become athletic director because they wanted a new football coach. Fond as I was of Bump and all he stood for, I did not think that was the right reason for making him athletic director. At that point I asked Mark Plant, who was on the Law faculty and who had for many years been the Michigan faculty representative to the Big Ten, to come and see me. I told him it was down to Bump and Don, and that since he knew them both better than I did, I would value his judgment of both of them as the new athletic director. He spoke very highly of Bump and the affection in which he was universally held. He said Bump would be the popular choice. He knew this was partly because many people wanted a new football coach but they also didn't want to hurt Bump. As to Don, he pointed out that Don had shown strong managerial ability in developing his own side-business in athletic training films, and that he was a highly successful track coach. If we thought we needed promotional and managerial ability in the business sense, he thought Don was probably the stronger choice.

Apart from everything else, my principal concern was that there never be any hanky-panky in our athletic affairs. Crisler had been a bear on that subject, and though having a good football team and filling the stadium were critical to our finances in supporting other team sports, I did not want our success to be accompanied by improper practices. When I finally met and talked to Don, that was our principal topic of conversation. Fortunately, he felt as I did.

Appointments of this kind come to the Regents, and they too are under the same pressures that the president experiences. In accordance with our practice, I took the names of both Bump and Don to the Regents, but recommended that Don be given the appointment. They accepted the recommendation but were concerned about a possible conflict of interest between the athletic director's position and Don's business. If he received the appointment, they thought he would have to put the business in a blind trust during the period of his service. This he ultimately agreed to do, and the appointment was made. After he had been in office a year, he laughingly commented that we should have put the university in the blind trust and kept his business!

Don's performance as athletic director made him the outstanding director of his era, and he promptly made Bump an associate athletic director with a view toward helping him take an athletic directorship elsewhere. Then, with advice from Bump, he spotted Bo Schembechler, and the rest is history. Bo filled the stadium with his teams. Meanwhile, within a very short time, Bump became athletic director at Iowa, where he not only enjoyed great success but upheld his usual reputation for decency and honesty in every respect. Sometimes things happen the way they are supposed to!

Another thing that happened during our first year in Ann Arbor was getting to know and work with city officials. There was then, as there is now, a professional city manager and an elected mayor. The mayor changed from time to time, but most of the time when I was in office the city manager was Guy Larcom, and he was, from my point of view, pure gold. Calm and collected, he understood that any city that contains a major university has some special problems. In the first place, public, nonprofit institutions don't pay property taxes, and, since they own a large share of the property in the city, this erodes the city's tax base. That is always a source of grumbling on the part of city residents. It is then aggravated, even in normal times, by the capacity of students to engage in practices that annoy the residents—like too much noise and too much beer.

The other side of the coin is, of course, that the university is the city's largest employer, that it attracts more outsiders to the city than anything else, that it makes Ann Arbor a world-renowned center, and that it includes one of the world's best medical facilities.

Despite the inevitable tensions, both sides understand the importance of good mutual relationships. We tried to sustain this through fairly regular meetings and accommodations. Because of the student turbulence that characterized the 1960s and early 1970s, the most sensitive point was, of course, the use of the police.

At the time I came, and through my years in office, the university did not have a police force of its own. It did have security officers who were unarmed and without the power to make an arrest. Their principal function was to protect our property against both thievery and fires. We needed the city police for other purposes, and we had a pact with the city with respect to their availability. Even so, the police force of the city of Ann Arbor is not large enough to cope with large numbers of students if they are engaged in destructive conduct. In such cases, the police have to be augmented by either the nearby county sheriffs or the state police.

Most of our needs could be met by the local police. In command was Walter Krasney, who, like Larcom, was superb. He was often caught between the local populace, who wanted him to stop all that student nonsense, and the practical fact that if students were doing whatever they were doing in large numbers he simply didn't have enough men to stop it. Accordingly, he courted good relationships with the students and acted in a restrained manner when the situation was explosive. The result was that he was respected by the students and he did a very effective job. The county sheriffs were a different kind of problem. Their constituencies were different, and were, by and large, annoyed with students and wanted something done about them.

In toto, the city of Ann Arbor and the university have worked together harmoniously, although there are occasional differences of opinion. I learned to have great respect for the city people.

Finally, our first year in Ann Arbor was capped off by a trip to Israel in the summer of 1968. Bill Haber, then dean of the College of LSA, had long been active in world Jewish affairs, and he arranged the trip for us. It was a fascinating experience.

Israel is small enough, and was at that time new enough, to make it possible to meet very important people, to tour the country, to comprehend the hostilities that exist in the Middle East, and to sense the dedication and the vitality of the residents.

Fanny Haber, Bill's wife, had gone to school in Milwaukee when Golda Meir, then prime minister of Israel, lived in this country and attended the same school as did Fanny. Accordingly, we spent about an hour with her one afternoon. Her office was quite plain, with none of the splendor one associates with heads of state. She was a very grand-motherly type to talk to, but one also sensed the steel in her character. Her dress was ordinary, she smoked constantly, and she talked casually but precisely. I had the feeling that she was weary, which, given her schedule, should have been true if it wasn't.

While we were in Israel, a leading professor of archaeology took us to the Wailing Wall, recently made accessible because of the Six-Day War, and explained its history to us. Another expert took us to Masada, near the Dead Sea, where, in the time of the Romans, a Jewish sect was surrounded and committed suicide rather than surrender. Looking down from the peak, one can still see the marks of the Roman encamp-ment. Masada has great symbolic importance to Israelis because it was, like Israel itself, surrounded by hostile forces that wanted to destroy it. We visited the recently captured West Bank and saw the permanent gun emplacements from which shells had been fired down on Israeli citizens in the valley below. Whatever one thought of the merits of the Israeli-Palestinian differences, it was intolerable for the Israelis to sit idly by under that kind of provocation.

We went to Bethlehem and visited the shrines that are so important to Christians. We were uneasy, as we had been around the Vatican in Rome, with peddlers pushing cheap religious mementos in the area around the shrines. We went to the Sea of Galilee. We visited the Yad Vashem Museum, and I was reminded of the horrors we found in going through Dachau at the end of World War II. And we visited and talked to many Israelis from all walks of life. Partly because of the victory in the Six-Day War, Israelis were upbeat, enthusiastic, hopeful and dedi-cated. It made me wonder if something of the same spirit hadn't per-vaded our own country at the end of the Revolutionary War.

I was particularly struck by the fact that, at dinner parties that often included high government officials and academics, there would be vig-orous arguments about the future. Then, as now, there were the hard-liners and the peaceniks. Even then, some people thought that at least some of the land captured in the Six-Day War would have to be given back in exchange for peace with their Arab neighbors. For others, this was the territory given by God to the Jewish people and must forever be held by them.

It was a stimulating trip, and by the time it was over we felt we better understood the dilemma of the Middle East. Now, a quarter century later, the same argument is going on, though a determined effort toward peace is once again underway. Can it succeed? One hopes so, but even if it does disruptive forces will remain and there is likely to be tension for a long time to come.

En route home from Israel, we were able to visit American University in Beirut, where our daughter Nancy had spent her junior year abroad. It was then a beautiful city, and the university was located on an apparently peaceful plot of land overlooking the Mediterranean Sea. While there we met with a large contingent of University of Michigan graduates over dinner. Among those graduates were both Muslims and Christians and they solved the problem of electing an alumni club president by alternating the choice each year between the two sects. In the days before the war that later so badly destroyed the city, that was the way they solved most of their political problems.

From Lebanon, we went on to Turkey and Greece, mostly to see the great cities of Istanbul and Athens. So much history is linked with both of them, particularly with the Acropolis, on which the Parthenon was built, that we would not have wanted to leave that part of the world without seeing both countries.

We came back refreshed, and ready to face our first full year in Ann Arbor. Student problems were still escalating, all the tensions that aggravated students were still unresolved, and the year ahead promised to be difficult. We did not know it at the time, but the problems would not peak until the spring and summer of 1970, which meant that discontent would continue for at least the next three years.

Chapter 12

Student Problems

Most of the difficulties during the 1960s and 1970s came during the period between 1964 and 1972. Trying to better understand it requires both some history and an appreciation of the context in which it occurred.

Unrest on campus is nothing new, as Howard Peckham has recorded in his history of the University of Michigan. In 1856, the so-called Dutch War took place. Two German-owned eating places downtown were favorite student hangouts. One was Hangsterfer's. One night, two noisy students were thrown out. The following night they returned with a gang of students and demanded a treat for all or "take the consequences." Hangsterfer's refused, and a fight followed in which clubs and knives were used, kegs and barrels were broken open, and furniture damaged. The police intervened and pushed the students back to the campus.

In 1876 and again in 1892, students tried to rush the entrance to a circus. Police and firemen were called, fire hoses were turned on the students, a side show tent was burned, and President Angell was called. The students later proclaimed that they had defended Michigan "honor" after being "attacked" merely because they had exercised the "right" to rush a gate. The students were arrested, President Angell provided bail, and money was collected to pay damages. No circuses visited Ann Arbor for years thereafter.

What those events tell us is that when we place large numbers of young people in a relatively small geographic area and subject them to a steady regimen of study, there are going to be occasional outbursts. Students are in the prime of their physical energy, they are removed from parental restraints, they are not yet fully mature in their judgment, they find a certain joy in challenging their elders, and alcoholic stimulants are bound to contribute to unruliness.

What made the period from 1964 to 1972 different was not the fact that there were problems, but that serious unrest in the larger society came on top of what might be described as the "normal" agitation. We were involved in an unpopular war in Vietnam, we were engaged in civil unrest over racial differences, and protesters had learned the advantages inherent in the tactics of civil disobedience. On top of that, our values were changing. There were severe strains on the traditional family structure; drugs, particularly marijuana, had entered the scene; premarital sex was no longer the taboo it had once been; and respect and civility were lacking. There were also a great many young "drifters" who wandered around the country. They were not students, but they were of student age and they found the campus climate to their liking even though they were not in school. They, along with juveniles from the local or surrounding high schools, were often on campus during periods of excitement. Thus, the context for unruliness was different than it had been in the past.

For purposes of analysis, our troubles at Michigan during the 1960s and 1970s could be roughly divided into three categories. There were those events that might be described as "normal" at any time on a campus; there were then those that were disruptive but not violent; and, finally, those that had a real potential for violence. Some examples will serve to illustrate the difference.

Normal Troubles

Traditionally, presidents at Michigan had held periodic student teas at the house. Freshmen were particularly welcome, but anyone could come. At the first tea in 1968, a number of students came, walked through the receiving line, and then went to the dining room for cookies and punch or tea. Before long, a little band of activists came along bearing gifts for me, which they insisted on presenting along with some well-chosen remarks. Their hope was that we would call security and have them thrown out, in which case the student newspaper would give the incident far more publicity than it deserved. Instead, we stopped the line, encouraged the other students to sit down on the floor, and invited the group to perform. They then made several presentations, including a bow and arrow, which the audience was told represented my domination by the military-industrial complex. Next came a round mold of jello, shaking on the plate, but said to represent the state of my backbone. At the end of their presentation, they sang a little song depicting some of the less-desirable aspects of my character. When they finished, we all clapped and suggested that they go out and get some cookies and punch. This they did, but it turned out that they had brought big brown sacks, into which they poured whole platters of cookies before departing. This did not endear them to the other students, but the event went off without trouble.

A second incident occurred at a later tea. This time, as we stood in the receiving line, two males dressed in evening gowns suddenly approached. One looked like a football lineman, and sported a great, hairy chest made even more evident by his low-cut gown. The other was slender, wore earrings in both ears and lipstick just below his mustache, and was dressed in a white gown. The big man said his name was Kitty, so that is what we called him. The other chatted a little with Sally about his gown, which she admired, particularly since he said he acquired it at a secondhand clothing store downtown. They passed through the line without incident except the astonishment expressed on the faces of many of the watching freshmen. Was it simply an act, drummed up for the fun of it? We never knew.

In 1969, the program committee at the Michigan Union contracted with a Broadway theater group to bring a current play, called *Dionysius '69*, to the campus. The play was then scheduled to go on to other campuses. As it turned out, the play did not do well in New York, so the cast decided to take off their clothes during part of the performance. The idea that this could happen in Ann Arbor shocked the local citizenry, but it also happened that there was a city ordinance banning public nudity. The local newspaper could hardly overlook such a promising issue, so it kept everyone informed of the matter. Given the outcry, the chief of police, Walter Krasney, came to visit the students. He told them about the city ordinance, and said that if the cast performed in the nude he would arrest not only the cast but also the students who contracted for the performance. Faced with this dilemma, the students worked their way through the university bureaucracy until they finally arrived in my office. They told me the story and asked what they should do. I responded that it didn't seem to me that it was my problem, and anyway they had been telling me for the past two years that they were all adults, capable of making their own decisions, and that they wanted nothing to do with the old rule of in loco parentis under which the university acted as a parent in residence. To this, one of the students responded that if he got arrested his father, who was paying his bills, might decline to continue the parental subsidy. I agreed that some parents might take this view. Another student said that there was a principle of freedom of expression involved in the decision of the cast to disrobe and that this freedom ought to be respected. I agreed that there were certainly some people who believed such a principle was involved in this case. The only advice I gave them was that when I had a difficult problem, I often took a tablet and wrote down all the pros and cons and then reviewed them until I could choose an answer. Perhaps they could do the same thing. Somewaht reluctantly, they left.

Happily, they resolved the problem by getting the chief to agree that if they asked the director of the play in writing to have the cast remain clothed and they did not do so, he would not arrest them, but he would arrest the cast. The play went on, the cast did remove their clothes, and they were arrested, booked, and released on $25 bail per person. They left town the next morning for their next destination, thereby forfeiting their bail. From their point of view, the publicity surrounding the incident was far more valuable in their future campus visits than the cost of the bail. Meanwhile, the local residents were pleased that someone got arrested, the students were pleased that it was not them, and we received no letters at all about the incident.

On another occasion, a half dozen seniors came to see me to talk about their coming commencement. This was at a time when, across the country, students were revolting against the traditional ceremony. Their idea was to abandon caps and gowns, dispense with a speaker, and bring their guitars for a kind of sing-along. When they finished, they asked what I thought of their proposal, and I said, "The trouble is, it isn't really your commencement, it belongs to your parents. If we do what you suggest, they will be disappointed. They like the dignity of the ceremony, the color of the caps and gowns, and they want to take your picture in your gown. It is a landmark in their lives, you should not deprive them of it." When they were silent, it occurred to me that this was a new idea to them, so I pressed further and suggested that they might clean up for the occasion (this being a time when student dress was decidedly subpar), and they might want to make it a "thank you" time for all their parents had done for them. One never knew whether advice like this would sell, but they left and we had a tradi-tional ceremony.

Finally, there was the little man carrying a brown paper sack who used to appear at our door periodically to announce, in a conspiratorial tone, that LBJ, Jackie Onassis, and other well-known luminaries were coming to town for a big rally in the Michigan Stadium. He wanted to alert me, because when the occasion came the caravan would pick me up. The date when the purported event would take place passed, but he appeared twice more with essentially the same message and a new date. The second time he gave me a password that I would receive so that I would know when to come out. Nothing ever happened. Only later did I find out that the same man had approached the presidents of Michigan State and Wayne State with the same message. I still wonder what was in the paper sack!

Disruptive Events

Because of the Vietnam war, our Reserve Officer Training Corps (ROTC) program was always under attack. To the activists, it represented our complicity in an unpopular war. To others, including many faculty, it represented a kind of program that had no place on the campus of an educational institution. This always made the problem difficult to deal with because it made allies of two groups, both of which would be happy to see ROTC disappear, but for wholly different reasons.

At the time I arrived in Michigan, the ROTC problem was already under review. Included among the options that the committee was considering would be termination of the ROTC program. The defect in that solution, whatever one thought of its merits, was that it represented a classic case of a conflict between the culture of the campus and that of the larger society. Even though the Vietnam War remained undeclared, everyone knew that it was a genuine war. For that very reason, cessation of our ROTC program would appear to be almost an act of treason to many off-campus folks. The Regents would be well aware of this, and would likely reject any such recommendation. The result would be a hazardous situation for a president. If he supported the faculty but the Regents refused to adopt the recommendation, he would lose the confidence of the Regents. If he refused to follow the faculty recommendation, he would lose their confidence. Fortunately, the committee did not recommend abolition of ROTC and we made modifications that were generally acceptable. This did not mean that the trouble was over. We had a number of instances of momentary takeovers of the building, rocks thrown through the windows, graffiti painted on the outside walls, and general harassment. Still, we managed to live through it without a major clash.

A particularly troublesome issue during all this time was the refusal of radical groups to allow speakers who held different views from

ROTC
MARCHES ON

The University of Michigan ROTC will stage a close-order drill demonstration in <u>Waterman Gym</u> today at <u>1:10 PM</u>. Everyone is invited to come watch the Army make their ROTC cadets march through simulated rice paddies on the gym floor.

The cadets turned out by Michigan's officer factory are among the finest of the 150,000 across the nation. ROTC, as everyone knows, produces the officers essential for continuing the United States' genocidal war in South East Asia. Over 50% of the Army's new officers, 35% of the Air Forces', and 20% of the Navy's are graduated and commissioned ROTC cadets. "Without ROTC," proclaims <u>Where the Leaders Are</u>, an Army ROTC recruitment brochure, "the rapid expansion of the American Army during the two World Wars, the Korean conflict and other periods of national crisis would be difficult if not impossible." The bloody involvement in Indochina is one of those "other periods of national crisis."

The United States government sees American universities and colleges as crucial places from which to recruit youth into the officer corps. ROTC now produces twice as many career officers for the Army as does West Point. For years the University of Michigan has supplied the Defense Department with North Hall plus secretarial and maintenance services at a cost of $430,000 per year.

In the past, ROTC has been a frequent target of anti-war demonstra ions. Last fall an extensive, though unsuccessful, effort was made to end ROTC. This spring after the Cambodian invasion, ROTC was again the target of attack – North Hall was occupied for 3 days. But ROTC still continues. This fall, SDS is waging a campagn against all University ties with the military – ROTC, military research, and recruiting by corporations with Department of Defense contracts. Join us in our effort – come to the ROTC demonstration.

Meet in the
FISHBOWL at 1⁰⁰
then we go to Waterman Gym
SDS

their own to speak without interruption. It was not a question of physical attacks, but the noise was disruptive. The tactic was, of course, totalitarian and antithetical to the freedom of expression that is valued in a university community. Fighting might occur between members of the audience, and calling the police could do more harm than good because radicals will always promote trouble and then claim police violence whether it occcurred or not, and students are likely to be sympathetic with their fellow students even when they are wrong. For the most part, we had to suffer through these events. Meanwhile, radical speakers of the most incoherent philosophy readily came to the campus under the protection of our policy of freedom of expression. This alienated conservatives and caused them to be critical of the university administration.

A different kind of disruption threatened when an activist group wanted to dig a bomb crater in the middle of the Diag to remind people of the bombs that were being dropped in Vietnam. I didn't mind the bomb crater, because there were already all kinds of holes around the campus having to do with new construction and one more would hardly be noticeable. The Diag, however, could not be used because there is so much plumbing and wiring buried beneath its surface that a dig there would be dangerous. The agreed solution was a different spot somewhere in the neighborhood of the Michigan League, where there were no problems. The hole was dug, a placard was placed there, little attention was given to it, and campus life went on as usual.

Not all confrontations could be dealt with so amicably. On another occasion, an activist group consisting of some students and some outsiders came to the office, insisted on seeing me, and crowded into the conference room next door. When I went in to see them, they promptly let loose with a barrage of obscenities over their "demands." After enduring this for a brief period, I told them I would be glad to talk to them provided the obscenities stopped and we used better English. It was not, I explained, that I was unfamiliar with the words they were using since I had served in the Army for three and one half years and had bargained with some rough-talking trade unionists, it was just that this group used the obscenities so ineptly. A good first sergeant would be ashamed of them. There was no color or flair to it. Obscenities, when used, were much better handled by experts. For whatever reason, the discourse thereafter was quite civil.

Mixed in with antiwar and civil rights protests were others more germane to the campus itself. Early after the start of the fall semester, a batch of small tents suddenly appeared on the Diag. They were occupied by students who alleged that they could not find housing in Ann Arbor. The housing director thought their claim was spurious, but it was taken at face value and the students were assured that the university would help them find housing and would, in fact, put them up in hotels until housing could be found. The offer was rejected. The student government was always sympathetic with any student complaint, and the *Michigan Daily* gave the situation great publicity. We then called a meeting of the student government leaders and some faculty people to discuss the issue. The university position was that the tents could continue until a "public health" problem developed arising out of the fact that there were no public toilets that would be available on a twenty-four hour basis for the use of the tenters. A day or two later, the county health officer made an inspection and reported that a "public health" problem was present. The original group of conferees was convened again, and when some of the students disputed the existence of a health problem, they were invited to tour the campus with the health officer. The latter reaffirmed his original conclusion, and it was supported by some of our own doctors drawn from the School of Public Health. The tenters were then told that they would have to remove both tents and belongings within the next twenty-four hours or they would be removed by the university. One of the student government members lagged behind the others as he left and quietly advised that the time to make the removal would be during the dinner hour at the dorms that evening. His advice was followed, and the tents were removed without incident.

There was an amusing aftermath. One of the tenters called that evening to protest that his only pair of jeans had been taken to the collection point, and he could not go to work the next day. One of our people who was suspicious of the claim offered to buy him a new pair, but the offer was refused. It turned out that the problem was not a lack of jeans, but the fact that there was some marijuana in the pocket of the pants that the student preferred not to have confiscated!

Potentially Violent Events

Quite understandably, the most worrisome events were those in which there was a potential for violence. Absent that factor, many things that were distasteful could nevertheless be tolerated in order to contain the tensions that lurked in the background.

Interestingly enough, the first such incident came in 1968 over a benign event. A coalition of students had been campaigning for a student-run bookstore in the Michigan Union. They alleged that the local bookstores were gouging them on book prices, and they pointed out that there were student-run bookstores on all the other Big Ten campuses. Our own studies of the situation didn't accord with the student view, but we had no objection to such a store. There were, however, two problems. One was that the local bookstores quite naturally opposed such a move, and the other was that the students wanted sole control of the bookstore but with the university accepting financial responsibility for it. The public, and therefore the Regents, could be expected to have some sympathy with the local stores, and the university could not accept financial responsibility for the store without having some control over it. If the latter problem could be resolved, we were prepared to recommend establishment of a store. The students were caught up in the concept of "student power," and they were unwilling to budge on the demand that they run the store with the university being the banker. The negotiations heated up, the activists saw in it the potential for disruption, and on the day the Regents met the students occupied the LSA Building across from the Administration Building. When they refused to leave at closing time, there was a question of what to do about it. Unlike the explosive but divisive Vietnam and civil rights issues, a student bookstore sounded benign to other students and it might draw very widespread support.

In the early evening, a very large crowd of students gathered outside the building. We had essentially three choices as to how to respond. We could allow the students to remain in the building and hope that they would tire of it and leave. We could seek an injunction on the ground that the students were trespassers and then use the police to evict them if they would not leave. Or we could simply take a police action against the trespassing, and hope that the occupants would leave without any resistance.

There had been building occcupations at other universities by that time, sometimes with lengthy and destructive stays. An injunction might or might not be available through the courts. A police action would be too big for the local police to handle, it was desirable at that time to keep the hostile Washtenaw sheriff off the campus, and that left

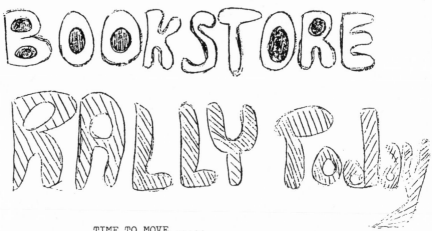

BOOKSTORE RALLY Today

TIME TO MOVE .....
THE ISSUE IS CLEAR. IT IS CONTROL OF THE INSTITUTIONS WHICH
AFFECT OUR LIVES. SOME OF OUR FELLOW STUDENTS SAY "WHAT DOES
IT MATTER". THE BOARD OF REGENTS (READ DADDY) WILL LET US
HAVE A BOOKSTORE . WHO CARES IF PIERPONT RUNS THE SHOW? THE
REASON IS CLEAR: IF THE ADMINISTRATION HAS FINAL POWER TO SET
PRICES, THEY WILL NOT COMPETE WITHU ULRICH'S OR FOLLETT'S.
IT WILL BE ANOTHER CASE OF THE ADMINISTRATION PLAYING FOOTSIE
WITH BUSINESS INTERESTS. ARE THE PRICES IN THE MUG ANY
LOWER THAN AT THE BROWN JUG? NO! WHY NOT ? BECAUSE THE
UNIVERSITY SETS THE PRICES AT THE MUG AND IS AFRAID TO ANNOY
THE MERCHANTS. PRICES WILL NOT BE LOWERED UNTIL A PUBLICLY
OWNED ANTI-PROFIT BOOKSTORE IS SET UP. WE WILL NOT BE
SATISFIED UNTIL THE BLOODSUCKING BUSINESS MEN WHO HAVE
EXPLOITED STUDENTS FOR YEARS ARE EARNING AN HONEST LIVING.
            COME TO THE RALLY TODAY TO ROTEST THE REGENTS ACTION
IN DENYING STUDENT CONTROL   OVER A BOOKSTORE FINANCED BY
STUDENT FEES. ONLY BY ACTION CAN WE BEGIN TO DETERMINE THE
COURSE OF OUR OWN LIVES.

DING 2:00

the state police as a last resort. They were the best disciplined and would be the most helpful.

We were reluctant to allow the occupation to continue because it would inevitably attract outsiders; an injunction might be useful if only in the sense that it would show our desire to proceed as peacefully as possible; and the other alternative was the state police. To use them, the support of the governor would be needed. As always, Governor Milliken was both sympathetic and helpful. The chief of the state police arrived shortly and joined the conversation. We had in the meantime obtained an injunction, but it proved impossible to serve given the large crowd outside the building.

When a decision was made, the city manager (Guy Larcom), the chief of police (Walter Krasney), many of our own executive officers, and a few faculty representatives were present. The decision was ultimately mine to make, but I was concerned about a clash between the police and the students. The chief of the state police said that he would not send in his troops without arms, but that they would be under strict orders not to use them unless resistance made it necessary. We agreed that the time to clear the building would be 4:00 A.M. when we thought there would be few people still around the outside of the building. Meanwhile, Sally had the staff at the house make a picnic supper for us and it was sent over to the Administration Building.

During the late evening, a strong contingent of state police was brought to Ann Arbor though they were not visible to the populace. At 4:00 A.M. they came to the LSA Building in buses, and the chief announced via bullhorn that the occupants, of whom there were by then about 100, must leave in the next five minutes or be arrested for trespass. Several of us, including Sally, stood on the roof of the Administration Building and watched, hoping there would be no resistance. Fortunately, there was none. A few students left voluntarily, but most of them stayed and came out singing Michigan's famous football fight song, "The Victors." They were taken downtown, booked and fingerprinted, and released on $25 bail per person. After a wait of a few months, they were tried in groups, some were convicted and others exonerated, all on essentially the same evidence, but with different juries. Shortly thereafter, a faculty committee persuaded the students to abandon their claim for financial liability on the part of the university without any participation in its governance, and a student-run bookstore was established. It ran successfully for a number of years in the

Michigan Union, then lost its lease in the face of an increase in rent and reopened in a nearby privately owned building. After operating there for a time, it sold out to a commercial business. There is now a privately owned bookstore in the Michigan Union.

Whenever an event took place in which the police were involved, there was always the potential of further agitation the following day. When I returned from lunch that day, many students wanted to talk so I sat on the ledge outside the building much of the afternoon visiting with them. They were not hostile and seemed, in fact, to understand why we felt obliged to clear the building. If there had been resistance, and some students had been hurt, their attitude might have been quite different. We were lucky!

Not too long thereafter, the anti–Vietnam War forces invited Rennie Davis to come and speak on campus. Rennie was a young man who had just finished his initial graduate work at the University of Illinois. He was very bright, full of energy, highly articulate, a fine public speaker, and totally opposed to the war in Vietnam. He had made periodic trips to Vietnam and come back with reports that were contrary to what we were being told by our government.

Once it was known that Rennie would speak right after one of his trips to Vietnam, a liberal faculty group came to see me to ask that I agree to speak on the same platform with him. Their fear was that Rennie, with whose views many of them agreed, would nevertheless so arouse the crowd that there would be violent demonstrations. They thought that if I spoke I could, with my known anti–Vietnam War views, hold the middle ground by a more objective statement than they expected him to make. The meeting was scheduled for Hill Auditorium, which holds 4,500 people, and is located in the center of the main campus.

After discussing the matter with the executive officers, I accepted the invitation. Knowing that having the president of a major university speak on the same platform with someone whom the public identified as a radical would draw radio, TV, and press attention, I wrote the speech and read it so that no one could successfully charge me with saying things that I did not say. It was a reasoned analysis of our involvement and why I thought it was a mistake.

The night of the meeting came. Hill Auditorium was packed and there was tension in the air. Activist students had filled all of the front seats and were prepared to give Rennie loud support. How they would treat me, I did not know.

There was a factor about this that no one knew. I had known Rennie since he was a small boy, when his father and I worked together in Washington right after World War II. They had been in our home a number of times, but I had not seen Rennie in recent years and I did not know how his entrance into radical politics might have changed him.

When Sally and I approached Hill that night, I went in the back door so that I could enter the stage at the proper time. It was empty when I arrived, but soon thereafter Rennie came in alone. He came toward me with a big smile and said, " Gee, it's good to see you again, my folks send their warmest greetings." I said, "Rennie, one of the last times I saw you, you threw up on our floor." We laughed and chatted before going out on the stage, and I felt confident the evening would end all right.

Rennie delivered a passionately anti–Vietnam War speech for which he was cheered wildly by many in the audience. Then I spoke. I got a warm reception, probably because many in the audience knew why I was there. There was no effort to keep me from speaking.

When it was all over, the activists swarmed around Rennie and I prepared to leave. I debated whether to intervene and say goodnight to him, but I understood that for the two of us to be friendly might ruin his reputation with the activists, so I started to leave. To my surprise, he broke away from the group and came over to say good-bye and say how pleased his parents would be that we had shared a platform.

There was no violence that night. The tension largely evaporated. The press made a good deal of it, and Vice President Spiro Agnew promptly blasted me for "gutless" behavior. The vice president was not yet at the point where he was forced from office for accepting bribes, but he was immensely unpopular with both students and faculty and nothing could have helped me more than his remarks.

A similar incident took place in front of the President's House. I think it was March 31, 1968, just after Lyndon Johnson had announced that he would not run for a second term. Around ten o'clock in the evening a large crowd began to build up outside the house. It turned out that Bill Ayers, a leading student activist at the University of Michigan, was leading them. I came out and they began to shout questions about the university's involvement in alleged war research, ROTC, and

REFLECTIONS ON VIETNAM

An address by Robben W. Fleming to the "Action Teach-In,"
Ann Arbor, Michigan, September 19, 1969

I accepted the invitation to be here tonight as a matter of personal conscience. I share the agony of all those who oppose the war in Vietnam. I happen not to agree with the views held by the radical left. Nevertheless, I am not here to criticize others who oppose our Vietnam policy, but to state my own views.

I am not an expert on Southeast Asia, though I have visited that part of the world twice for limited periods. Nor do I purport to speak for the University of Michigan, though I recognize that my title will be of more interest to the reading public than will my name.

In the days immediately after World War II we were obsessed with the idea that communism was a monolithic evil which threatened not only the countries which immediately bordered on Russia, but our own existence. Viewed objectively it can perhaps be said that Russia did little to alleviate that fear. But surely the years since 1945 have taught us the error of this greatly oversimplified analysis of the communist world. The strains of nationalism were patently stronger than the communist ideology. Marshall Tito showed us that a communist neighbor to the Russians could successfully pursue an independent policy. The Poles have slipped in and out of orbit. The Chinese and the Russians are at each others' throats. The Albanians have thumbed their nose at the Russians for some time. The Rumanians are not wholly integrated into the communist orbit. The Czechs are a living example of the brutal hand of force, but also of the unreliability of a forced ally. In short, the communist world has been no more able than the rest of us to pursue an absolutely unified policy to which all of its members adhere. From this I draw the conclusion that it is not a disaster for us if Vietnam ultimately becomes an independent communist country. There is historic animosity between the Vietnamese and the Chinese, and if our preference is for an independent Vietnam, it may well be that peace furthers that objective, whereas war is forcing an alliance.

Secondly, I do not see a world in which the United States can afford, either economically or in terms of manpower, to be the policeman. The day when a few thousand well-trained marines can land and take over is gone. Against a determined band of guerrillas everyone now seems agreed that we cannot win unless we are prepared to invade the North, mount an all-out air attack, or use atomic weapons. These things we will not do, not only because of our own morality and world opinion, but because we do not care to run the risk of retaliation at the hands of other powers. If none of these alternatives holds any promise for us, we must reconcile ourselves to the fact that a great many things will go on in the world which we will not like.

We have also the rather naive notion that our political institutions have served this country so admirably that they must be applied to every other country in the world. Perhaps we are the victims of our own acute consciousness of the genius of those young revolutionaries who wrote that extraordinary series of documents on which our country was founded. It is, incidentally, a rather sad truth that when public opinion surveys are taken of the principles set forth in our Bill of Rights—without identifying the source—there is great doubt on the part of American citizens as to whether they subscribe to the truths contained therein. When the same principles are stated to be from the Bill of Rights, the acceptance of them promptly goes up.

In any event, to suppose that one can impose the American concept of democracy on countries which have no democratic traditions, no heritage like ours, no organized political parties, too few educated leaders, and strong military traditions defies rationality. With respect to the South Vietnamese government, there is little in the record that inspires confidence in the minds of many of us that it is a representative government, that it could remain in power in a genuinely free election, that its views on continuing the war go beyond a concern for a rather privileged class. If the Saigon government had in fact won the war, one suspects that the model of government which would emerge would look as little like our idea of a democracy as some of the models which are sure to emerge if and when there is a successful peace negotiation. Put somewhat differently, a bad government is not made good simply because it is not communist.

There is another factor which must be considered. Our own revolution is now far behind us. All of us have grown up reading of the tyranny of the British during the period of our fight for independence. By and large we do not question the righteousness of our cause, though others may. As a matter of fact, I had the rather sobering experience last spring of watching the film about the American Revolution which is shown at historic Williamsburg, Virginia. I had seen it before, and the only thing that was novel about it this time was that I saw it in the company of a number of vice chancellors of British universities. Our conversation afterwards left me with the impression that there might be a slight disparity between American and British textbooks on that subject! I use this example only to suggest that possibly our view of the cause of revolutionaries in other countries which are foreign to our culture may be less accurate than we suppose. Is it not possible that the real explanation of why the incumbent government in Saigon has seemed to generate so little popular support is because it does not represent the hopes and aspirations of the people?

If I am right in what I have said so far, I do not see how one can avoid the conclusion that our present involvement in Vietnam is a colossal mistake. Here I must pause to say that while I label our involvement a "colossal mistake" I do not share the view which is so popular in the radical left that it is all the result of evil and corrupt forces which govern our society. My own life experience is that honest mistakes can be made. A great many men and women in America were and are obsessed with a fear of communism. A great many wise and independent statesmen fear that if we withdraw from Vietnam it will have a disastrous effect in all of Southeast Asia. I simply do not share that view.

When I weigh in the balance the arguments for continuing the war versus those for ending our involvement, my scale tips distinctly in the latter direction. The economic, human, and spiritual costs of continuing the war seem to me unbearable. I start with the economic costs, not because I think them most important, but because they are perhaps most readily disposed of.

Support for the war in Vietnam now takes a large share of our national budget. We concede that we cannot win a military victory without using tactics which we are unwilling to use. Meanwhile, we see daily the desperate need for funds at home and abroad in the cause of peace and human betterment. Demographers freely predict that the Malthusian Law is finally catching up with us and that we will see mass starvation in the world unless we learn how to control our population and expand our food resources. The polluted state of our air and water is more evident daily. We are becoming more conscious every day that we cannot even keep up with removing rubbish in our major cities. Massive injections of funds are essential if we are to pay more than lip service to the stated objective of racial justice. The poor may inherit the earth, but unless we take a different course than we are presently pursuing, they will do so while ill clothed, ill housed, and ill fed.

It is not just that our military expenditures in Vietnam are enormous, it is that the whole experience contributes to a condition in which war and the weapons of war dominate our economies to the detriment of all of us. And so long as that condition continues it tends to diminish the chances that we can avoid a world wide conflict.

So much for the economic aspect of the war. Let us turn now to the human equation.

A year ago I talked at some length one evening to a senior American statesman whose name you would know well. In the course of our conversation we talked of Vietnam, though with some reluctance on his part. Engrossed as he was in what he considered to be the larger problems of world politics, he said to me with some annoyance that our casualties in Vietnam did not even equal our traffic accident losses here at home. As to the statistics he is doubtless right. But I could only think of Lord Tennyson's "Charge of the Light Brigade" which made such magnificent reading until one came to realize that the men who rode into the valley of death died with so little reason. Death on the battlefields of Vietnam is not a statistic, it is a tragedy in the lives of a whole network of human beings. If it is justifiable at all surely it can be only because there is visible benefit to America and to the world. I do not see that benefit in terms that outweigh the destruction, devastation, and death.

The youth of a country are always the wave of the future. Vietnam is not the only cause of alienation between the generations, for if it were one would not expect to find alienation in countries which have only a peripheral interest in that sad area of the world. But if it is not the only cause, who can deny that here in America it is a major cause. Those who burn their draft cards, go to prison, refuse to serve, or simply drop out of society are not by such acts cowards or traitors. History reminds us that in the early thirties the students at Oxford and Cambridge swore that they would never fight again, and thereby caused great uneasiness among their elders as to their courage and fortitude. But when World War II came, and the freedom of England was at stake, they fought magnificently. Americans who see no useful purpose in a war in Vietnam do not thereby automatically rule out all wars for all possible reasons, though increasingly all of us must see that war is futile.

Another of the human costs of the war is the inequity with which it falls on various segments of our society. Strangely enough, this is in a sense attributable to the fact that it requires so little, rather than so much, of our total manpower. In a period of total mobilization, like World War II, all manpower becomes subject to military and civilian allocation. This being so, all are subject to government mandate, though inevitably some will enjoy better conditions than others. When a limited war comes along the services do not need all the manpower that is available. A Selective Service System uses block deferments lest the system produce far more men than are needed. The result is that we set up rules which have varying justifications, but which contain the seeds of inequity. College students may be deferred because one can show that the flower of French youth were killed in World War I and it has affected that country ever since. Unfortunately, the reason one young man goes to college and another does not may be totally unrelated to his intellectual capacity. Innumerable studies show that a high proportion of those whose I.Q. warrants continued study do not attend an institution of higher learning, while others, with less capacity do because their parents are able to send them. Moreover, there is no way under such a system to avoid the likelihood that those who are less privileged in our society will be most likely to find their way into the service. There are racial overtones here which only serve to exacerbate the injustices which flow from that cancer in the larger society.

There is perhaps another societal casualty of the Vietnam War. Older generations are frequently troubled by what they regard as the great increase in obscenity in our national life. Historians are inclined to tell us that this is a phenomena which is cyclical, but who among us—when offended by some particularly inappropriate or offensive bit of material—has not met the argument that the killing of women and children in a far off part of the world is even more obscene? So long as the war goes on, how do we cope with that argument? It is not enough to respond that the other side is guilty of the same tactics. One must believe completely in his cause before he can accept the death and destruction of war, and it is evident that few of our people believe that deeply in the need for our presence in Vietnam.

Finally, let me speak of the erosion in values within our universities since that is the world that we know best. Those who asked me to speak tonight particularly stressed the propriety of the university as a forum for debate for all kinds of views. But let us be candid. If a strong proponent of the war in Vietnam were asked to occupy this platform tonight, I doubt that he would be permitted to speak without interruption, however sincere and intellectually honest he might be. The interruption would be justified on the grounds that he could not morally believe in such a position. For those of us my age who know the evils of the Third Reich first hand, such tactics smack of the Brown Shirts. I count this one of the casualties of the emotion, the hatred, the suspicion, the tragedy of the Vietnam War. No one would be foolish enough to suppose that only Vietnam could cause such an erosion of the values of the university for it has happened before under other circumstances and it will doubtless happen again. Nevertheless, it is dangerous to the climate of free inquiry.

When the human cost of the Vietnam War is assessed there are those who conclude that the war was started and continues only because American imperialistic interests require it. I know from personal experience in many parts of the world, both during World War II and afterward, that there are those who are war profiteers, that there are the cynical armaments manufacturers who supply the weapons of death to both sides, that the military-industrial complex in this country is enormously powerful. Still I say that it is nonsense to suppose that this is the reason the war continues. So ambitious a politician as Lyndon Johnson did not, in my view, destroy his political career and his place in American history for these reasons. Richard Nixon will not, in my view, allow his career and his place in history to go the same route for such reasons. Both men were and are, I suggest to you, trapped in the web of two powerful considerations. The first is the political dilemma at home: it is not nearly so clear as those of us who think the war ought to end believe, that the bulk of our citizens agree. And the second is a concern for what will happen to the South Vietnamese who have worked with us and what will happen to Southeast Asia if we simply leave that beleaguered area of the world.

As to the second problem—our stature in Southeast Asia and how to protect our friends among the South Vietnamese in case of a takeover—I do not have an answer, but I do not feel guilty about this since my reading indicates that there are genuine experts, including some of our own from this university, who believe that this problem is manageable. I am prepared to accept a conclusion that we can find ways to solve that aspect of the problem.

The home dilemma is a different one. University communities are notoriously unrepresentative of the society at large. Doubts about and hostility to the Vietnam War are so widely voiced within the academic community that those of us who inhabit the community tend to forget that our views are frequently at odds with the noncampus world. The labor union hierarchy, for instance, would express grave doubts about a withdrawal from Vietnam. Radical analysts dismiss this as a crass concern for jobs and high wages, but they forget that sons of working people are being killed in Vietnam every day and these personal tragedies influence the home just as they do in other segments of the society. The truth is, in my view, that an enormous number of Americans, perhaps a big majority, would like to get out of Vietnam, but they do not know how to do so. Nations, like individuals, do not like to lose face. Nations, like individuals, do not lightly abandon their allies to an unknown fate. Nations, like individuals, do not find it easy to admit that they have made mistakes.

Having explained to you why I am against the continuation of the war in Vietnam, I feel some obligation to tell you what I think should be done about it. At the same time I am conscious of my inadequacies on this account. Some of the best minds in the world, many of them possessed by people whose knowledge of the situation far exceeds my own, have not yet produced a formula for ending the war. I am therefore not so presumptuous as to suppose that it is within my power to voice the magic solution. I can only tell you what I see as the major elements which are involved.

If, as I believe, we have made a major mistake in foreign policy, we must say so, or at least admit it to ourselves, rather than continuing along the path to disaster. The countless white crosses which dot the path of the past cannot be changed, but we can avoid adding to the list. For those who are concerned with military pride, we have not been defeated, indeed we have shown that the tide of sure takeover of four years ago was reversed. It was our unilateral decision to avoid the use of tactics which would wipe our opponent from the face of the earth, and that decision, whether made for the right or the wrong reasons, leaves no one confused on the question of pure military might.

It might now be apparent that short of military conquest, which we are not willing to undertake, we are not going to impose a settlement on Vietnam. The North Vietnamese, for what seem to them to be good reasons, are apparently prepared to go on indefinitely with the war.

Speaking for myself, I would be willing to support three basic propositions.

1. An announced unilateral decision to withdraw from Vietnam.
2. Massive troop withdrawals, by which I mean Clark Clifford's goal of 100,000 by the end of 1969, and McGeorge Bundy's formula for removing 100,000 to 150,000 per year for the next two years until we ultimately are down to 100,000 volunteers serving on a rotating basis.
3. Advice to our friends in both Vietnam and Southeast Asia that we

will make the above moves and that we must therefore reevaluate, with them, our position in that area of the world.

My framework is much too simplistic to settle the problem, but I believe that it is the frame on which a new policy can be erected.

I have only a few final comments. You are here, these two days, to hear other speakers, many of whom may know a good deal more than I do about the problem. You will consider a variety of tactics, some of them internal to the university. Anything I say on this point is suspect, of course, on the ground that it potentially raises problems with which, in my administrative capacity, I must deal. I can only express my own conviction that activities which arouse the public against the university do more to harm than to help the cause. It is a sobering thought that all of the minority left candidates got less than 230,000 votes in the last election, while George Wallace tallied about 10,000,000.

Let me leave this thought with you. Following the Kennedy and Martin Luther King assassinations, we set aside the 11:00 A.M. to 1:00 P.M. period to express our anguish and concern. We did so with dignity and compassion. We authorized professors to cancel classes insofar as it was possible during the period of observance. If this idea is attractive to those who will be discussing Vietnam and wish to have the university show its posture on the war, I shall see that the university provides the facility in the weeks ahead. Hill Auditorium holds 4,000. The Events Building holds 15,000. If there are enough concerned students and faculty to fill the latter, I shall be glad to carry their message to Washington. If this effort is supplemented by individual letters to Senators and Congressmen, I suspect that it will do far more to advance the cause of peace than other activities which may reinforce our own opposition to the war, but which have no noticeable impact on the outside world.

I can, and I will, express to my colleagues who are presidents of other academic institutions my concern about the war, and my hope that their campuses, like ours, will find a vehicle through which faculty and students may bear witness to their convictions.

In the discussions which will follow during the course of the next two days, I wish you success and fulfillment.

all the usual issues. Bill had a bullhorn, as did I (one was kept at the house!). There was so much noise that it was impossible to answer questions, so I suggested they sit down in the yard and quiet down so I could reply. They did, and the crowd grew bigger until the entire street was closed off. Draft cards and flags were being burned, antiwar signs were all over the place, and, to my horror, a Confederate flag suddenly floated out of a third floor window of our house. We had a Virginia girl living with us as a companion for our high school age daughter. She was not really a Southerner, she certainly was not rascist, and what caused her to produce the flag, except perhaps the excitement of the occasion, I will never know. Fortunately, the crowd was focused on Vietnam, not civil rights, and the flag was soon withdrawn without incident.

Questions and answers went on until around 11:00 P.M. The crowd was restless, there was tension in the air, and the police were present but not taking any action. Suddenly, Bill Ayers put his bullhorn down to his side and said to me, "Would you like us to go home, you must be tired?" I replied noncommittally that I would be glad to talk as long as they wanted to. He then picked up his bullhorn and said, "All right, we are through here, let's go over to the Union and continue." At that the crowd broke up and the evening was over.

Again there was a fortuitous factor, unknown to anyone but Bill. His father and I were good friends. The father was a Michigan graduate, the chief executive of a major utility in Chicago, and one who had been in the forefront of the fight for racial justice in Chicago. I had arbitrated a number of labor disputes between his firm and the union. Was that the reason that Bill drew the audience away from the house that night? I don't know. Anyway, there was no violence.

Sooner or later, our luck was bound to change, and we did have an incident that got out of hand. I never really knew how it got started. Relatively early in the evening, there was some trouble on South University, in the block below the Engineering Arch. My impression was that it involved some juveniles and perhaps some of the drifters. Suddenly, perhaps around nine in the evening, there was a banging on our front door and students shouted that they were being tear gassed. We opened the door and, sure enough, the air was heavy with tear gas. There were perhaps twenty students, and we brought them in, sent them to the nearby kitchen to wash out their eyes, and closed the door as rapidly as possible. When I asked what had happened, they professed not to know, saying only that sheriffs had come across the campus throwing tear gas.

We waited for the gas to subside, and then I went out. At that moment, the Ann Arbor police were marching west on South University and had reached the Clements Library, which is next door to the President's House. Captain Olsen, Chief Krasney's second-in-command, was leading them and I knew him to be a fine policeman. He halted the march as I approached, and I asked what was going on. He told me that there had been some trouble down the street, that some cars had been set afire, that there were bonfires in the street and so on. I told him that insofar as I knew there was no university involvement at all, but that the sheriffs had come across campus above the point of the trouble throwing tear gas. I suggested he withdraw his police to the block in question, and I would then come out and walk the entrance to that street in an effort to keep university students away. Douglas Harvey, the county sheriff who was anathema to students, was there and was itching for a confrontation. Fortunately, he was not in charge, and he later complained to the newspapers that I had no courage in dealing with students. (In later days he would sometimes fly over the Diag in his helicopter and students would throw rocks at him). By midnight the situation was calm, university students did not get involved, and the situation was under control.

It was foreseeable that trouble might resume the following night. Sure enough, the activist group, made up partly of outsiders, called for a mass meeting at high noon in front of the General Library on the Diag. Their strategy was always to try to build on prior incidents, and the best way to insure a crowd would be to meet in front of the library just as classes broke at noon. Once I knew there was going to be a rally, I had my secretary call and say that I would appear and wanted to speak. They said the "people" would have to decide whether or not I could speak. The "people" were the masses of the downtrodden whom they felt they represented. Knowing that not many of the students who would constitute the bulk of the audience felt very downtrodden, I told them to go ahead and ask the "people."

The rally began right on time. Both campus and off-campus radicals harangued the audience about alleged police brutality the previous evening and exhorted the crowd to assemble that evening at the same spot and confront the police. When they were finished, I was still there waiting and, perhaps because they didn't know what else to do with me, they asked the "people" if they wanted me to speak. To my astonishment, a cheer went up—the best I had expected was silence. I recited the events of the past evening, saying that, to my knowledge, it had no university involvement whatsoever until the sheriff had come across the campus throwing tear gas. I suggested that students stay away from the street that night.

Following my remarks the radicals made another try. They twice asked the audience in vain to respond affirmatively to a call to arms that night. When both efforts failed, they resorted to an old radical tactic that I had seen before. They asked everyone who favored taking to the streets to stand up, knowing full well that everyone was already standing because there were no seats. This failed to fool anyone, and the audience laughed.

This did not mean that there would be no trouble that night, so we worked with the city in cosponsoring a rock concert several blocks north of South University. There the mayor and I both spoke, the band played, and the evening went off without incident.

Still ahead were two other incidents that had potential for violence. One was the Black Action Movement (BAM) strike, and the other was a visit from the President of Israel, which was protested by the large Arab community in nearby Dearborn. Neither was within the usual framework of problems that we had, and each was unique in its own way. The BAM strike was much the more extensive and is deserving of its own chapter, therefore let me turn to the Middle East dispute.

In 1975, the President of Israel, Ephraim Katzir, was invited to come to the University of Michigan to receive an honorary degree. Normally such degrees are given only at commencement, and this had been the original intention in this case. Unfortunately a foreign policy crisis kept him home, and he came at a later date. We decided to go ahead with the ceremony while he was in the United States, and it was slated to be held in Rackham Auditorium with about a thousand people in attendance.

Ceremonies of this kind attract little attention, and certainly not for students. Given the ever-present tensions in the Middle East and the size of the Arab community near us, we anticipated a possible protest. Since it was not the kind of event that drew a large student audience and was not within the ambit of their current protest interests, we could prepare for problems without being concerned with students.

Shortly before the ceremony was to begin, several buses drove up in front of Rackham and discharged passengers in Arab dress. They entered the building quietly, but made no effort to take seats, contenting themselves with standing at the rear of the hall in the wide space that exists there. Meanwhile, those of us who were to go on stage were lining up by two's preparatory to walking on the platform. Both the Israeli and American Secret Service people were in attendance. The Israeli president was a small man who came just above my shoulder. As the Secret Service people viewed us, they positioned him so that he would be shielded by me and we walked on stage. I remember thinking that I had not anticipated this role as a part of my portfolio.

When the ceremonies began, I did the preliminaries and then introduced him. The minute he started to speak, the Arab group made so much noise that he could not be heard. I came back to the podium and explained to the audience the university practice of allowing all points of view to be heard, and I then asked them to accord the speaker this courtesy. They listened quietly as long as I spoke, but the minute he resumed they again made it impossible to hear. I returned to the podium and said that this interruption was intolerable and that unless they permitted him to speak we would have to evict them. They listened to me, but promptly interrupted him. I then said that I was sorry, but there would be a brief intermission while they were evicted. At that point, the police streamed on the stage from a door that led downstairs. They were in riot gear, with shields, and they started walking up the aisles. None of us knew what would happen. Fortunately, the Arab group, probably by prior agreement, backed off and left the auditorium. They had apparently made their point and gotten the desired publicity. As we stood there watching, President Katzir said to me, "So this is the way you do it here. We have this problem all the time at home, and we throw them out right away! May be we ought to try this method."

Student strife reached it zenith in 1970. That was the year in which student protesters were killed by National Guardsmen in a clash on the Kent State campus in Ohio, when radicals blew up a building, killing a graduate student, at Wisconsin, and when deaths also took place on campus at Jackson State in Mississippi. Those tragedies sobered the campus outlook. Before these events took place, but only slightly earlier the same year, we had the BAM strike. It is to that event that I now turn.

Chapter 13

Open It Up or Shut It Down

In 1970 we had the Black Action Movement (BAM) strike. It was to be the most difficult of all issues because it was a racial matter and the feelings were intense. Since the strike was twenty-five years ago and is shrouded in myth, it is important to supply some background.

Civil rights legislation was a major focus of federal attention all during the 1950s and 1960s. The school desegregation case of *Brown v. Board of Education* was decided by the Supreme Court in 1954. The battles in Congress over additional civil rights legislation continued for the next two decades, evoking animosities dating back to the Civil War. Those of us who saw the televised confrontations of blacks and whites in southern cities will never forget their brutality. Martin Luther King, Jr., the preeminent black leader and a man of peace, was assassinated in 1968. His death set off violent demonstrations all over the country. In the same year, the Kerner Commission reported that the United States "was moving toward two societies, one white, one black—separate and unequal."

Against this background, it was not surprising that some of the black students, faculty, and staff at the University of Michigan began to organize and to campaign for changes in the status of blacks at the university. Ultimately, their "demands" included: enrolling 10 percent of the total student body from black applicants, thereby equalling the proportion of blacks in Michigan's population; recruitment of more black faculty and administrators; financial aid for black students to attend the university; further development of the Afro-American studies program; a center at which black students could congregate; and a few lesser items. Labeling such matters as "demands" was, I should note, entirely consistent with the actions of other student groups of the time. I always insisted on using the term *requests,* but this did not change their label.

The university administration was well aware of the need to take action in some of these areas long before Sally and I arrived in the fall of

STRIKE
OPEN IT UP or SHUT IT DOWN

This afternoon, the Regent's agreed with the Bam goal of increased black and chicano enrollment but made no concrete committments to implement that demand. The Regents also convenientyly misconstrued and disregarded the black faculty's support of BAM demands. Regents are not willing to redirect U funds, or to change the priorities of this U.
18% of college age Michigan youth are black
3% of U of M are black
Between 1960-65 only 1 black graduated from U of M Law School.
The propsed budget for 1970-71 does not include A SINGLE PENNY for increased minority admissions.
THIS IS RACISM AND THIS IS BULLSHIT

The Regents cannot deal with people who confront them about the racism at this University. So they called in the pigs this afternoon. One black woman, and black men and one white man were busted. BAM and its supporters have called fir a strike of all classes.

SUPPORT BAM
SMASH RACISM
STRIKE

SUMMARY OF B.A.M. DEMANDS
1. 10% black enrollment of Fall 1973
2. 900 new black students by Fall 1970
3. An adequate supportive services program including financial aid to finance black students' education.
4. Graduate and 9 undergrad recruiters to recruit black students
5. A referendum on March SGC ballot to have students vote on assessing themselves $3.00 for 1 year for the Martin Luther King Scholarship Fund.
6. Tuition waivers for minority group students who are residents of Michigan and admitted under special programs.
7. The establishment of a community located Black Student Center
8. All work of a permanent nature on the Black Studies Program to be haulted until a community-University forum and effective input is fully developed.
9. The creation of a University-wide appeal board to rule on the adequacy of financial aid grants to students.
10. A revamping of the Parents Confidential Statement
11 There should be one recruiter for Chicano students to assure 50 Chicano students by Fall o970
12 Black students are to be referred to as black not as Negro or anything else.

STRIKE

1967. Nondiscriminatory programs with respect to the employment of personnel were in place, as were financial aid programs for disadvantaged students. Still, progress was slow, and, in the mood of the times, faster action was demanded. We had an internal committee, headed by Stephen Spurr, who was then dean of our graduate school and later president of the University of Texas at Austin, which was working on the kinds of responses we might make. Our black enrollment at that time was about 3.5 percent of the total enrollment, and the demand was for 10 percent. There were no specific percentage demands for faculty and administrators, but there was pressure to increase their numbers. Meetings between the Spurr committee and the by then established BAM committee took place periodically during the fall of 1969. We recognized the merits of some of the black proposals and we were anxious to make appropriate changes.

Our study indicated that we could double the proportion of black students to 7 percent within a reasonable period, but we were very dubious that we could reach 10 percent without other societal changes over which we had little or no control, and we were reluctant to promise something we thought was unachievable. Our reluctance appeared to the blacks to be racial bias, and we were gradually reaching an impasse.

All of my experience in the settlement of disputes suggested that a showdown was going to be inevitable, and that when it came it would be very difficult to contain. There had been a terrible riot in nearby Detroit in the summer of 1967. There would be strong white activist sympathy for the blacks, though the blacks were unlikely to want to make common cause with radical groups if for no other reason than that they wanted to control their own affairs. Radical groups would, nevertheless, do whatever they could to escalate the tensions that were sure to develop. The faculty would be split, but would oppose violence. The Regents would be uneasy if intimidation was resorted to, but they would be favorable to changes that seemed reasonable.

While I was involved in discussions of what to do about the forthcoming crisis, I deliberately stayed out of the direct negotiations because, if my instinct that there would be a showdown was right, I would ultimately have to become involved, and at that point I would be a last resort that ought not to be exhausted too early.

As I tried to analyze the problem, I realized that the way in which the BAM people looked at the dispute and the way we looked at it were totally different, and therein lay the difficulty. It might be impossible to bridge that gap.

Seen from BAM's standpoint, this was a straight-out racial discrimination issue. Black people had been brought to this country as slaves, they had been denied an education from the beginning, they had been discriminated against in the job market, their housing was both poor and segregated, their schools were underfunded, the environment was hostile to them, they were seething with anger, and they were almost totally distrustful of the white establishment. From their point of view, those of us who represented the university could be expected to move only if forced to do so and, even then, unwillingly. We could not be expected to understand either their anguish or their distrust of the white community.

We looked at the matter quite differently. We wanted to be helpful, we wanted a society in which blacks and whites were no longer separate and unequal, and the problem was not one of willingness, but of dealing with some very difficult practical problems. The problems had to do with finding qualified black students in the numbers required to meet the goal, recruiting black faculty and administrators who had the necessary background and experience, and then finding the money to support the effort.

During World War II, black residents of the south had migrated north to the great industrial centers, like Detroit, to find employment. That meant that Detroit, like so many other big cities, had a large black population. At the same time, whites had increasingly moved to the suburbs. As the tax base for the city eroded, the urban schools went downhill because, as in so many other states, property taxes were used to support the schools. High unemployment in the black community, poor housing, and an increasing crime rate contributed to the problem. Large numbers of black students were not graduating from high school, thereby eliminating any chance of qualifying for college. Those who did graduate were often not well prepared. This meant that, quite apart from any question of race, only a limited number of the high school graduates were going to be able to qualify for admission at the University of Michigan if they were chosen on a strictly competitive basis. If they were taken on a preferential basis, two problems would arise. One was whether it would be fair to ask them to compete with the other admitted applicants, practically all of whom came from the top of their high school classes. If they then failed, it would be a sad end to an academic career that might have succeeded in a less competitive milieu. The other problem was that, since blacks represented only 10 percent of the total population of Michigan, there were, in fact, far more white than black high school graduates who would be turned down for admission to Michigan on the basis of grades and test scores.

From the black standpoint, our emphasis upon taking only students who could qualify was simply a device for excluding blacks and was therefore racially discriminatory. They could point out that we accepted athletes who could qualify within the NCAA standards and that we then gave them tutors to help them complete their academic work successfully. If we could be that solicitous about athletes, why couldn't we be equally concerned about helping other black students?

Possible solutions to this dilemma were discussed, including remedial work, but this only raised the question of whether such work would be given credit toward graduation. Our conclusion was that, while we could give academic counseling and assistance to those who needed it, we could not give program credit without diluting the degree and thereby identifying such students as second class, which would help no one.

I had another idea that, when it was adopted twenty years later at one of the University of California campuses, was hailed as a significant first. The idea was that we would identify marginally qualified black students and help support them for the first two years at Washtenaw Community College. They would have to take the liberal arts curriculum and maintain a B average, and we would then admit them automatically at the junior level at the University of Michigan. We had enough experience with WCC two-year students to know that students who met those criteria could succeed at Michigan. We would also try to find ways to involve them in UM affairs during those first two years so that they would be familiar with us before they came as juniors. The idea was rejected on the grounds that "you just don't want black students at the University of Michigan." It was not, from their point of view, a time for any kind of compromise.

As to black faculty and administrator recruitment, there were also many problems. In many disciplines, largely because openings had never been available to them, there were almost no trained people and it would take years to change the situation. There were, of course, some "stars" who were already established at other universities, and this fact set up a bidding war among universities faced with the same problem we had. Again, our concern for quality was viewed by blacks as pure discrimination, though more sober analysts recognized the dilemma. Trying to convince the BAM group that there was any merit in our position was like telling activist students that we had no control over the government's conduct of the war in Vietnam. They were distrustful of the whole white establishment, and they had to exert pressures where they could, not somewhere in the off-campus world.

There was also the question of where to find the necessary money for additional student aid. We could raise part of it by increasing tuition for all students, and then using some of that increase to aid the new black students. This was not something new to the academic world because, since the very beginning, colleges in the United States had transferred some part of tuition revenue to needy students. To do so would, however, focus more public attention on the practice, and this would doubtless fuel racial antagonism, though that storm could be weathered. Our other source of money might be the Michigan legislature, but it was already pressed for resources and any violence at the university might doom our chances.

By the spring of 1970, the BAM folks were talking about a strike that they hoped would shut down the university. I saw no way of avoiding the strike without making promises the university could not keep. In the long run, I thought this would be worse for all of us than to face the troubles we would have by refusing the demands. Yet I viewed a strike with great apprehension. I was confident a strike could not shut down the university, but I also knew it might become violent. If we had to use the police or the National Guard it could become a nasty racial brawl that would be a disaster for all of us.

The matter came to a head in March of 1970. We had kept the Regents apprised of the situation and we had prepared, for their consideration, what we regarded as the maximum offer we could make in settlement of the various issues. It included the following major points.

1. We would establish a *goal* of 10 percent black students to be reached by 1973–74.
2. The criteria for the admission of disadvantaged students "should be continuously studied and experimented with in such a way that increased enrollment may be achieved *while at the same time preserving a satisfactory probability of successful completion of the educational program at the university.*"

3. Enough student aid money would be guaranteed to support the enrollment goal if attendance was not possible because of financial reasons.

4. Additional funds would be provided to recruit additional black faculty and staff, to continue the development of the Afro-American studies program and the initial development of a Black Students' Center that would be open to all minority students.

The Regents were prepared to approve this offer and they did. It set a *goal* of 10 percent enrollment rather than making it an absolute *commitment* because our review of the available high school market led us to believe that we could not find that many students who could qualify. We thought the 7 percent figure that came out of our studies was more realistic, and we did not want to be accused of promising something we could not achieve while being consistent with our standards. In an effort to lend credibility to our offer, we specifically provided that we would not fail to reach 10 percent because an otherwise qualified student did not have the financial resources to attend the university.

When the public meeting of the Regents took place on March 19, 1970, black students crammed the room beyond its capacity, crowding up tight against the chairs of the Regents. They insisted on making a statement of their demands, including a threat that they would close down the university if the demands were not met. The room was tense, there were police around—they were under instructions not to interfere, and once the black statement was made the group withdrew. Before leaving, one of their spokesman said, "It is a battle of political realities . . . of self-interest. You can't win. If we are on a collision course, so be it." The Regents then went through their agenda, including approval of the plan we had offered to them.

BAM promptly rejected our proposal, principally on the ground that it did not *commit* us to reaching the 10 percent goal. The papers reported that there were a thousand students outside the Administration Building who then engaged in a melee with the police, as the result of which four students were arrested and some police officers were hurt.

The strike began under the slogan, "Open It Up or Shut It Down." On Friday afternoon, March 20, participants blocked traffic at the intersection of State and South University and broke some car windows.

There were some arrests and the police reported four bomb threats to university buildings, but no bombs were found. The following day the BAM group complained to the city that, in making arrests, the police had singled out only blacks despite the fact that white radicals had committed some of the offenses.

On Saturday, March 21, some five hundred members of the faculty published a full-page advertisement in the *Ann Arbor News*, the *Michigan Daily*, and the *Lansing State Journal* saying, "It is time for voices to be raised against the actions of the few who are driving the university community into chaos."

On Monday, March 23, pickets appeared in front of several of the colleges but made no attempt to prevent students from attending classes. That night, representatives of BAM attended a meeting of the Ann Arbor City Council demanding an immediate investigation of the city Police Department, charging brutality and discrimination during the skirmish on March 19.

On March 24, there was still no physical problem. Class attendance was somewhat down, and the strike was not very effective. As a matter of fact, throughout the period, the strike principally targeted the Main Campus rather than the North Campus across the river.

If the strike was not achieving its objective, I knew from my experience in the labor field that one of two things had to happen. Either the strike would fail for lack of support, or it would become disruptive. In either case, I was confident the university would not be shut down, simply because they did not have the personnel to spread all around the campus. My strategy was to make the best offer we could and then wait it out, hoping that we could withstand minor violence without having to use either the State Police or the National Guard. I consulted with Governor Milliken, and he was in support of this position and promised help if we needed it.

BAM chose the disruptive path, and on Wednesday, Thursday, and Friday of that week there was a good deal of turmoil. Roving bands of students entered buildings making noise and disrupting classes, caused ammonia and stink bombs to be released, threw some books off library shelves, and broke some furniture. Black students claimed, doubtless with justification, that it was radical white students who were doing some of the damage.

The press had a field day covering the campus. A good deal of indignation was being expressed around the state, and the Regents were becoming increasingly concerned. I had been telling them that, if we could hold out for a week or ten days, I thought we could survive without anyone being seriously hurt and with only minor damage to the university. Nevertheless, under constituent pressure, some of the Regents were thinking seriously of the National Guard.

To avoid any disruption that might occur if the Regents met in Ann Arbor, we met in Dearborn on Thursday, March 26, to discuss the situation. The radio reported that morning that two of the Regents had said that I was going to be fired. Paul Goebel and Bob Brown were particularly upset, and when the meeting convened it was Paul Goebel who spoke first. He had been an All-American end on the football team in the 1920s, a former Republican mayor of Grand Rapids, and one of the university's most devoted alums. Angry as he was over what was happening, he nevertheless leaned his considerable bulk forward at the outset of the session and said, "I have two things to say before we start. First, did any of you say that the president was going to be fired today?" As he spoke, he pointed at each Regent. No one admitted saying this, although I always thought it quite possible that one or more of them had made the statement. Paul then resumed, "I have one other thing to say. At the end of this meeting we are going to make a statement. I do not know what it will say, but I do know what the last paragraph will say and it will be that we are 100 percent behind the president!" Good old Paul. He was one of the great men I have known. Unhappy as he was with what he saw, he was willing to take a chance that I was right and that we could get matters under control. Following Paul's remarks, we had a good meeting and the Regents issued a conciliatory statement. I told them that I thought we were near the end of the strike.

On behalf of the faculty, SACUA did yeoman work trying to calm their colleagues and in helping to bring about a settlement. At a special meeting on Wednesday, March 25, the university's Senate Assembly unanimously approved a resolution urging the university's eighteen schools and colleges to make "admissions and budgetary decisions to achieve at least 10 percent black enrollment by 1973–74." The various deans, who had been meeting with the vice presidents, convened their faculties and obtained approval from them for budgetary adjustments in support of the effort to enroll more black students. This support was critical to our efforts, and, understandably, it was not attained without strong differences of opinion. In the course of the LSA faculty meeting, one very distinguished and highly respected member of the faculty said: ". . . today the truth lies in chanting, marching columns. . . . And so, we will now submit in one way or another to all the demands of BAM. In doing so, we will admit, explicitly or implicitly, that we are indeed a repressive, racist institution—but that is *still* a lie." He continued, "I was never so ashamed [of the university] as I was this morning . . . when my students came to ask me why we were not having class. I didn't know what to tell them. I still don't. Unless it is this— there is no reason; there is only power." But when it was all over, he had both the courage and grace to say, "I was clearly wrong in predicting that BAM would win all of its demands. In essence, as I see it, BAM ended its strike having won little or nothing beyond what had already been determined before the strike began. . . . Nevertheless, as I look around the country at what has happened . . . I conclude that the ability of this or any university to preserve the values which most of us know and cherish still remains highly questionable." His words on both occasions undoubtedly expressed what a number of other faculty people felt.

On Saturday, March 29, I entered the negotiations. We talked all afternoon and into the evening. The talks ended about 10:00 P.M. when the students went to Rackham Auditorium for a meeting. We had agreed that no statement would be made about our progress. To my horror, one of our public relations people, who apparently did not understand the agreement, released a statement. This infuriated the BAM group and they demanded an apology. They were right, we were wrong. I made the apology. I have never understood why an apology under such circumstances is regarded as a sign of weakness.

That same day a meeting had taken place between BAM leaders and Vice President Pierpont, his associate, Jim Brinkerhoff, and the Ann Arbor police in which it was agreed that the aggressive picketing would stop. Black faculty members joined in urging the students to pursue peaceful approaches, and black legislators were also quietly urging restraint.

On Monday, March 30, the talks resumed. The pickets had been removed and class attendance began to increase toward normal levels. We met very late that night. With me was only Herbert Hildebrandt, who was then secretary of the Regents, and one or another person intermittently. The sticking point in the negotiation was always our refusal to make a commitment to 10 percent enrollment as opposed to setting it as a goal. We were not prepared to take just any high school graduate in order to achieve a 10 percent figure, and all of the data we had gathered convinced us that we could not reach the goal without doing that. The BAM group insisted we were only using this as an excuse, and we argued that to accept a student who would only find the path too difficult would be to stamp that individual as a failure when this need not be true if the competition was less severe.

Finally, at 4:00 A.M., when our conversations seemed stalled, one of their spokesmen said that he had to make a telephone call. It seemed to me an unlikely time for a call, but he went to the adjoining room where there was a telephone. In a few minutes he came out and announced that I had a call. I knew this could hardly be true at that hour, but I didn't know what he had in mind. He came in the room with me, and when the door was closed, he said, in a perfectly calm and friendly voice, "We've got to get this thing over with. What is the best offer you can make?" I repeated what we had been saying, "We will set 10 percent as our goal, we will provide the financial aid to make this possible if the student has need, and we will do the other things we have already told you about. Beyond that I cannot go, nor do I think the Regents will go further." He said, "All right, let's go back in the other room. I will ask you the same question, and you give the same answer. Then I will say that we must consider it until morning. We will then meet at 10:00 A.M. in this room to end it." We returned to the bargaining table and went through the required conversation. They then left, as did I, and I was sure that the break I had been waiting for had finally come. We met the following morning for the formal agreement.

Public reaction to the settlement of the strike was mixed. The conservative *Detroit News* intoned, "When a great university, guilty only of excessive tolerance, goes begging on its knees for the forgiveness of arrogant radicals it's time for someone with authority and guts to step in and call a halt to the farce." But the liberal *Detroit Free Press* said, "The University of Michigan's regents have chosen the path of wisdom in supporting President Robben Fleming and in trying to live up to the commitments which have brought the student strike to an end. Let us hope their decision will help to still the angry clamor and will permit all of us to see President Fleming's actions in some kind of perspective."

President Nixon's vice president, Spiro Agnew, weighed in with this comment: "In a few years' time perhaps—thanks to the University of Michigan's callow retreat from reality—America will give the diplomas from Michigan the fish eye that the Italians now give diplomas from the University of Rome." That comment was immensely helpful to us, not only because he unnecessarily insulted the University of Rome and made Italians angry, but because Agnew was himself so unpopular in university circles. Even my most severe internal critics blasted the vice president.

When the vice president criticized me it was fodder for the media, and I was immediately asked to comment. I said simply that "the vice president is apparently badly misinformed about the commitment the university's Regents, faculty, and administration have made to provide educational opportunity to disadvantaged young people, particularly blacks."

My comments prompted a prominent Michigan executive who had good ties to the Nixon administration, and was a friend to the university, to call one of our Regents and offer to get an appointment with the vice president so that I could explain the situation. I expressed a willingness to do so if the vice president wished, but I also said that I didn't really think his comments had anything to do with either understanding or wanting to understand our situation. I thought it was pure politics. No meeting ever took place, and it was not long after that the vice president was drummed out of office for irregularities in the conduct of his own affairs.

My own mail during this period was immense, the majority of it hostile. But Governor Milliken, gracious and understanding as always, endorsed the BAM goals and praised me for being "sensitive to the needs of black students." On the other hand, one of the BAM leaders was quoted as saying, "The university will do anything to survive. It will even do right."

We were not helped by the press, which never understood the intricacies of the agreement. It was a time when the words *goals* and *quotas* were being bitterly debated, with many people insisting there was no difference in their meaning. We had used the word *goal* deliberately to avoid committing ourselves to a *quota*. In our view, goal meant that we would try our best to reach 10 percent, but we would not do this at the expense of taking just any high school graduate. To us, quota meant a commitment, no matter what the problems.

The press and media still persist in saying that we did not in subsequent years fulfill our agreement to reach 10 percent. We did reach 7 percent, and since then the university has made further progress under successive presidents. (Parenthetically, one of the ironies of "planning," as represented by our 7 percent figure, is that if you reach it you are then accused of a "self-fulfilling prophecy.") No amount of explanation that a goal was not a commitment unless we could find the requisite number of qualified students has ever caused the members of the press to change their line.

Later in the spring of 1970, student protests brought death to students on three campuses as the result of an activist bombing at one university and bullets fired by those who were brought in to restore order at the others. This was what I had long feared would happen, and why I thought a maximum effort had to be made to restore order without resorting to force. Sad as these events were, they apparently did bring second thoughts to students who believed that violence could resolve campus problems. They probably also helped in gaining greater understanding of our restraint during the BAM strike.

The University of Michigan alumni magazine received an enormous number of letters about the BAM strike. It reported that "a major concern evidenced in alumni letters was that there might be a compromise with or lowering of either admission standards or performance quality at the Universiity."

By 1971 the worst of the campus difficulties was over. Disruptions continued, but the revolutionaries were largely gone. Some of the tactics would linger, such as protest marches and confrontations, but the violence was mostly in the past.

Looking back on the BAM strike today, I would change little that we did. The bottom line was that we avoided serious violence, we established much-needed programs for the advancement of black people, and no one would argue today that the image of the University of Michigan as one of the great universities of the world was diminished by what happened then. If we were indeed successful, there were many contributors. The governor was a major source of strength and assistance, the Regents stood firmly behind us when they were under severe pressure, the faculty rallied overwhelmingly behind us despite provocative incidents, and the majority of the students always went about their business even in the face of turmoil. Finally, Sally was always a source of great strength. She didn't like what was happening, and she was fearful for me, but she understood and approved what we were trying to do. She never let the tension get her down, even when groups of students followed us around campus shouting, "Open It Up or Shut It Down!"

Given the state of race relations in our country, it is not surprising that there are still tensions between black and white students on campus. Black students resent the fact that too many of the white students look upon them as if they were all recipients of a special favor in being allowed academic admission. It is a curious commentary on our society that black athletes, who heavily populate our outstanding football and basketball teams, are worshiped by the public while they are in uniform but become black again when they are in street clothes. How deep is our prejudice! Twenty-five years ago I thought we might, in the next twenty years, rid ourselves of much of this prejudice, at least on campuses. Now it is apparent that we still have a long way to go. We have made progress, and we will make more, but we will never reach our goal until we can do something about the abysmal conditions that surround the schooling and social and economic conditions of minorities and their families in the inner cities.

Perhaps the way to end this account of student problems is to tell a story about a meeting I had with Professor William Paton on the occasion of his 100th birthday. He was a famous professor of accounting at Michigan and was a genuine leader in his field. His students were prominent in all types of business ventures and they were very loyal to him. But he was also a first-class curmudgeon who always said exactly what he meant. Since he regarded what he said as factually true, he never saw any reason it might offend anyone.

Professor Paton was already retired when we came to Michigan in 1967. It was not long thereafter before I got my first blistering letter indicting me for my tolerance of student shenanigans. Since I didn't know who he was, I inquired and was told that I would receive many such letters, as did other officers of the university, and that I should not respond in kind. The result was that I always answered his letters with moderation, although this had no visible results in terms of his next epistle. I got to know him a little better when the Business School was raising money for a building in his name and I helped with that effort. Our relationship was always friendly enough, but his criticism never ceased.

After I was retired, and toward the end of the 1980s, I saw an announcement in the paper that the Business School was going to have a reception in honor of his 100th birthday. Sally and I thought we ought to go and we did. It was a large reception and a great many of his former students, now famous in their own right, were there. He was not very strong, so he was seated on a loveseat with room for a companion to sit down beside him for a minute while greeting him. Neither his sight nor hearing was very good, and when I sat down I said, "Professor Paton, I'm Bob Fleming, and I came to congratulate you on your birthday." He said, "Bob Fleming, Bob Fleming, I know that name. Who are you?" I responded, "I was president for a long time." He said, "President of what?" and I then said, "The University of Michigan." He sat silent for a few seconds, and then said, "Weren't a very good one, were you?" A few more seconds elapsed, and he then said, "They have another one now. He's not very good either!"

All of which is to say that I was never without critics! Still, I am proud of the fact that we never had anyone hurt badly during the course of an incident, we had no residue of hate and bitterness arising out of our conflicts, and the university remained the great institution that it had always been. Since the human instinct seems always to be one of retaliation in force once there is trouble, those who counsel peaceful negotiation have a hard time gaining much credibility.

Chapter 14

A Restrospective on Student Unrest

Is there anything we can learn about successfully coping with student unrest in light of the experience of the 1960s and 1970s? Certainly not if one envisions an all-purpose, magic formula that will have universal application. If, however, one can devise a way of thinking about such problems, then there is hope. Let me try to do that, using a large, public university as a model.

The Milieu

In the 1960s and 1970s, the University of Michigan had, on its Ann Arbor campus, about forty thousand students. Roughly 60 percent of them were undergraduates, about 23 percent of whom were from out-of-state or foreign countries. Forty percent were graduate students or were enrolled in the professional schools. A selective admissions policy existed, which meant that almost all of the students had done very well in their previous academic endeavors. Sixty percent of the students were male, 40 percent female. As a general, but not universal rule, students in the College of Literature, Science, and the Arts, Social Work, Education, Music, or Law would be more liberal in their social and economic views than would those who were enrolled in Engineering, Business, or Medicine. Student governments existed in each of the schools and colleges and functioned quite well within that limited mission. The overall student government did not work well, partly because of lack of student interest in it and partly because it was easily captured by splinter or purely capricious groups.

The city of Ann Arbor had about 100,000 residents and the old shopping district was immediately contiguous to the campus. The city was well run by an elected mayor, an appointed city manager, and an elected city council. Relations between the city and the university were harmonious, with occasional inevitable lapses resulting from actions on the part of one or the other that might momentarily annoy the other.

The university had no police force, but it did have security officers, without police power, who monitored buildings for security purposes. The city police force was under the control of a chief, Walter Krasney, who understood the nuances of working with students, but his force was not large enough to cope with a major problem on campus. In this case, the surrounding county sheriffs were able to come on campus without our permission, and they were, in general, less understanding of students than were the city police. The state police, under the control of a governor who was wonderfully understanding of campus problems, was a very fine and well-disciplined body under the command of a first-rate officer who, after his retirement, became the head of our security force at the university.

Not all of our security problems were caused by students. Footloose young nonstudents, usually male, drifted in and out of campuses throughout the period and readily involved themselves in campus disputes. Juveniles within the city likewise sensed the excitement of being on campus and showed up regularly during outdoor demonstrations. In terms of serious crime, a serial killer was loose in the area. He murdered several young women before he was caught, and though none of them were UM coeds and the culprit was not connected with the university, we received some of the blame simply because of the unrest on campus. One bereaved parent even suggested that his daughter be buried in the front yard of the President's House. There was, in addition, a deranged student arsonist who set a half dozen fires in our Graduate Library before he was apprehended. Fortunately, none of them did serious damage. Bomb threats against buildings were frequent, but nothing ever happened and we largely ignored them. In the midst of a few campus demonstrations, rocks were thown through windows at the President's House, once breaking a lamp near where we were standing. I never thought this was done by students.

Among the students, there were only a few genuine revolutionaries. They were shrewd in the use of radical tactics; that is, they played the media with skill and they staged their meetings at times and places where there would be a ready crowd. They made advance dates with TV cameramen, and they reserved their most vehement rhetoric for the microphones. But they were not good tacticians. They were so caught up in their own machinations that they always imagined they had much more influence than they really did. The problem the radicals posed was not so much in their acts as it was in how best to respond to them. If the police intervened, deliberate efforts to bait them would be made, and any arrests would be followed by allegations of police brutality. When force was used, it was almost a foregone conclusion that some curious onlooker would be hurt and this would incite other students even though they were not sympathetic with the radicals.

Federal government officials were unpopular, principally because of the Vietnam War. It was the albatross that hung around the necks of a series of presidents, finally coming to rest most severely on Lyndon Johnson. He could not accept withdrawal, and world opinion was against an all-out assault by a giant on what was perceived to be a relatively primitive nation. We poured in more and more men and equipment and were given a series of reports that were untrue as to the results being achieved. Undergraduate students were protected from the draft as long as they remained students, but this left them uneasy about their preferred status.

Meanwhile, the civil rights movement pressed forward, only to have its leader, Martin Luther King, assassinated. This in turn led to serious racial conflict and to campus demonstrations in support of the movement. The tactic of nonviolent resistance, which King had demonstrated worked, became a standard part of the campus repertoire. The result was sit-ins, building occupations; and resistance to ROTC, to research funded by the Defense Department, and to recruiters from weapons companies who appeared on campus to interview candidates for jobs. Interest in these issues extended beyond the radical fringe and, therefore, made dealing with them more hazardous in terms of tactics.

When Richard Nixon became president, he found a way to withdraw American forces from Vietnam, which relieved that pressure, but he destroyed himself over Watergate. His deliberate lies ultimately forced his resignation. Unfortunately, it also furthered the image of government officials as untrustworthy. This only encouraged student distrust of all authority.

Within the state of Michigan, we were extremely fortunate to have a moderate Republican governor, William Milliken, in office. He would serve for almost all of my years and he was superb. This was critical to us because the governor is in command of the state police, and he has the power to call out the National Guard. If he had decided to do this on

A SIT-IN
HAS BEGUN
AT THE
L.S.A. BDLG.

A SIT-IN IS TAKING PLACE AT THE L.S.A. BUILDING PROTESTING:

    A.   THE CONTINUING EXPANSION OF THE INDO_CHINA WAR

    B.   THE ARREST OF 2 PERSONS ATTEMPTING TO ENTER AN "OPEN"
         REGENTS' MEETING LAST FRIDAY

    C.   THE LACK OF DECISION-MAKING POWER OF THE UNIVERSITY
         COMMUNITY

IN ACCORDANCE WITH THE ABOVE, THE FOLLOWING DEMANDS ARE BEING
MADE OF THE UNIVERSITY:

    1. AN END TO THE ON CAMPUS RECRUITING OF RACIST AND
       SEXIST CORPORATIONS.

    2. THE ESTABLISHMENT OF A 24-HOUR DAY CARE CENTER
       RUN BY THE PEOPLE WHO USE IT AND WORK IN IT.

    3. AN END TO WAR RESEARCH.

    4. OPEN UNIVERSITY FACILITIES TO THE ANTI-WAR MOVEMENT.

    5. STUDENT CONTROL OF THE COURSE MART.

    6. END R.O.T.C.

TO DECIDE THE FUTURE OF THE SIT-IN
MEETING: 4:30 AT L.S.A.

GUESS WHO'S COMING TO CAMPUS

GUESS WHO'S COMING TO CAMPUS?

    Du Pont Chemical, that's right folks, old Du Pont Chemical—
the better living through chemistry people— are coming here to
recruit a few of you all for some of this so-called better
living.

GUESS WHAT DU PONT OWNS?

    Besides the Continental United States, the Du Ponts own
such notables as Remington Arms, Phillips Petroleum, and
Uniroyal. They used to own General Motors, but they were forced
to trade it. Instead of General Motors, Du Pont now owns the
state of Delaware.

GUESS WHERE DU PONT HAS ITS HOME BASE?

    Wilmington, Delaware, you all remember Wilmington folks,
that's the town that was placed under martial law from April of
68 until January of 69. That's the town where the black ghetto
was occupied by white troops so all those people wouldn't get
too upset about the assassination of Martin Luther King. And
just so the National Guard would be protected, the state legislature gave this here White Guard legal immunity from any and
all prosecution. Hot Damn, Vietnam.

NOW TRY REAL HARD AND GUESS WHO CONTROLS THE GOVERNMENT OF
WILMINGTON?

    Give up? DU PONT, that's right folks, old Du Pont Chemical
(the same one that's going to be here, without the National Guard)
has its little synthetic hand wrapped tight around the government;
in fact, that little synthetic hand is the government. How about
that folks, kind of knocks the breath right out of you don't it,
kind of makes you think twice about this here corporate structure,
don't it?

GUESS WHO OWNS HALF A MILLION DOLLARS WORTH OF DU PONT STOCK?

Who else? Your very own University of Michigan, the Auschwitz
of the Midwest.

JUST THIS LAST ONE: NOW GUESS WHAT WE'RE GOING TO DO WHEN
THIS REPRENSTATIVE OF MR. DU PONT COMES HERE. TAKE A WILD GUESS.

 MEET IN THE FISHBOWL THURSDAY AT 11 AM

Go to the Reparation Conference this Weekend

Better Living Through Revolution
sds

his own without consulting with us or without our consent, our power to cope with demonstrations according to our own best judgment would have been destroyed. He never exercised this power, and it is a tremendous tribute to him that he did not because there were times when public sentiment was clearly hostile to the way we were handling things. Not only did the governor keep hands off, he supported us in what we did and with the state police when we needed them.

At the immediate governance level were, of course, the elected Board of Regents. They were all well-known citizens, mostly UM graduates, and with a true devotion to the university. A majority of them were Republicans when we first came, though this later changed in the opposite direction. They worked well together, they did not vote in party blocks, and they stood up under great pressure when times were hard. They accepted the indignities that were visited upon them because they understood that it was an inevitable part of the service they were rendering.

Leading the university was, of course, the president. That was the role that I occupied. I had been hired, in significant part, because the Regents thought, based on my Wisconsin experience, that I might be able to cope with student unrest. They thoroughly explored my views on this in the course of early interviews. They knew that I had publicly expressed the view that our presence in Vietnam was a mistake. My reasons did not accord with those of the radical left, I simply thought that we had undertaken to do battle in the wrong place, for the wrong reasons, and at the wrong time. Knowing that confrontations, incivility, and a certain amount of civil disobedience could not be avoided, all of my experience in the dispute resolution field led me to believe that the use of force was not useful as long as there was any other tactic available. Following that path would nevertheless anger many people outside the university community because they would read it as a sign of weakness.

The faculty and staff were also critical components of the university community, and, if we were to succeed, we had to hold them with us. The staff was always composed of two components, one being the long-term employees who saw it as a career and the other being those who only sought temporary employment, often in support of a spouse who was going to school. Because of their difference in status, their loyalties would differ as would their sympathies.

The faculty was enormously diverse, not only in its social and economic views, but in its interests. Given the size of the university, faculty members did not know one another well across school and college lines. Many were relatively removed from any probability of disruption, while others were very exposed. Aside from their individual school, college, and departmental governance structures, they had an elected universitywide body headed by an elected executive committee called the Senate Advisory Committee on University Affairs (SACUA). As in most major universities, there was a strong tradition of faculty governance. This made it imperative that the relationship between the president and SACUA be good, because without their support such policies as we might pursue would be extremely difficult to enact and enforce.

Finally, there were the alumni and alumnae (a distinction in title between men and women that, to my knowledge, applied only at Michigan and is now largely abandoned). They were, and always have been, an extraordinarily devoted group. Some are conservative in their views and some are liberal, but all are proud of their tie to the university. They would hold different views about how we should deal with students, and it was therefore important that we maintain a close tie with them and that they understand what we were trying to accomplish.

This then was the climate within which we would approach student problems for the next several years.

The Objectives

Given the setting, we had then to decide what our objectives were. Preventing violence was essential, but there was a great deal more to it than that. Coping with student unrest, however much time and energy it took, was, after all, not the main mission of the university. The University of Michigan had, over the years, acquired the reputation of being one of the country's premier academic institutions and its reputation was worldwide. If we won the battle of handling student unrest but lost the battle of maintaining a superb university, all our efforts would have been to no avail. Student unrest would pass, but the university would endure.

The objectives I set for myself were the following.

1. Maintain the excellence of the university. This would not mean simply a continuation of the status quo, because no university can remain great without adapting to new times and circumstances. It would mean that we would not abandon our emphasis on quality.
2. Preserve the intellectual integrity of the university and the freedom of expression for all points of view. We could not bow to the demands of either the radical left or right in what we did or said, but neither should we cut them off.
3. Carry the bulk of our major constituents—the students, the faculty, the staff, the alums—with us. We could not satisfy everyone, but neither could we succeed if we could not hold the majority support of those who were closest to the problem.
4. Insofar as possible, contain student unrest without the use of repressive force. To do this, we would have to be willing to endure insulting behavior, premeditated provocation, minor disruptions, and harassment. We would also have to make it understood that there were limits beyond which we would not go without using the police.
5. Hold the state legislature and the public with us sufficiently to permit all of these objectives to be fulfilled without retribution.

While I did not publicly articulate these objectives in the form they are stated here, they were the guideposts by which I intended to govern my own conduct. Inherent in them were the values that, for better or worse, I held. I had been brought up in a family that believed deeply in fairness, courtesy, concern for others, and humility. I was not a theorist, I was a pragmatist. I had lived for twenty years in academic communities, and I knew a good deal about the habits of the academic world. I had also lived for a similar period in the world of conflict resolution, and I knew a good bit about how people behave under stress and how to identify real, as distinguished from staged, behavior. I knew that sometimes one would be faced with options that were all bad. The choice might simply be which was the least bad! And I already knew that the deck was filled with wild cards. The best-laid plans can go astray if an individual who is out of control suddenly enters the scene and commits some lethal act. Given the tension of the time and the prevalence of drugs and alcohol, this was always not only a possibility, but something over which we had little or no control. There was, for instance, a deranged man who, in the midst of campus disputes, would show up with a giant slingshot made from a branch of a tree with a sling made from automobile innertubes. He specialized in shooting bricks through windows, but if his aim had gone bad he could have hit and killed someone.

If we thought we knew the milieu in which we would have to operate and what our objectives were, what were the strategies that might hold out the best hope for success?

The Application of a Strategy

Though our overriding objective was always the maintenance of the high quality of the university, my focus here is on student unrest, and for that reason I shall not attempt to assess our success or failure in achieving other objectives. That is, in any event, better left to others. In this connection, I should note that the recently republished version of Howard Peckham's history of the University of Michigan, done by historians Nicholas Steneck and Margaret Steneck, covers this period in far more detail than I could in this memoir. I am gratified by their conclusions.

The beginning of wisdom in dealing with student unrest is surely trying to understand student attitudes toward it. They do not like violence, and they do not like having their education disrupted or property destroyed. On the other hand, they are more tolerant of deviant behavior than their elders, they tend to take the side of students in any given dispute, they resist authority, and peaceful disobedience often appeals to them.

On their side, quite naturally, will be their own student governments and the student newspaper. Students will, in episodes like tenting on the Diag, the digging of a bomb crater on campus to oppose bombing in Vietnam, the holding of a silent vigil during halftime of a football game as a protest against the war in Vietnam, or similar incidents, see no reason to intervene. They will tend to oppose any restrictions on them that would not be imposed on the rest of the population outside the university.

The student newspaper will almost always be a thorn in the side of a university administration. If it uses language no other daily commercial newspaper would use, it will enrage substantial portions of the public and the alums, but it will be protected by the First Amendment of the Constitution. If it reports on a speech, it will pick and choose which portions it wants to report, and it will often take what is said out of context. It will, as it did in the case of my inaugural remarks, quote what I said about "allowing controversy to flourish," but it will leave out the rest of the sentence about doing it "in an atmosphere of dignity and respect for others." In short, like most of the commercial press, it has a point of view that is not always encumbered by a need for accuracy! It will dare the administration to suppress it, knowing full well that the press, the media, and the American Civil Liberties Union will support it, however bad it is. Despite the annoyance of the student newspaper, it is easy to take it too seriously, and there are some steps that can be taken to cope with it.

We had an Advisory Committee composed of faculty and outside journalists who could exercise some restraint. When the *Michigan Daily* was at its very worst and the Regents were tempted to abolish it, the Regents realized that this would accomplish little because, aside from the vigorous attack that would be made upon them by the commercial press and the court action that would follow, we would only have to start another paper and there was no reason to expect that it would be better. In addition, though the paper could be very annoying, it was not that influential. Its limitations were well known to both students and faculty. The result was that the marketplace began to exercise its influence. Advertisers kept coming to us, saying that they did not like the language the paper used, and couldn't there be some alternative paper that they could use for advertising purposes? Since the *Daily* was wholly self-supporting and not dependent on a university subsidy, a loss of advertising could be serious. We did not want to start a competitive paper, but we did find a way to get the *Daily*'s attention. It did not publish on Mondays. We therefore started the *University Record*, which published only on that day and was designed to provide the university community with accurate factual information. Advertisers would have gladly supported it rather than the *Daily*, but we did not want the *Daily* to go out of business. If it did, we would then have to start and subsidize another paper. Accordingly, we told the *Daily* what we were going to do and why, and then let the market forces take over. The result was that the *Daily* improved, certainly in its language, and the *Record* became a respected source of information.

Lest it sound like the *Michigan Daily* was a disaster, it was, in fact, one of the better student newspapers, and it gave a number of now well-recognized journalists an opportunity to learn their trade. Its limitations were a product of the milieu within which it operated and the immaturity of some of the judgments its editors made.

If one recognizes at the outset the unsurprising fact that the student body, its government, and the student newspaper are likely to be sympathetic to the student point of view, it immediately says something about how one can deal with student unrest. A premium is placed on two strategies, one being to listen carefully to what students are saying, and the other is to see that they are not hearing only one side of a policy or issue that is in dispute. I found this out more by experience than through any cerebral process. The only way to avoid protesters who came to the president's office during that period was to either lock them out or shunt them off on someone else. If you locked them out, you left the impression that the primary authority figure in the university either feared them or would not listen or could not defend whatever item they were protesting. Either way, you lost with the bulk of the students. If, on the other hand, you met them, listened and made changes where you could and explained why if you could not, you gained points. In the audience were always a large number of people who were simply attracted by the dispute. If the only voices they heard were those who were protesting, they were not getting a balanced view of the problem. When protesters favored abolishing ROTC, if no one in authority told them that ROTC was entirely voluntary and therefore represented freedom of choice on the part of students, that the scholarships it offered made it possible for a number of students who might not otherwise be able to go to school to attend, or that essentially civilian army officers were important to the future of our democracy, those arguments were lost.

If students came to you and asked for some financial support in order to run a student evaluation of teachers and you made some funds available contingent on their willingess to accept advice from the university's respected Institute for Social Research as to how to conduct the evaluation, why not do it? There would be those who would say that the result would be worthless, but the students were trying to be constructive and the process would be educational.

If the students wanted to change the conduct of their commencement, and you could explain how important the traditional ceremony was to their parents it might give them a different outlook on the problem.

If they wanted to talk about the secrecy attached to certain kinds of research, why was this not a topic that ought to be discussed? If the university was, in fact, doing things that were indefensible, why was it wrong if students raised the issue?

If activists found infrared technology research unworthy of a humane university because it could detect hidden military equipment and make it vulnerable to bombing, wasn't it important that students also know that the same technology could detect disease in forests or in growing crops?

If radical students were exhorting students to continue a showdown with the police on South University following an evening of confrontation with the police, why was it not important that someone tell them that the dispute had nothing to do with the university and that they ought to stay away?

If a speaker who is coming to campus may cause an ensuing riot by condemning our participation in the war in Vietnam, is it not important that a president speak on the same program expressing a more balanced view in an effort to contain emotions?

Run-of-the-mill disruptive events were annoying, but not difficult to meet. The make-or-break decisions were always those where violence could break out, and there was no guarantee that any decision one made would work. When the LSA Building was occupied and the students refused to leave, we had to decide whether to let them stay in the building or use the police to clear it. Good arguments could be made on both sides. The bookstore was not a radical issue, and it had widespread support among students. If we used the police and there was resistance during which someone was hurt, student anger might escalate. If we didn't remove the demonstrating students, experience elsewhere suggested that the occupation could continue for some time and that nonstudent radicals would be attracted to the area. We were hearing from our security people inside the building that some offices were being entered, and that a wastebasket fire or two had been set.

My own conclusion was that we ought to take back the building that very night. If we did it at a late hour, like 4:00 A.M., the crowd would be small. If we gave students a chance to leave without arrest, some of them probably would. If we tried to use the legal injunction process and it was not successful, we could at least demonstrate our good faith in wanting to avoid violence. By using the state police we could rely on their disciplined restraint. If there was no resistance, it would be apparent to the students that we would not always be tolerant of what was being done and this might induce restraint in the future. If they were arrested and then tried, it would take months to complete the trials and this would leave students uncertain about how seriously a jury of Ann Arbor citizens might take their acts.

As it turned out, we guessed right. The eviction went smoothly, there was no resistance, there were arrests, and after months of waiting there were trials. I had to testify in the trials. Had I not done so, the police would have felt let down. They had done their duty, why wouldn't I do mine?

The other occasion when the use of force had to be contemplated, and when it could have turned into a total disaster, was during the BAM strike. If we had felt we had to use the police on that occasion, it would have been considered as purely an issue of race by the black community. The fact that some of the tactics, including disrupting class-rooms, intimidating students who wanted to go to class, and throwing books off the shelves in the library did occur made the period very hard to endure. True, white activists were involved and certainly committed some of the acts, but black students were very proud of the fact that this was their strike. Public feeling was running high, city and state officials were under pressure to intervene, and the Regents were receiving all kinds of communications hostile to what was going on. We were near the end of our ability to settle the strike without using force, but so were the black students. Black faculty were counseling them that it had gone far enough, some of the black legislators came to campus to try and cool things down, and the governor was holding with us. Working with our people, the black students agreed with the police and the city officials to stop the intimidation, and at my level we were still trying to find a settlement. It came in terms that I have already described and, in re-strospect, it has worked well, though at the time the public attitude was clearly against us.

None of these things could have happened without the support of the majority of the faculty and staff. During the bookstore fracas, the faculty came out in large numbers to exert whatever influence they could against violence, and they worked out the details of the ultimate settlement. While the BAM strike was on they worked with their deans and departmental chairpersons to identify cuts in their budgets that would guarantee that we could finance aid for qualified black students. During our "tenting" and "public health" dispute, they worked with us to find a solution that ended the occupation. Staff people, particularly those in secretarial positions and those working with grounds maintenance, held up under a good deal of harassment and kept their tempers under remarkable control. This happened, I think, because, quite apart from student unrest, we tried to build a participatory relationship with both the faculty and the staff. It was a way of governing a university that they liked because they were involved. We could have differences among ourselves, but when we were in trouble we came together.

We did less well with the public. It got its information largely from the press, and the nature of both newspapers and the broadcast media is to focus on the spectacular. Even so, there were good reasons for people to be angry with what was going on, and, when they are angry, they are more interested in striking back than in trying to take a longer view. On several occasions, we pushed the public's level of tolerance to the limit. We did, however, have some public support. Michigan tends to be a centrist state politically, perhaps because big industry and big labor had struck a balance in which they could live together despite their differences. They understood what we were going through, and they were often supportive.

Like the rest of the public, our own alumni were ambivalent. They hated what they were seeing, but they were also parents and they tried to understand the turmoil that was going on in the younger generation. I remember an evening when I was talking to an alumni group in a very conservative part of the state. I had been warned in advance that I would probably get many hostile questions. I made a talk in which I tried to explain why we refrained from using the police or the National Guard in the face of major problems. When I finished, one man stood up and said that this was silly and that we ought to immediately call in the National Guard. I asked whether he would be willing to run the risk that, if we did so, an entirely innocent student might be killed, and he said, "Yes, they ought to be shot." His answer so shocked the audience that there was an immediate change in the tenor of the meeting. Distraught parents might not like what their children were doing, but the idea that they might be killed was totally abhorrent to them. (This was before the incident at Kent State, when students were killed in just such a situation.)

The director and the board of the Alumni Association held firmly with us, though the pages of the Association's magazine were always open to critical letters. An occasional donor would send word that no further support would be forthcoming, but we were not hurt in that category generally.

At the national level, both the president and Congress explored the situation. President Nixon held a dinner at the White House one evening to which a number of us were invited. The president was present only for cocktails, but Henry Kissinger, then the president's National Security Advisor; Robert Finch, the secretary of health, education and welfare; Paul McCracken, the chairman of the president's Economic Council (Professor McCracken was on leave from the University of Michigan); Erik Erikson, psychoanalyst from Harvard; William Hubbard, dean of medicine at Michigan; and a number of others were present.

At about the same time, the president appointed a Special Committee on Student Unrest, which was chaired by Governor Stratton, a moderate Republican from Pennsylvania. A number of us were asked to testify and a voluminous report was published. Just before that a congressional committee, chaired by Edith Green of Oregon, also conducted hearings at which a number of us again testified. Those proceedings were also published.

Finally, President Nixon sponsored a White House Conference on Education that, it was anticipated, would be held in Washington. I cochaired one of the planning groups, along with a black student from the University of Virginia. By the time the meeting approached, the folks in Washington were apprehensive and decided to change the venue to Estes Park, Colorado. I remember that when I was first told of the change I remarked that we used to vacation in that area and that if they held a conference there on the dates suggested there might be a blizzard. All I got in answer was knowing smiles. The conference was held, there was a blizzard, press coverage was minimal, and neither progress nor trouble took place.

Unrest inevitably runs its course, and the violent deaths that occurred on campus during the spring and summer of 1970 hastened the end. The Vietnam War would end with our withdrawal, and racial tension, though unresolved, was at least finding an outlet under civil rights legislation.

Some of the tactics of the 1960s and 1970s would remain, and civility would still be strained, but the agenda changed. Equity across racial, ethnic, and gender lines would become major points of dissension, and the gay-lesbian issue would emerge and be confronted, but the threat of violence was largely gone.

What did we learn out of all this that is worth remembering?

My list would include the following items.

1. Accept and recognize that students will, in the normal course of events, often have a different point of view than that of their elders, and that their views should be treated with respect.

2. Analyze and respond to their demands objectively, no matter how flawed or inflammatory the presentation may be. They may be right in a substantive issue, even if they are wrong on their tactics!

3. Understand that in dealing with divisive issues, the university must hold with it the majority of each of its constituents, i.e., relevant government authorities, the university's governing board, the faculty and staff, the students, and the alumni. Success in doing this is not going to be achieved by appeals in times of emergency unless an ongoing pattern of cooperation is already in place.

4. Recognize that the use of force in terms of the police or the National Guard is a measure of last resort. They may be an indispensable ally if the need is unavoidable, but restraint, even in times of great public pressure, is preferable in the long run.

Chapter 15

Reflections on a University Presidency

For the five-year period between 1965 and 1970, much of my time at Wisconsin and Michigan was taken up in dealing with student unrest. Nevertheless, we all knew that the unrest would pass, simply because energy devoted to causes always ebbs and flows and time and events bring changes. The more important task was always to protect the academic side of the university and to maintain and enhance its quality.

One finds in the literature about university governance a good deal of rhetoric about the relative lack of power in the hands of a president. Whether or not that is so always seemed to me to lie not so much in the lack of power as in the way power is exercised.

It is true that the legal power to govern invariably belongs to the governing board which, at Michigan, is known as the Regents. It is also true that the faculty regards the curriculum as residing in its domain and that many faculty members will have tenure and be protected from interference in what they do. The staff is indispensable in carrying on the daily routine of the university and a significant part of that staff may be organized into unions and be working under collective bargaining contracts that restrict management's right to change working conditions.

To assume that these restrictions on the president's power will thwart necessary changes overlooks a number of other factors. One of those is the power over the budget. The budget is made by the central administration, often largely through the academic vice president and the finance vice president. In that budget is a certain amount of "free" money, that is, money that is unrestricted and can be used anywhere at the direction of the budget makers. That money is much sought after.

A far more important factor than money, however, is the potential in a harmonious working relationship with the Regents, the deans, the departmental chairmen, the faculty, and the staff because this can result in common goals that are mutually beneficial. Achieving that degree of harmony is not easy because the Regents will differ among themselves both in philosophy and personality, and there is a high degree of autonomy in the schools and colleges. Counterbalancing this, however, is the fact that the tent over the schools and colleges is the university, and its name has considerable value to them.

The beginning of wisdom for a president is the realization that he or she cannot possibly succeed without high-quality people around him or her. The organization is too big for a single individual to manage, it requires expertise in many different areas, some of which are beyond the principal competence of the president, and it requires trusted advisors who can supply perspective on problems. It also requires a strong enough person in the presidency to rely on his or her own judgment in critical situations while at the same time inviting, and listening to, the advice of others before taking action. Perhaps this can be best illustrated through examples.

Governing boards of public universities usually meet monthly, except in emergencies. They cannot micromanage the university, and for that reason they must trust and follow the lead of the administration most of the time. This fact nevertheless places a special responsibility on the administration to gain the respect and confidence of the board. To do this, it must be sensitive to the kinds of issues that will be of particular concern to the board and see that these are fully discussed before a decision is made. The BAM strike well illustrates that point. The disruption on campus was being widely publicized, off-campus opinion was split but predominantly hostile to our posture of tolerance while pursuing a settlement, and there was enormous pressure on the Regents to use the police or the National Guard. They refrained from ordering that step because, in the course of our long discussions, they understood the peril in using outside force and they were willing to go to the brink with us in exercising restraint. The BAM strike is equally illustrative of the necessity for good relations with the faculty. In that hour of peril, they were willing, through their schools and colleges, to find ways in which they could reduce their budgets in the interest of finding funds to provide more student aid for minorities.

There are other examples of working together to solve problems. They are interesting mostly because of the diversity they exemplify.

After World War II, the Willow Run properties, famous for mass production of airplanes during the war, became surplus. At the same time came the Cold War, and our government began pouring immense resources into research. The best source of research talent was to be found in the universities, and University of Michigan faculty members were highly competent in certain areas that were of major interest to the Defense Department. By the mid-1960s and thereafter, weapons research became highly unpopular because of the Vietnam War. It was also true that the facilities at Willow Run, which were temporary in the first place, were deteriorating and would have to be replaced either there or elsewhere. If they were to be replaced, the logical thing to do would be to bring the facility into Ann Arbor where it could be contiguous to our North Campus, thus making it easier for faculty who enjoyed dual appointments to participate.

By the time this debate was taking place, many of the personnel at Willow Run had worked for the university for years and it was important that we try to find some way to save the facility and their jobs even if, in doing so, we spun-off the organization.

Ultimately, we determined within the administration that the facility should be spun-off and made into a nonprofit organization under nonuniversity management. This was acceptable, and even to some extent welcomed by personnel at Willow Run, provided financial security could be guaranteed. The latter was always precarious because the agency lived from contract to contract and would have difficulty retaining essential personnel between contracts if it did not have some reserve on which to rely. Continuation of the facility was important to the state because unemployment was becoming an increasing problem and the preservation of jobs was an important political consideration.

Working with the state and an always helpful governor, we found a way to have the state pension fund loan money to a newly incorporated nonprofit successor to the Willow Run labs and for it to continue in existence. The Regents were fully informed of the progress of those negotiations and the solution appealed to them. The deal was consummated in a way that was satisfactory to all of the interests that were involved, and the entity has survived.

A far more risky and controversial problem involved the building of a new hospital allied with the Medical School. Our hospital was obsolete, its accreditation was threatened, and the construction of a new hospital was essential. Bringing that about would be a very complex problem. In the first place, it would be enormously costly (ultimately the most expensive public building ever constructed in Michigan). In the second place, planning for a new hospital is always highly controversial, partly because of internal forces at war over space and partly because of the ever-changing nature of science and equipment.

In recognition of these facts, we had employed outside planners for several years to help us develop a project. Because the project was disputatious, no acceptable plan ever emerged and the Regents became restless. They finally issued an ultimatum that unless we came forth with a plan, they would do so. They knew, of course, that this would be impossible for them, but they also knew that we would have to do something in the face of their threat.

At the level of the central administration, we knew that the lack of a plan was not the problem, it was an inability to arrive at decisions that were acceptable within the complex. The only way for those of us in the central administration to cope with that problem was to become intimately involved in the decision-making process. That would be hazardous for us because we could be legitimately charged with knowing less about it than did the professionals in the field. At the same time, one factor that would make intervention easier was that the Medical School and Hospitals, probably because of the type of work they do, tend to be more authoritarian in their management than does much of the rest of the university. We therefore made the decision to intervene. We created a new committee, of which the president would be chairman and the vice presidents of academic affairs and finance would be members. The balance of the members would be drawn from the Medical School and the Hospitals. We then went a step further and created the kind of outline of a report that we thought the Regents would expect in considering the project. The medical personnel were then told to supply the planning information that fitted into the outline. With that information at hand, I then wrote a tentative report, which, after review by my immediate colleagues at the central level, was given to the medical and hospital authorities. They were to review it, make changes where they felt they were required, and then resubmit it to us. This was done in short order. They were then told to submit it to the medical faculty for comment and suggested changes. When the document ultimately came back relatively unchanged, it was submitted to the Regents and they examined it thoroughly. We were all aware of the hazards it contained, and even if approved there would be a long path ahead in order to gain funding and the approval of both state and federal authorities, but at least we would be on the path to success.

To my great relief, the project succeeded in getting all the support necessary to achieve approval by the Regents. It would be almost ten years before the new hospital would be completed, and it required great talent from Presidents Smith and Shapiro and their financial advisors to bring it to completion. In the end, the project succeeded because of the cooperation of the faculty, staff, administration, Regents, and the state. That kind of cooperation does not just happen, it has to be cultivated.

One final comment on Regental relations. At the time I retired, the customary retirement dinner was held at the house, and I received an assortment of presents. One of the mementoes given to me was a copy of *Roberts Rules of Order,* encased in a new binding entitled *Robben's Rules of Order.* In it was an amended second paragraph on "Motions," sec. 3, page 22, which had been altered by Regent Thomas Roach.

No motion shall be in order until the subject matter has been introduced by the president and all members desiring to do so have spoken to the issue. In this way, debate following the motion will be minimized or nonexistent, and the outcome of the vote on the motion will be reasonably predictable. If it appears from the remarks of the members that the wrong result will be achieved by a vote, the president shall announce that the subject matter is an item for information only, and will come to the board for action at a subsequent meeting.

I did, indeed, do what the altered rule said. The fact that the Regents, any number of whom were very familiar with Roberts Rules, let me do it speaks, I think, to the cordial relationship we had with one another.

I have already spoken of the great aid and assistance the faculty gave to us in dealing with student unrest. Of more long-run importance to them would always be those items that touched on the academic side. Two examples, in the field of research, illustrate the point.

When Geoff Norman was vice president for research, he came to me one day with a very unusual proposal. One of our well-known psychologists was studying high-risk decision making. To do this, he needed a venue within which to work. One possibility was the military, but it had declined. A second was a study of gambling in Las Vegas. The proposal was that a table be established at one of the gambling casinos, and that the faculty member study high-risk decisions there for two or three years following which he would write a book on the subject. There was a reputable foundation sponsor, appropriate measures could be put in place to cover losses or winnings, the subject was legitimate, and the faculty member was responsible. The trouble was that one could immediately envision the newspaper headlines: University of Michigan Runs Gambling Table! That kind of publicity we did not need, nor would we ever be able to counteract the fun the press would make of the venture. But there was another side to the coin. The governance of a university is always seen as an annoyance by the faculty, allegedly because it is too timid in accommodating legitimate demands. If we could not find a way to authorize a piece of research that was substantively valid, that would be the charge we would hear from the faculty. The solution we found was to subcontract the table to a university in Nevada, where the state's economy and culture is so reliant on gambling that the operation of a table would be acceptable. The result was that the project was carried out, the book was written, and a conflict with the faculty was avoided.

A far more serious problem came about when the new and exciting biogenetic research was just getting started. Tampering with genes was a very scary idea to many people and even the National Institutes of Health were studying what the allowable limits of such research should be. Our own scientists were impatient to proceed, but they did understand the opposite point of view. Another faculty group, composed largely of humanists, was strongly opposed. In addition, city governments in places such as Ann Arbor or Cambridge, Massachusetts, were also showing concern about the safety of such research. Thus we had both an internal faculty dispute and a potentially hostile city government on our hands.

At the suggestion of Charles Overberger, who was by then the vice president for research, we decided to hold hearings on the subject as a means of educating all of us about the potential gains and hazards from the proposed research. If we did that, the scientists would be a bit unhappy because they wanted to get on with the task and be among the first to achieve results. On the other hand, the faculty faction that was in opposition would have a full opportunity to present its arguments, and city officials would also have a chance to adjust. If we held the hearings before the Regents, they too would learn a good deal more about a subject on which they were going to have to act.

We proceeded with that plan, it worked well, and a faculty committee came up with a proposed policy that closely resembled a policy being considered by the National Institutes of Health. The Regents were able to approve the recommendation without rancor among the faculty, and the research went forward. The plan worked because all those who were interested had an opportunity to participate in the debate, and an answer emerged that everyone could accept if for no other reason than that the procedure had been fair.

A third example of cooperative planning with both students and faculty involved the construction of new recreational facilities. Over the years, our facilities for student recreation, as distinguished from intercollegiate sports, had become woefully inadequate. They were built at a time when the student body was much smaller. Our problem was not disagreement over need, but how to finance the new construction. The legislature, which financed much of our building program, would not fund recreational facilities because they had all they could do to keep up with our academic needs. It was true that they had been good to us in this respect, and we did want to continue receiving funding for a series of academic projects. Raising money privately was an option and we tried it, but the results were unsuccessful. We could find a number of donors who wanted to give us money to enhance intercollegiate facilities, but not for student recreation. The only solution we could find was to impose a student fee. This would be opposed by students for obvious reasons, but we also had reservations about increasing the cost of attending the university. If we did go ahead with a fee, it was entirely foreseeable that students would complain if we imposed a fee while constructing the building because they could legitimately argue that they were funding something they could never use. In short, we were stymied. Even so, a student-faculty planning committee had gone ahead with some plans worked out in cooperation with the construction people under the financial vice president. We were ready to go if we had the money.

The result was a project for which a number of people could claim credit. I thought I started it by deciding that the time had come to test student opinion about a fee, but one that would not be imposed until the building was completed and available for use. Bill Pierpont, who was then the vice president for finance, found a way to work out a delayed fee while still proceeding with construction, and his committee worked with the student-faculty committee to perfect the plans. The Regents approved the plan, there was no significant protest, three new facilities were built on different parts of the campus, and our capability was enormously improved. Two of the buildings were financed by the fee, and a third was built for the joint use of intercollegiate athletics and student recreation with funds the athletic director, Don Canham, supplied. We went, in one fell swoop, from inadequacy to very high quality. More important, all those who participated were convinced that it was their effort that was the primary contributor to the result!

Some Pleasures in the Life of a President

If there were hazards in being the chief executive of a major university during this time of stress (or, indeed, any other time), there were also some wonderfully satisfying benefits. One of the most pleasurable was the opportunity for foreign travel.

We had, beginning with our first around-the-world trip while still at the University of Illinois and continuing with visits to Southeast Asia during our time at Wisconsin, become aware of the benefits of foreign travel. All of this continued at Michigan.

There are many reasons why a university president has opportunities to go abroad. All of them revolve around the fact that, after World War II, global interaction increased enormously. The Marshall Plan brought closer cooperation with Europe, and the occupation of Japan necessitated more involvement in Asia. The Cold War with Russia, and the concern about Communist China, along with the dominance of the United States as a world power, caused us to view the rest of the world differently. In this effort, the universities of America became assets to our government because they had the expertise needed to cope with many of the problems of a war-torn world. The result was American university involvement all over the globe. Agriculturalists, economists, engineering experts, political scientists, public health scientists, educators, and a host of others were called upon to assist in other countries. President Kennedy's invention of the Peace Corps appealed to both students and middle aged or retired experts and they offered their talents abroad. In this scramble, university presidents became important because their good will in cooperating with requests for personnel and assistance was important, and one way of encouraging their cooperation was to invite them to see the progress that could be made with the help of their people. Some of our foreign aid, particularly in underdeveloped countries, came in the form of improving their educational systems, and in that respect presidents had their own expertise to offer. In any event, given the prominence of the University of Michigan, any president at that institution would have many opportunities to travel. Almost all of that travel was financed by the U.S. government, as a part of a program with which the University of Michigan was cooperating, or by a foundation that, for one reason or another, supplied the funds. Over the years, we were able to cover a large part of the globe and to thereby immensely expand our own comprehension of the world we live in. Some of those trips are worth recounting because they were to places that then and now command world attention, while others were simply a culturally broadening experience or a joyful visit.

South America

In the early 1970s we were privileged to take a trip at the expense of the Danforth Foundation. At a time when presidents of universities were an endangered species because of student unrest, Danforth announced a program under which it would finance a leave of up to three or four months for a few besieged presidents whose institutions would grant them leave and continue their pay during that period. A condition of the grant was that the president and his wife leave the local premises and go somewhere else. We were a lucky invitee and we went to South America. We had not been there, it was a part of the Americas, and we thought we ought to know more about it. We had no official business there, but Sally was on the board of Youth for Understanding, which had many programs there, and I was on the Chrysler board and the company had a number of plants in that part of the world. Through both organizations, we had many contacts that would be helpful to us.

We chose to be gone for only about six weeks, and we went during the coldest part of the winter, when things would be slow at the university. We started in Mexico, then went to Colombia, and from there around the perimeter to practically all of the countries in South America. We witnessed the struggles of the Indian minorities, and realized once again how repetetive this phenomenon is in countries all over the world. We noted the prevalence of military governments and the instability of democracy in most of the countries. We saw the dominance of the Catholic Church, and at the same time the turmoil within its own ranks as it tried to satisfy both an urban elite and a disenfranchised peasantry. We found that many of the public universities were closed because of violent conflicts between the police or the Army and the students. And we heard a great deal about graft and corruption in government.

Fortunately, we also had an opportunity to view the treasures of the early Indian cultures, boated on beautiful Lake Titicaca, and saw some of the marvels of the Inca civilization, including the unfathomable construction genius made evident in the remains at Machu Picchu.

Following our trip to South America, Russia, China, South Africa, and England were among our most interesting and enjoyable experiences.

Russia

The first time we went to Russia was in 1978, when the Communist Party was still in power. The International Association of Universities, to which Michigan belonged, was meeting there and opportunities to visit Russia were not easily come by, so we went.

The meetings were held in Moscow, we stayed in one of the boxlike hotels the regime had built, we were warned that our rooms were probably bugged, and we were kept busy with the official program. University people from all over the world were there, there was entertainment every evening, and there was not a lot of time to free-lance. It was interesting to hear some scholars from communist countries subtly suggest in their lectures that some of their cherished ideological beliefs were nonsense.

A magnificent cocktail party was held at the Kremlin before we left. The Great Hall, in which the reception was held, was built during the time of the czars and was gorgeous. Set in the Great Hall were long tables loaded with caviar, vodka, and a great variety of other goodies, all in plentiful supply.

When the conference was over, visitors had the option of taking one of several package trips. We went to Leningrad (now and previously St. Petersburg) and Kiev. Away from Moscow, the foreboding atmosphere seemed more relaxed. The siege of Leningrad by the Germans during World War II had left an impression on the citizenry that will endure forever. Not only was the city nearly destroyed, but an enormous number of people died before relief came. By the time we got there, the city was again beautiful and we were privileged to visit the magnificent art galleries of the Hermitage.

It was also during the visit to Leningrad that a very funny incident took place. On an afternoon when the Russians apparently had nothing else to do with us, they took us to visit the Medical School at the University. When we got there we were ushered into a large auditorium where an announcement was made that we were about to see a film on thoracic surgery, which would be quite bloody. If any of us would prefer not to see such a thing, we were free to leave. Few of us were doctors, even fewer had any desire to see the film, but we could not avoid the challenge. No one left, and the room was darkened. The film started and, within minutes, there was a sound of someone falling off his chair. The lights flashed on, white-coated figures dashed to the fallen figure, and, wonder of wonders, it was the Russian public relations man! There was a pause while he was carried out, probably to a new assignment in Siberia. We were so pleased with what had happened that we settled back in our chairs and watched the rest of the film without interruption.

China

China was a different kind of experience, even though it was also a communist country. We had a strong China program at the University of Michigan, as a result of which some of our faculty members had been involved in the very earliest of the Nixon administration's efforts to open up China. Once this came about, China offered to host a group of university presidents from America in 1974. The invitation came to the American Council on Higher Education, of which Roger Heyns was then president. That organization chose a group of about a dozen presidents, and I was lucky enough to be included in the group.

Mao Tse-tung and Chou En-lai were still in power, though both were ill. Deng Xiaoping was heading the government, though after we left he was ousted and then returned to office.

When we arrived in China, all the old symbols were still in place. The Little Red Book, containing the sayings of Chairman Mao, was much in evidence, loudspeakers broadcast exhortations daily, and our activities were restricted. We were, nevertheless, treated graciously and with great kindness. We did all the usual things, i.e., visited the Great Wall, the Forbidden City, communal farms, schools, and factories, and talked to various officials. If they did not want to answer a question, or if they did not want us to visit a given facility, they would stall, never saying no, but never saying yes. Nightly we would see some kind of entertainment, usually acrobats or dancers but sometimes a Ping-Pong match.

Jay Rockefeller, then president of Wesleyan College in West Virginia but later governor of the state and now in the U.S. Senate, was one of our group. We teased him a good deal because there was so much Chinese propaganda about wealthy landlords, and we would frequently see people throwing darts at pictures of Chinese landlords handily posted for that purpose. Later on, when we were the sole passengers on a small DC-3 propeller plane that was carrying us to a new destination, he got back at us by saying, "All right, you guys, if this plane goes down the *New York Times* will have a headline saying, 'Rockefeller and Eleven Other Presidents Killed in China in Plane Crash.'" He was, of course, right.

With all its restrictions, China was absolutely fascinating. One might see a field in which a hundred people with hoes were walking down the field together, hoeing as they went. In our eyes, a single tractor with an appropriate attachment could have done the same thing much quicker. But China has no shortage of people. What would they do with them if machines came in and took over?

The children were beautiful, the people were friendly, and the enormity of the population would become evident every time our cars stopped because hundreds of people would appear out of nowhere and crowd against the cars to look at us.

One thing that intrigued us about Communist China was the strict hierarchy of people. Before we came, they wanted the leader of our group to identify the presidents in the order of their importance. Naturally, no leader of ours was going to do that, so the list was submitted in strict alphabetical order. They noticed this and insisted that it be changed. Our fearless leader, Roger Heyns, formerly the chancellor of the University of California at Berkeley and then president of ACE, kept a straight face and insisted that the list was in the order of the importance of the individuals. Ultimately they dropped the subject, but then they wanted us to ride in the same cars each day, presumably so that they would always know who was present in any given car. (We always suspected that the drivers and guides who were assigned to each car were reporting daily on what we said while traveling.) We paid no attention to this rule and rode with different people every day. That too bothered them, though they came to accept it.

In the course of our visits to universities, we had many opportunities to talk to both students and faculty. We tried to do so outside buildings, because we suspected that the rooms in which we met were bugged. Even so, if we asked students what they wanted to do when they graduated or where they wanted to live, the answer was always the same: "Whatever the government wants me to do, or wherever they want me to live." That was a standard answer simply because they had no choice. There were not enough openings in universities to allow all qualified students to attend, and government studies decided what kind of training was necessary and where the jobs would be. If you wanted to attend a university, you accepted the system. It was, and is, a tightly controlled society. That control, however, was widely believed to favor the children of military and government figures.

In some ways, the highlight of our visit was a long discussion with Deng, who was then the leader of the country. He invited us to the Great Hall and gave us a surprising amount of time. He did not speak English, though one suspected that he understood a good deal of what was said in English. His interpreter was an American-born Chinese woman who had been, as I recall it, Mao's interpreter. We all sat in comfortable chairs arranged in a big circle, and we were served tea as Deng talked. Much of what he had to say was about the perils that Russia posed, which reminded me that when we were in Russia they always talked about the "Yellow Peril"! Deng wanted to be sure that we stood firm against Russia.

One other memory of China pleases me greatly. When we came out of China and entered Hong Kong, the sole delegation to meet us was a group of Chinese who were University of Michigan graduates, and they were waving a Michigan banner and singing the famous football fight song, "The Victors." I could not refrain from calling to the attention of my distinguished colleagues which university it was that received a welcome! Incidentally, a year after my visit, Sally went to China with a delegation of our Regents, and she shares my fond memories of the country.

South Africa

In the course of the civil righs disputes that raged on campuses during the 1970s, one of the major issues became the investments that many university endowment funds held in businesses operating in South

Africa. The practice of apartheid, through which the races were kept apart in that country, was abhorrent to most Americans, and a campaign was mounted to demand withdrawal of all such investments so long as apartheid continued. On the merits, as distinguished from the emotional considerations, the argument continued about whether this would help blacks more than it would hurt, because it might cause the loss of jobs for blacks if foreign investments were withdrawn. Nevertheless, the pressure continued and many states ultimately forbade such investments on the part of public entities.

Since the University of Michigan's endowment fund did include such investments, it was the object of considerable pressure to divest even before the state acted. Because of the agitation, the interest of the university in what was going on in South Africa escalated.

Both Sally and I were invited to go to South Africa in 1978 under the auspices of the United States–South Africa Leadership Exchange Program (USSALEP). The trip was funded by the Carnegie Foundation, and I had for several years been a member and then chairman of the Carnegie Fund for the Advancement of Teaching. The USSALEP program was funded on the South African side by business interests opposed to apartheid. Because of the prestige of the organizations backing the program in both countries, we were given complete and open access to all factions, and we were allowed to visit such places as Soweto and the Homelands. When we talked to black leaders, they told us that they were probably the last generation with whom peace could be made because their own children now thought that only violence would solve the problem. Given the power of the army, open resistance would result in a massacre, but guerrilla warfare would be a long and bitter struggle.

When we visited the Homelands, to which various tribes had been assigned, it was more like viewing a movie set on which a group of actors were playing the role of various government officials. I had the feeling that their biggest problem might be who got to play president.

We visited universities all over the country. Students were always reluctant to talk inside a room (shades of Russia and China), so we tried to take them outside.

Our talks with white government officials were, at the time, not very hopeful. They recognized the problem, but they could not face establishing a democratic government in which blacks would far outnumber whites and in which they believed they would lose control. The white population felt that it was they and their ancestors who had really settled and developed the country. Waiting to face the inevitable nevertheless made less likely a satisfactory compromise, because the younger black population was prepared to revolt.

South Africa has, of course, by now taken the critical step of freeing Nelson Mandela, and of working out a transition in the government that incorporates the black population. There are enormous problems ahead in trying to quickly fulfill the expectations of the black population for a better life. It is further complicated by the question of whether, given Mandela's age, there is anyone waiting in the wings with his prestige, wisdom, and power who will therefore be able to hold the nation together. Whatever result history ultimately records, South Africa is a magnificent land, full of opportunities for all if only the racial and ethnic differences can be overcome. If it succeeds, it will be a model for all the world to envy.

The British Isles

It is not surprising, I suppose, that so many Americans cherish visits to the British Isles. We share a language (or at least we can mostly understand one another!), our ancestry is often the same (Sally with Welsh or English, and I with Scottish ancestors), we have democratic governments, our cultural interests are largely shared, we have been partners in two world wars, and we are relatively comfortable with one another. Thus, we think of our repeated visits to the British Isles as one of our great pleasures in foreign travel. On one occasion, when we were meeting with academic colleagues from all over the British Commonwealth, the meetings were in Scotland at a time when the Queen and Prince Philip were in residence at Balmoral Castle and where the Prince hosted a reception. It was a lovely summer day, and the color of the occasion reminded me of the Astor racetrack scene in *My Fair Lady*. Quite by accident, we were thrown into direct contact with the Prince and enjoyed a few minutes of conversation with him. Skeptical as we Americans tend to be of royalty, it was an easy meeting without any of the royal formalities.

Following the Scottish meetings, we Americans were transported with our English colleagues to a further meeting in south England for a few days that would be devoted more to our particular interests. We traveled, courtesy of the Queen, in a private train.

In the course of such meetings, the Lord Mayor of whatever city we were in would always have a dinner for all of us. There were certain ceremonial features at such a dinner, including entry introductions where a formally clad major domo would intone, "My Lords and Ladies, I have the honor to introduce President and Mrs. So and So from the University of X." We felt a little silly, but it was fun and no one outdoes the British in graceful and impressive ceremonies.

Our lives were enriched by the travel, we had a far better under-standing of other cultures, and we were always glad to come home, even when it meant facing some unpleasant problem! We shall always be grateful to the universities and foundations that made our travels possible.

Chapter 16

Leaving the Academy

Mother, who meant so very much to me, died in September of 1972. She was eighty-six and, since her remarriage late in life, had been very happy. Her husband, Paul Boutwell, died in 1971. Neither of them had been in good health, and Mother came to live with us in Ann Arbor after Paul's death. She and Paul had several wonderful years together, and this gave the children of both families enormous satisfaction.

In her last months, Mother was largely confined to her room and her hearing was bad. When I came home from the office in the evening, I used to go to her room for a little chat before dinner. On one occasion, Sally told me a story about a conversation she had had with Mother, and when Mother saw me laugh she wanted to know why I was laughing. The story was that Sally had said to Mother, "We are having some students to dinner tonight." To which Mother, obviously not hearing correctly, responded, "Yes, I like tuna fish!" When I leaned closer to Mother's ear to tell her what had made me laugh, she said, "Don't you like tuna fish?" And the following day, when Sally by accident brought her a tuna fish sandwich for lunch, Mother said, "Oh, left over from last night, I see." Since Mother had a great sense of humor, she would often carry on a conversation she had heard properly as if she had not heard it. So I don't know whether she really didn't hear or was just teasing us.

Mother's death was not a great sorrow, because she had lived a full life and was no longer well. On the other hand, we had been very close and I missed her. We had always written to each other weekly and there was now a great gap in my life. Also, it reminded me of my own mortality for I was now, but for one cousin, the oldest surviving member of that wonderful extended family with whom I had grown up.

When we came to the University of Michigan in the fall of 1967, I had said to the Regents that, if they didn't fire me in the meantime, I would probably not stay in the presidency more than ten years. Ten years seemed like a long time when I said it, and I genuinely thought that ten years was about the right length of time for one to serve.

By fall of 1977, the ten years was up and we began to think of whether we should do something else. Other opportunities kept coming up, some of them interesting and flattering. The State University System of New York was looking for a president of the system and asked me to talk about it. I told them from the outset that I had little interest in a system presidency because we liked life on campus, where we had a faculty and student body. They pursued their call with a visit, but at my request we spent most of our time talking about other people they might contact.

Robert Hutchins, who had been a distinguished if controversial president of the University of Chicago and was then the president of the Center for Democratic Studies in Santa Barbara, called and started the conversation in typical Hutchins fashion by saying, "Bob, is there any truth in the rumor that you are about to succeed me as president out here?" We were not close friends, but I knew him well enough to know that this was his way of asking if I was interested, so I said there was nothing to the rumor as far as I knew. He then pursued the question further, and I told him there was almost no likelihood that I would do it. He went further and asked an emissary from Chicago to come and see me in Ann Arbor. The visit took place, but I was still negative. At that point, Hutchins called me again and asked me to come out and talk to them and to bring Sally along. I told him that, much as we liked Santa Barbara, I would be embarrassed to have them pay for a visit when there was little chance we would accept. He insisted that he would be at ease even if we rejected the bid, so we went.

Hutchins was not well, but he was still both an impressive and imposing figure. I spent the day talking to people at the center and we had dinner with them that night. They were interesting, attractive people and I remember that Elizabeth Mann Borghese introduced us to her dog, which she had taught to type certain letters on a typewriter fixed with pads for keys. The dog was not a conversationalist, so I suspect she was merely trying to prove that this kind of teaching was possible.

The next morning Hutchins and I had breakfast and he tendered a formal offer. By that time I was even more certain that I did not want the position. In the first place, the organization was in serious financial trouble and a new president would have to spend most of his time fund-raising, which did not appeal to me. Second, there were serious personnel problems arising out of a life-contract policy that had been given to some now very senior staff people who should have been retired. Third, Hutchins was a very proud, able man who would always remain on the board and it was clear to me that he could never play second-fiddle to a new president. More important than anything else was the fact that the programs the center ran were not exciting to me. The visit ended amicably but without results. They later hired Malcolm Moos, who had been president of the University of Minnesota. Within a few years the center largely ceased to exist.

There was another call from California. Charles Hitch, who was president of the multicampus University of California and who had come to office at the same time I had, called. He was retiring, a search for his successor was on, and he said the board really wanted me. Would we come out and talk to them? I said it was hard for me to see why I would leave Michigan to come to California, particularly since I had never wanted to preside over a system (as distinguished from a campus). He persisted, and we finally said we would come out. A date was set, but the day before we were to go I was half-sick with flu and I called to tell him we would have to cancel the date. He said plans had gone so far that if it was at all possible could we come and simply stay at the hotel where the meeting would be held and where I could rest in the interim. I had a temperature and felt badly, but we went. There were periodic meetings during the day we were there, and we then returned to Ann Arbor with an agreement that we would come back later. We did so a week or so later only to find a quite different situation than the one I had anticipated. Now I was supposed to be a full-blown candidate for the position, to be interviewed by all sorts of groups, and to explain why I thought I ought to become the president of the University of California. My impression had been that they were to try and convince me that I should come!

Quite apart from everything else, the governor was in the picture. Under California law, the governor is a member of the Governing Board of the University. During Ronald Reagan's time, he had regularly attended board meetings and had, in fact, been instrumental in forcing Clark Kerr's resignation. (With his usual capacity in coining a phrase, Clark said, "I started my career as I ended it, *fired* with enthusiasm.") Now Jerry Brown was governor, and he too attended meetings. Since he was already acquiring his "moonbeam" reputation, I said to the university representatives that if I were to think seriously about coming out there I would want to sit down and talk to the governor about his views on higher education. They agreed to this, and the governor and I had a private luncheon. It was, from my point of view, totally unsatisfactory. I couldn't find out anything about what he thought of higher education. California had a long-established three-tier system of higher education in which there was the University of California, with its many campuses, the state colleges and universities, and then the community colleges. There had been rumors that Governor Brown did not favor continuation of this system, and I wanted to know whether this was true. I could not get any meaningful comment from him.

It then turned out that there was also an inside candidate, David Saxon, who was the vice chancellor at UCLA. He was a very able physicist, he had worked in the system for some years, he knew much more about their problems than I did, and he seemed to me a very logical choice. I had no desire to campaign for the position, and I certainly did not view myself as one of several candidates. Sally and I discussed the turn of events, talked to one or two members of the board, and then said that we did not wish to be considered further. David Saxon became president, it was a fine choice for them, and it turned out to be the best result for all of us.

Probes of one kind or another continued to come along, including one from the Aspen Institute and a letter from an old friend who was then chairman of the board of the Corporation for Public Broadcasting. He was asking about possible candidates for the presidency of CPB. He ended the letter by asking if I would consider it. I told him I knew little about broadcasting except that I liked it, and that while I was in office we had public stations at both Wisconsin and Michigan and that, to this extent I knew something of their operations. We agreed to talk, and active conversations then ensued. When it was obvious that this was serious, Sally and I had to make the decision as to whether or not to leave Michigan. This was difficult. The university had been very good to us, we loved the academic world, we loved Ann Arbor, and we were among many old friends.

But there was another side to it. Retirement at Michigan was at age seventy. I had nevertheless persuaded the Regents to establish sixty-five as the age for major administrators to retire. I was sixty-two, three years away from retirement, and I would not want to have the rules changed for me. Difficult economic times had already come to Michigan and it was evident that, if we remained, it would be necessary to find ways to reduce the budget. Cycles of this kind are not unknown, and are part of the job of a president and his associates, but if we stayed I would have to retire in the midst of the process and and it might be better to install a president who could deal with it over a longer period.

An additional consideration was that if I wanted to work beyond age sixty-five, it would be better to make a move before I reached that age because sixty-five is so fixed in the public's mind as the age at which one normally retires. Since I also held a law professorship, I could leave the presidency and go back to teaching law, but that might make it awkward for my successor.

There was also the fact that both Sally and I were a bit tired of the presidential routine and the many demands it imposes on the president and his wife. We were clear in our minds that we would like to return to Ann Arbor to live, but we had always enjoyed Washington and we thought that if we took the CPB job but didn't want to remain in Washington we could always use my age as an excuse for retiring after three years.

With a good deal of reluctance, but also some excitement at doing something new, we decided to go to Washington as of January 1, 1979, just over eleven years after we had come to Ann Arbor.

The Corporation for Public Broadcasting is the "banker" for the federal funds that are invested in public broadcasting. Federal participation in funding of this kind dates back to President Johnson's time, and it was initially thought of as largely an investment in educational broadcasting. The TV and radio stations around the country that comprise the system are all nonprofit entities, usually owned by universities, educational systems, or foundations. The balance of their support comes from state appropriations, foundations, outside donors, and, more recently, a limited amount of advertising. Federal money was new to the field and was something that had been long sought.

CPB does not own any stations itself, nor does it produce any programs. It was set up as an independent, nonprofit, nongovernmental agency into which public money could be channeled, thereby placing programming beyond political interference. The actual programming is done by the stations, and most of them belong to the nonprofit private associations known, on the radio side, as National Public Radio (NPR) and, on the TV side, as the Public Broadcasting Service (PBS). The stations retain their independence, but they pool some of their funds in support of certain programs, such as *All Things Considered* and the *MacNeil-Lehrer News Hour*. CPB funnels much of the money it receives to the stations according to a formula mandated by Congress, but

CPB can retain some money that it may use to generate programs of its choice to be produced by others. Stations can then decide whether or not to use those programs.

The commission that proposed federal support for public broadcasting recommended that CPB be governed by an independently selected board, but that was unacceptable to both the president and Congress, so members are appointed by the president with the consent of the Senate. The legislation requires some balance in the appointments in terms of political parties, but presidents from both of the major parties tend to appoint people who share their philosophy regardless of which party they ostensibly represent.

Public broadcasting had been described to me before I went to Washington as being much like a university whose colleges stand on their own bottoms, but it is in fact quite different. In the academic setting, there is a tent over all of the schools and colleges called the university. While the schools and colleges do have a great deal of independence, they nevertheless greatly value the name the university bears and they have a loyalty to it. In public broadcasting, there is a tent, called CPB, but its name has no value to its constituents, and they view it as purely a source of money. If the stations had their choice, the only function of CPB would be to meet on January 1 each year, allocate all the funds to the stations according to a formula approved by the stations, and then disappear for a year until it was time to distribute more money. Even within their own associations, the stations are more like the United States under the Articles of Confederation rather than under the Constitution. This all adds up to saying that public broadcasting is a badly organized entity. The trouble is, it is hard to figure out how to improve it within the limits the political process will allow. Stations greatly value their independence, though they desperately need the federal money. They resist a common time format for programming, even for the most popular progams. There are some practical reasons for this, including different time zones across the country, regional tastes in programming, or the need to cater to local interests. But there is none of the discipline that made the British Broadcasting Corporation (BBC) the model for excellence, nor can there be.

The British started with a government-supported system and there were no commercial stations. We went the opposite route, which meant commercial stations supported by advertising. That system is very strong. It approves of public broadcasting because such a system will do educational and quality programming that an influential segment of the public wants but which is not profitable for commercial broadcasters. Now entrenched in that system, the commercial stations, quite naturally, like things just the way they are. An excellent argument can be made that, since the broadcast spectrum is limited to the number of stations the spectrum can accommodate, the government ought to charge a license fee for the use of this resource. The commercial broadcasters vigorously oppose this. Every time an effort is made to identify a tax that would fall on the broadcasting industry, it mobilizes its full strength to avoid this, and, like so many of our very powerful lobbies, it has always prevailed.

On the political side, neither the president nor Congress are enthusiastic about a public broadcasting system that can freely criticize them. It is no different in other countries in which public funds support broadcasting. It would be surprising if it were otherwise. In addition, various private organizations become self-appointed watchdogs over the content of public broadcasting, complaining vigorously about alleged biases. President Reagan particularly opposed public broadcasting and would have abolished it except for the fact that Congress, including members of his own party, did not agree.

Finally, there is always infighting between radio and TV. The latter is much more expensive to operate, but radio has seniority and would like more of the total funding than the comparative audiences or costs of the two would justify. Both NPR and PBS lobby Congress independently, often against each other and against CPB. In short, it is a curious nonsystem, yet it manages to do some great things and we are better with it than we would be without it. Some of the states, of which Wisconsin is a prime example, do a superb job with their statewide systems.

It is not hard to figure out how this nonsystem could be improved, but efficiency is not the hallmark of a democracy, and the chances that the political problems that surround the issue can be resolved are zero. Perhaps it is best viewed as an example of the old adage that democracy, with all its contending forces, is the worst form of government there is, except for all others.

We had been at CPB only a little over a year when an untoward event occurred. While taking a shower, I found that I had a small lump about the size of half a pecan in the area of my appendix. Since we are all constantly exposed to advice about the cancerous nature of lumps, I promptly went to the doctor. He looked at it, assured me that there was not one chance in ten thousand that it was cancerous, and advised that I go home and put some heat on it and return in another week. I did this and the lump had not changed. It did not hurt, I felt fine, and there was no problem except there it was! On the second visit, the doctor reiterated his conclusion that there was not one chance in ten thousand that it was malignant. I told him I would feel better if he did a biopsy. He made the arrangements, and the biopsy affirmed that I had a lymphoma. This conclusion sent me off to the oncologist, who did a series of tests that indicated no spread of the malignancy. I was given a choice of radiation, chemotherapy, or surgery, and I accepted chemotherapy on the theory that if, despite the tests, there was any spread elsewhere in my body it would best be dealt with by chemotherapy. This would mean that my hair would fall out and that I might feel badly. Since there would be no way to hide this, I preferred a public announcement to having rumors spread about what was wrong with me.

The treatments started and I was fortunate that they did not make me sick. I worked every day, I walked several blocks from the hospital to the office after receiving chemotherapy, and I could eat a hearty lunch. It did zap my energy to some extent, more in the sense that I would be abnormally tired at night, but not so much that it impaired my work. We even went to business meetings in France, England, and Italy during that time. Being relatively bald (I did retain a fuzz) was less embarrassing to me away from Ann Arbor than it would have been on campus because most of the people I met with did not know me. There were other occasions on which I would be asked by someone I did know how I felt, and I would reply, "Fine, except that I have lost all my hair," only to discover that the person I was talking to was permanently bald! After one or two such occasions, I realized that this was not the most diplomatic comment I could make.

My doctor had said from the outset that he was confident at the 85 percent level that my recovery would be complete. I took him at his word, concluding that I was in the 85 percent! Still, I knew that it might be fatal, and I thought about Sally's future. If I did not survive, I thought it would be better for her to be back in Ann Arbor among friends, though I never discussed this with her. I would be sixty-five by the end of 1981 and this would be a logical time to retire, so I advised the chairman privately that I intended to resign not later than the end of 1981. This was announced, and a successor was then sought. We made our plans to return to Ann Arbor when I left office.

Meanwhile, I felt I had made some contribution to public broadcasting. At an early meeting with the board, an occasion on which I felt confident they would not fire me, I managed to get the board to establish a Program Fund to be run by a professional director and into which all of CPB's remaining program funds would be channeled. This would prevent the board from dabbling in specific programming as opposed to establishing overall areas in which it wished programming to fall. The proposal went through by a split vote and we brought in Lewis Freedman, a distinguished producer who had worked with both commercial and public radio and television. He did a superb job, and the Program Fund still exists.

The other accomplishment was bringing the $150 million grant from Walter Annenberg to CPB to be used for educational broadcasting. I first heard of this possibility from Newton Minow, who was practicing law in Chicago but had been head of the Federal Communications Commission under President Kennedy and was serving as chairman of the PBS governing board. Newt had been at a dinner with Walter Annenberg at which the latter had talked about his interest in art and expressed the wish that a much wider audience could enjoy art in the way he did. Newt promptly suggested that this could be done through public television and Mr. Annenberg said he might be prepared to invest $150 million in such a venture. Newt called me, told me the story, suggested that he could arrange a meeting, and asked me to figure out how to manage such a project. That was the beginnning of a very interesting venture. We arranged a meeting at the Cosmos Club with Newt, Walter Annenberg and his wife, and a few others from CPB. There were three obstacles in the path of reaching an agreement. The first was the question of whether the gift would be tax deductible, a matter that would have to be cleared up with the Internal Revenue Service and would take some time. The second question involved the role the Annenbergs could play in participating in the decisions about how the money would be used. They could not, under the tax law, have a controling interest, but they could participate. If they could participate, this raised the third question of how this could be made compatible with the CPB board's authority in such matters.

We solved the first problem by jointly hiring the Caplin, Drysdale firm in Washington to represent us. Over the course of the next year, they managed to get a favorable ruling. Tom Troyer, a Michigan law graduate, did the actual work although we did not set out to hire someone from the University of Michigan.

The second and third problems were related because how we re-solved the matter of the Annenberg participation had to be acceptable to the CPB board. I worked out the formation of an Annenberg Council on which would be represented two people each from CPB, PBS, NPR, and the Annenbergs, plus two public members who would be named by the other members of the council. There would be a director of the project who would be chairman and that individual would make rec-ommendations about which programs would be funded. The council could negate any of his or her choices, but it could not mandate funding for a particular program. This seemed to me to resolve the problem of keeping council members out of micromanaging the project. This mech-anism was acceptable to me, as president of CPB, and to the other entities, so the only remaining problem was selling it to the CPB board. I knew that would be difficult, because the CPB board delighted in get-ting into details and it already regarded its authority as undermined by the resolution in favor of a Program Fund. Still, in the last analysis, as I pointed out to them, a condition of the grant was some form of mean-ingful participation by the Annenbergs, and there would be no gift unless this condition was met. With some mild dissent, the board ac-cepted the $150 million. Thereafter, the director of the Annenerg/CPB Project, as it came to be called, would report regularly to the CPB Board on the progress of the project.

Since I was still president of CPB when the Annenberg/CPB Project got started, I acted as director of it in the early days. The idea was for it to produce educational materials that could be used by in-stitutions of higher education for credit toward their degrees. This would be a formidable task because faculties have a vast distaste for materials they do not produce. Some of this feeling is justified, espe-cially if it is based on quality considerations, but some of it is also the threat of displacement. Our intention was to produce excellent products that could not be challenged on quality grounds.

Walter Annenberg did not come to the idea of education via tele-communications as a neophyte. He owned a number of radio and TV stations and he had experimented with educational programs. He was anxious to go further with the idea. He did, however, have one convic-tion that was right in theory but wrong in practice. He thought of such distance-learning as a way for traditional college-level students to at-tain a degree without having to spend as much time and money in residence on a campus. All of the studies of students who participated in this kind of learning showed that they were primarily older adults who were working and who needed additional training but who did not have the time or resources to be on a campus. As our negotiations proceeded, I realized that he was under the impression that the "boys and girls," as he referred to them, were the traditional-age college students, when in reality they were not. I was very uneasy about leaving him with a false impression, even if this meant that he would withdraw the projected $150 million that was on the table. Just before one of our periodic meetings, I wrote a very short memorandum to him telling him the truth about what kind of students we would be helping and saying that, though he apparently had the wrong idea of who they were, there were nevertheless very large numbers of people who would immensely benefit from his generosity.

When we met, it was usually at one of his homes, either in Colorado or California, rather than in his main residence or office in the Philadelphia area. His jet would pick up those of us who were coming to the meeting from Philadelphia or Washington and we would then go west for the meeting. Once we arrived, the routine was always the same. Walter would meet us with a station wagon and drive us to a nearby motel that was not far from his home. We always came in mid-afternoon and would then meet for dinner at his home. It was understood that there would be no business talk that evening, it was purely a social event. The formal meeting would come the following morning. He would meet first with his own people (who did all the negotiating with us) and then we would meet together. On the way out, on this particular occasion, I had shown my memo on the projected students to his advisors and I had asked them whether they wanted to give it to him or wanted me to. They wanted me to do it, but they warned that this might cause the whole project to fall through. I told them I knew this, but I did not want to deceive him about a critical fact. I chose the conclusion of the dinner party, as we left that night, to give Walter the memo. I did not say anything about its contents, only that I hoped he could read it before we met in the morning. After we returned to our motel that night, Newt Minow and I talked and agreed that if he was upset we would try to convince him to continue anyway.

The dinner parties, incidentally, were always great fun. Walter and Lee, his wife, were great hosts and they were widely knowledgeable about events all over the world. Their stint at the Court of St. James, as ambassador to England, had given them ready access to the royal family and they could give interesting insights into social life at that level. They had also been friends for years with many of our presidents, particularly Ronald Reagan who, even after he became president, spent the New Year's holiday with them. The dinner conversations were stimulating, and his homes always displayed millions of dollars worth of the world's great art.

When we met the following morning to discuss business, the first item, quite naturally, was my memorandum. Newt and I didn't know what to expect. But then Walter said, "I have read your memo, and it gave me quite a shock. But I have talked to my people, and I have been wrong before in my life and I will be wrong again. So let's go ahead!"

From that moment on, it was just a question of working out the other problems I have mentioned. There was a last-minute delay, brought about by the fact that Ronald Reagan had just become president and it was known that he favored getting rid of CPB. There would be no point in making a grant to CPB if it was to be put out of business. Congress, including Republican members, soon made it clear that it did not agree with the president, and we were then able to conclude the agreement. I found it a little confusing that the fact that his good friend, the president, wanted to get rid of CPB did not seem to influence Mr. Annenberg once he knew CPB would continue to exist.

The most delicate part of achieving success in administering a huge grant, like the one CPB was about to get, is to demonstrate as soon as possible that it was a good investment. In our case, speed would not be easily achievable. First of all, we had to organize the staff, then we had to decide how to proceed (remembering that CPB cannot produce programs itself), and then, having selected the projects we wanted to fund, get them produced. At a minimum, it would be likely to take two years from the time of commitment before a given program could be put on the air. Meanwhile, after all the publicity given to the project, people were going to get impatient about what was being done with the money. As I thought about how to cope with that problem, I had an idea about something we might make happen fairly quickly. Fred Friendly, who had worked for years with Edward R. Murrow, had been running private seminars, but they were not televised for the public. His method was to bring together well-known people of great stature, give them a hypothetical problem that nevertheless suggested real situations known to everyone, and then have them interrogated by a skilled law school professor. I knew about these sessions because I had participated in one of them on student problems, and I was impressed both with the level of the discussion and the fact that it might make good television. Even if I was right, however, we would have to put together a series of such programs and give them a common theme so that they would be worthy of academic credit. A solution to the theme problem might be to build the programs around the first ten amendments to the Constitution. This would fit in with the forthcoming 200th anniversary of the approval of the Constitution, and would focus on those amendments that guaranteed citizen rights.

Having tried out the idea on my CPB colleagues, I called Fred to discuss it with him. He said that they had not previously tried to televise their seminars for fear that, in doing so, they would lose their spontaneity. I offered funding from us if he would experiment. He agreed to come and talk to me, we did so, he became very interested, and the result was a great series that attracted wide public attention and got very fine reviews. It also fulfilled our need for some early, high-quality product. Since they were not rehearsed and were simply well-known people spontaneously having a dialog about difficult questions, they could be televised live or put on tape. It was also helpful that Fred, being the showman that he is, made an occasion out of the live filming by inviting a number of important guests, including the Annenbergs, to sit in the audience. Since the filming would extend over one and a half days, in order to have three separate programs, there could also be a wonderful dinner on the first evening at some special spot. Independence Hall, in Philadelphia, was the obvious choice for conducting the programs and that hallowed building gave a special feeling to all who attended. Sally and I had the good fortune to be present at almost all of them.

In subsequent years, the Annenberg Project produced a large number of memorable courses, some on TV, some on radio. It also financed research into how best to use such things for educational purposes, and encouraged new electronic methods for disseminating the products. Some of the most memorable TV productions included *The Brain, Planet Earth, War and Peace in the Nuclear Age,* and *Mechanical Universe,* but there were and are a long list of others prepared for TV, radio, and even interactive computers. Almost all of them were produced in collaboration with well-known universities and broadcasting stations. Two of the most heavily used courses, one in French produced at Yale and another in Spanish prepared by the University of Illinois at Chicago, are now given for credit by hundreds of colleges and universities across the country.

After I left the presidency of CPB and returned to Ann Arbor, I once again served as interim director of the Annenberg/CPB Project for a period on a part-time basis and then, when Mara Mayor became the permanent director, I remained as senior educational consultant for them. Mara did an outstanding job with the program and there is no doubt in my mind that the program has enormously enhanced the possibilities for higher education through electronic means. University faculties still find it hard to accept the concept, but, with the advance of computers, the opposition is eroding and in the years ahead we are going to see more use of electronic communication devices in the world of education.

Chapter 17

Over and Out

In 1981, during my last few full-time months at CPB in Washington, Roger Heyns, who was then president of the Hewlett Foundation in California, called me about a new venture they were about to undertake in collaboration with the MacArthur and Ford Foundations. It involved the creation of the National Institute for Dispute Resolution (NIDR), and it was something we had talked about before, except that now it had gone beyond the planning stage and was about to be launched. All three foundations had been interested in alternative ways of promoting the settlement of disputes, particularly those that would otherwise result in costly and prolonged court proceedings. I knew about this venture because Roger and I had talked about it over the course of the previous year or two, mostly because he knew of my background in the settlement of labor disputes. Now that I was retiring from CPB, he wanted to know if I would consider being president of the new nonprofit agency. I was not interested in being president because I did not want a full-time job, but I did agree to be chairman of the board and to organize the proposed agency. This task, along with remaining an active consultant to CPB on the Annenberg/CPB job and some ad hoc assignments, would keep me busy. I was sixty-five years old, my health was fine (the cancer had disappeared), and I was too used to being busy to simply retire. Over the course of the next eight years, I remained chairman of the board of NIDR. The three foundations had committed $15 million to it over a five-year period, with a promise that they would likely continue this funding for at least another five years if progress was being made. The timing was good for such a project, because public attention was being focused both on what was alleged to be a "litigious society" and on the great delay in getting cases heard and decided by the courts.

How much NIDR has contributed to the current widespread use of alternative methods of dispute resolution in our society is hard to judge because, as the subject became popular, so many others joined in the effort. It did satisfy its foundation supporters and NIDR is still in existence. In the early years, we used the money to encourage the offering of alternative dispute resolution courses in law and business schools, in helping government agencies develop such procedures in connection with the writing of administrative rules, in the promotion of conferences among court personnel to acquaint them with available procedures, in publishing otherwise unavailable materials, in helping states to establish mediation agencies for nonlabor disputes, and in promoting research in the field.

When we returned to Ann Arbor, the Law School needed an additional labor law professor, and I was invited to teach again. With some misgivings, I agreed to do so on the basis of one course during one semester each year. My reservations had to do with whether I had been gone from the field too long (I had not taught Labor Law in almost twenty years), and whether I was still sufficiently interested in it to make the course attractive. Many professors-turned-administrators have found that their fields have passed them by when they return to the classroom. I knew this might be so in my case, but, on the other hand, I had retained my general interest in the field and I thought that, unlike the sciences, it might be that little had changed. Once into it, however, I found that I wasn't teaching with the same enthusiasm and skill that I once had. Labor Law was neither the same field I had known, nor was I now arbitrating labor disputes, which had always enabled me to bring the sparkle of the real world into my classes. With the decline of unions, collective bargaining, which was at the heart of my interest, was now only a part of a course that included pension law, antidiscrimination legislation, and affirmative action. I understood the importance of those laws, but they did not hold the same interest for me as collective bargaining did. The upshot was that I taught for three years and then stopped. The decision was easy because a number of other interesting opportunities kept popping up.

Over the next few years, I served a term on the Harvard Graduate School of Education's Visiting Committee, a term as chairman of the Educational Testing Service's Advisory Committee, on an East-West Center committee at the University of Hawaii, as chairman of a Cornell committee to study their Extension Service, as a troubleshooter on a management problem for the five-college public radio station complex at Amherst, Massachusetts, and as a conferee for a Fulbright program in Spain. Mixed in with these were a four-year consulting assignment for the MacArthur Foundation, and an eleven-year membership on the S. C. Johnson Foundation board in Racine, Wisconsin.

From 1985 to 1990, at the behest of Governor Blanchard in Michigan, I served as his representative in an effort to find a more acceptable solution to medical malpractice problems. Working with a colleague, Jay Rosen of Lansing, we had the difficult mission of trying to find a formula that would satisfy doctors, lawyers, hospitals, and insurance companies. A consensus was needed because each of them had a powerful lobby that could make passage of the necessary legislation improbable. The doctors invested their financial support in the normally Republican Senate and could get the legislation they wanted in that body but not in the House. The opposite was true of the lawyers, where the trial bar poured its financial support into the normally Democratic House, with the intent of maintaining the status quo. Both the doctors and the lawyers blamed the insurance companies for unnecessarily high rates, while at the same time the state Department of Insurance insisted that the insurance companies raise their rates lest they go bankrupt! In short, each of the groups loudly proclaimed that troubles in the malpractice field were all the fault of one or more of the other constituencies. In that situation, I was doubtful that we could make any progress unless the governor took a firm stand, which he was reluctant to do in an election year. Somewhat to my surprise, we did come close to an agreement twice, once when the hospitals turned it down and the second time when the trial bar was unwilling to make any concessions.

The whole effort made clear one of the most serious problems in the effective functioning of our democracy. It is not that better solutions to so many of our problems cannot be devised, it is that heavily entrenched interest groups spend enormous amounts of money in supporting candidates who find that they, in turn, cannot be elected without spending lavishly on their campaigns. Until we reform our campaign practices, there is little that is going to change. How hard this is to do is made clear by the lack of success of public interest lobbies in persuading legislatures, both national and state, to curb the financial contributions of interest groups, to shorten the election period, to provide public financing for candidates, to insist on a certain amount of free television time for candidates, or to do anything else that sounds promising. Not surprisingly, the interest groups do their best to picture their activities as merely supporting what is best for the populace.

In 1988, at the request of the Regents, Sally and I returned to the presidency of Michigan for an eight-month period between Harold Shapiro's departure for Princeton and the selection of James Duderstadt as the new president. It was during this period that alleged racial, sexual, and gay-lesbian discrimination cases were drawing a good deal of attention, as a result of which it was important to address that problem. It was the practice of the Regents to reserve one hour each month at which anyone could ask for five minutes of time to address them on any topic. The gay-lesbian group would appear each month and have one or more people testify. Some of the recitations were heartbreaking, as both men and women told of discovering their own sexual preference and learning to live both with the reaction of their own families and public hostility. Others were ugly in their abuse of the Regents. This seems to be the history of all activist groups. They can never control all their allies, and they differ within their own ranks as to what tactics are effective. It has never been my experience that the nasty, combative approach results in much progress, but neither have I ever succeeded in convincing those who use such tactics of this truth! The reason, no doubt, is that there are many people who are combative in all their social relationships.

In 1988, we tried to construct a system of adjudicating discrimination cases of all kinds. Our effort failed when a federal district judge held that it violated the First Amendment freedom of speech provisions of the Constitution. The American Civil Liberties Union brought the case, but their lawyer, who was a Wayne State University law professor, was then helpful in working out acceptable changes. Subsequently, in the last year or two, a new set of principles has been adopted in place of the original, and they seem to be working fairly well, although the scene is always blurred because of alleged doctrines of "political correctness." That issue is, from my point of view, exaggerated, but there is no question that finding a solution to speech that offends, demeans, or vulgarizes is difficult. As educators, we have long known that the climate of learning is as important to an education as the classroom content. Yet if through speech or nonviolent harassment life is made intolerable for such groups as minorities or gay-lesbians, efforts to change that kind of conduct are immediately pounced upon as violating the right to freedom of speech. Though I have been a member of the ACLU for many years and received an award from it for protecting freedom of speech during the years of student unrest, I have never agreed with the hardline position some of its leaders take with respect to linking action and speech.

Inside the classroom, if a student disrupts the class by insisting on talking during a lecture, or monopolizing the conversation, or insulting classmates, there is no problem in barring him or her from class. No one, to my knowledge, has ever argued that this violates the First Amendment because there is recognition that there must be "order" in the classroom. But if, *outside* the classroom, a student pins a sign on another student's door saying, "Nigger, go home," and he or she is then disciplined for this, the immediate claim will go up that this violates First Amendment rights because it "chills" freedom of speech. Yet no one who has any understanding of the educational process would deny that the climate of a campus is as important to a student's success and survival as is the classroom instruction. Why, then, should it be impossible to discipline a student who disrupts the learning climate? The answer First Amendment devotees would give, I assume, is that so-called codes of conduct, which go into great detail in trying to define any and all types of possible offenses, greatly endanger the principle of free speech. I agree that there is this danger, and I am concerned about it. I would keep the codes as simple as possible, and I would stress counseling rather than punitive discipline. In the last analysis, however, I would not shrink from expelling a student for egregious and continued action that erodes the learning climate.

The freedom of speech problem is exacerbated by extending student conduct restraints to faculty and staff. This is, I think, a mistake. Because faculty and staff are employees, rather than students, there are other ways to deal with them. We are now in for a period of uncertainty with respect to what the Supreme Court will hold is violative of the First Amendment. It is unlikely that any answer it gives will please all of us.

In 1991, I chaired a four-person committee charged with looking at the North Carolina system of public universities and suggesting directions for them over the next decade. A periodic review of the missions of these schools was a part of their regular routine, and each school had already prepared a comprehensive statement of its aspirations for the next decade. Having outsiders review documents of this kind is often preferable to calling on in-staters because the latter inevitably have ties to one or another of the institutions that are under consideration. Our committee visited each of the campuses, several of which were historically black colleges and one which was historically for American Indians. North Carolina is noted for the quality of its system of higher education, and Chapel Hill rates with the best American universities. We spent a good deal of time on our report, which, like the one I had done in New York in 1973, had as one of its major objectives devising rules for the development of graduate programs. We made recommendations to the governing board that presides over all schools in the system, and they were adopted. Not every school in the system was entirely happy with our conclusions, but that would be too much to expect. The fact that the board adopted our report speaks for its overall acceptability.

In 1992 I participated, along with a retired judge, in the settlement of a multi-million-dollar lawsuit that had been pending before the courts for years. This was done at the request of the parties and with the approval of the judge before whom the case was pending. After a series of meetings, we worked privately with the parties, narrowed the range of potential damages, and suggested a way for them to cope with those damages. They liked that approach, worked with some technical experts on resolving some of the problems, and ultimately settled the case.

In 1993, I participated in preparing a higher education report that was issued by the Wingspread Group with sponsorship by the S. C. Johnson Foundation. The group consisted of sixteen accomplished individuals from different walks of life. It concluded that *all* colleges and universities, whatever their present quality, are going to have to undergo substantial changes in the years ahead. The changes will be different from place to place, because we have a wide array of colleges and universities. No one remedy can be applied to all institutions, but it is the undergraduate program that requires the most attention.

There are a number of reasons why these changes must take place. More sophisticated jobs will require education beyond high school; demographic changes, due in part to the influx of immigrants, complicate the schooling problem; the chronic underfunding of inner-city schools, plus a tragic social milieu, continues to erode the quality of the K–12 system; escalating tuition costs have to be brought under control and this is going to require internal cuts because state and federal sources of support are badly stretched now; the quality of teaching, including greater use of modern technology, needs improvement; and ways must be found to restore some of our values of tolerance, civility, and concern for others in place of the obsession with what is best for "me," at the expense of "thee." Doing all of of these things, or at least the things that are particularly relevant to a given school, will be difficult. If they are not done, however, our economy will suffer a lack of properly trained employees, and our society will become ever more divisive. The great selective universities of the country may be disposed to think of these problems as characteristic only of the lesser schools. It is true that the students in selective universities are, by definition, drawn from those who have demonstrated their talents early on. This does not mean, however, that such institutions are without problems, one of which is the shortage of money to continue their present programs. Tuition cannot keep increasing at a rate considerably higher than the cost-of-living even when it can be demonstrated that this is not an appropriate yardstick against which to judge the increase. Both federal and state governments are in financial difficulties and are unlikely, by any estimate, to pour large additional amounts of money into higher education when they have so many other calls on tax revenue. All universities are, as a result, mounting vigorous campaigns to raise their endowments, but this is not going to be a complete answer. The return on investments is, in the current economic climate, not high enough to sustain the demand for new money. If one accepts these facts, it means that colleges and universities are going to have to look internally for ways in which they can maintain their quality while at the same time making better use of their funds. This will be unpopular, and will be difficult for presidents, executive officers, and deans. It will also be hard for faculties and staff to accept. Some of the points of attack are likely to be the following.

There are schools considering a three-year undergraduate degree. This is, in my view, worth serious consideration. Such a degree might offer fewer course options to the student because, to maintain its integrity, it would likely have to be more prescriptive, but that is not all bad. We know that there are already some students who manage to complete the undergraduate program in three years, and it would, at a very minimum, be worth looking to see how, and with what kind of program, they do it. If a significant part of our concern is to adequately train people for a more sophisticated world of employment, while at the same time reducing the cost of doing this, it is likely to be demonstrable that this can be done in three years.

Modern technology can be used to aid and improve the total teaching function. Innumerable studies have shown that teaching of this kind can be effective, though it needs to be supplemented by personal contact. An internal study of what kinds of things best lend themselves to the use of technology would almost certainly produce some useable results and some cost savings in terms of faculty time.

Time allocated to research and teaching also needs reexamination.

In the best of all possible worlds, it may be that the best teachers are those who are also fine research scholars. Under present circumstances, research universities tend to build into every faculty member's time a research component. This can be justified only if all faculty members are productive scholars, and this is not universally true. Some would, in fact, prefer to teach; others are superb teachers but not good research scholars; and still others lose their interest in research as time passes. Sorting all of this out is very difficult, yet it could be done and, under financial pressure, it may have to be. A step in the right direction is a willingness to grant tenure to first-rate teachers regardless of their research. A further, and essential step, is joint exploration between the faculty and the administration of how to best allocate faculty time.

A nagging irritant and weakness in almost all large universities is in the use of teaching assistants. It is not that all teaching assistants are bad, indeed many of them are first-rate. More often, it is hard to find American teaching assistants in some disciplines, and this gives rise to the use of foreign graduate students for whom English is a second language. The result is a perennial complaint that students either cannot understand the accent, or work so hard trying to understand the words that they lose the content. This is an inexcusable state of affairs, yet it remains a practice and shows an inappropriate lack of concern for students.

Yet another area for close attention is the proliferation of courses that has taken place over the years. Once again, it is not so much that the courses are lacking in substance as it is that, in an era of tight budgets, some are less essential than others and the time used on them could be better spent elsewhere.

Finally, there is the question of counseling. At the undergraduate level, students often fail to get the help and advice that they need. Over the years, the tendency has been to hire professional staff counselors, and this is certainly helpful. It may nevertheless leave the student feeling that no faculty member has any interest in his or her success despite the fact that the faculty is at the heart of the enterprise. This does not, in the language of technology, constitute a user-friendly university. We can either wring our hands and say that, unfortunately, there is nothing that can be done about it, or we can change some of our priorities and find a way to do something about it. There are institutions that demonstrate this is possible.

My friends in the academic world will smile ruefully and say that these are the words of a retired administrator who may be right but who does not have to face reality and bring about the kind of changes that need to at least be considered. I do not underestimate the difficulties in bringing about change, nor do I envy current administrators who face resistance to change. But, as one of our ablest vice presidents used to say to me when I was bemoaning the difficulty of a given situation, "What do you think you get paid for?" Fundamental changes do not occur easily or rapidly, but they do not occur at all unless they are attempted.

Twice in the last two or three years, I have served as an expert witness in cases involving universities elsewhere in the United States. When Massachusetts Institute of Technology chose to resist the claim of the Justice Department that it was violating the Antitrust Act by joining with Ivy League schools in agreeing upon the allocation of student financial aid packages, I served as a witness for MIT. The federal district court held against MIT, but the court of appeals remanded the case and it was ultimately settled to the mutual satisfaction of MIT and the government.

In 1994, I participated as an expert witness for a federal judge in a desegregation case involving the Alabama higher education institutions. It revolved around Alabama's historically black colleges, the resources and status they enjoy as compared with the historically white colleges, and the possible remedies, if any, that might be mandated. That difficult question has been in and out of the federal courts since desegregation was ordered in *Brown v. Board of Education* in 1954, and it is enormously difficult to find satisfactory solutions. A further decision in the Alabama case is expected in the summer of 1995, but whether it will settle the dispute remains to be seen.

As I bring this memoir to an end, and as my active role diminishes as it must with age, I worry about the future of our country. When such a wise and insightful an observer as George Kennan, who was the principal intellectual architect of our containment policy in dealing with Russia, speculates about whether our democratic society can survive in the years ahead, it is time for all of us to think seriously about that subject. High on the list of worries is the lack of confidence in our government that is now so widespread.

We have a two-party system in which neither party has a coherent political philosophy. Both parties consist of members who are conservative, moderate, or liberal. One sometimes wishes that they could all be thrown in a pool and then sorted out so that meaningful political parties could emerge. For reasons of history and geography, that seems to be impossible. Democracy inevitably implies compromise, because there is no way in which a country as large and diverse as ours can avoid genuine differences, but at the present time we find it difficult to arrive at even reasonable compromises. Party discipline, which we once more nearly had, is lacking.

At the very time when we most need an efficient government, the problems are of unusual difficulty. Profligate spending has imperiled our ability to commit resources to domestic problems. Health care costs are out of control, but various interest groups squabble about how best to preserve their own turf and political parties vie for who will get credit for what the people very much want. A presently incurable disease, AIDS, is decimating portions of our populace and imposing enormous financial costs on society. A bitter debate over population control measures divides our people at the same time that it becomes ever more obvious that the world is becoming overpopulated. We spend more and more money on the construction of prisons that nevertheless remain overcrowded and cost far more per person than it would to educate occupants better and concentrate on employment for them. We see an international scene in which ancient hatreds erupt all over the world, featuring butchery, rape, religious warfare, and a mockery of civilized behavior. We suffer from environmental problems that are the product of long years of neglect. And we face a host of ethical problems arising out of such things as life-extending health care for the aged, genetic manipulation, and punishment for juveniles who commit crimes without any apparent remorse, all of which call for attention. The list could go on and on. In the last analysis, it is not the problems, difficult as they are, that worry me. It is whether we can organize ourselves to deal with them. We are left with the impression that the people who really govern our lives are the powerful interest groups.

As we get older, I suppose all of us tend to look back on our own lifetimes with nostalgia, and to think that it was a better world than the one we now have. Sally and I were both children of the Great Depression of the 1920 and 1930s. We were surrounded by loving familes. We thought we were lucky to find jobs that enabled us to go to school, and it was possible then, as it is not now, to earn enough to pay all of one's own expenses. We were overtaken and parted by World War II, but we survived. We raised three children, of whom we are very proud. The academic world came to us by surprise, but we loved it. The law was always my first love as a discipline, and I had the good fortune to serve as a law professor for several years. We were caught up in the years of student unrest, but my experience in the tumultuous field of labor relations made it easier, and Sally's ability to endure that period was of enormous importance. In retrospect, we were lucky!

The world of our children and our grandchildren is different. The family milieu we knew no longer exists for an enormous number of children. At the other end of the life cycle, those of us who are aging are living longer and using more of the nation's resources to support us. The standard of living we have enjoyed may not be sustainable, despite the rhetoric of the politicians.

Still and all, in spite of what may seem to be a recitation of all the troubles of our current world, I am an inveterate optimist. The materialistic world we have so emphasized in recent years is far less important than the care and concern we ought to have for each other. The question is going to be whether we want a society that cares, not whether it is possible to have one.

If I had to make a personal choice as to where best to start in assuring the future of our democracy, I think I would concentrate on creating jobs. The drive for increasing productivity is going to continue, and that means that many traditional jobs will be eliminated. Meanwhile, we have enormous deficiencies in an aging infrastructure, in housing, in schools, in highways, with the environment, and in other categories. We say we don't have the money to fund things of this kind, but that is a matter of priorities. If there were more jobs, welfare costs would go down, crime would almost certainly diminish, health costs would be more manageable, tax revenues would expand, the destructive impact of unemployment on families would be alleviated, and racial and ethnic tensions would be modified. In a climate of relatively full employment, we would, I think, be more disposed to care for one another. It does not trouble me that this might involve a kind of government-private collaboration that private enterprise devotees find so distasteful.

Do we have the will to change our ways? Not if we continue to allow the gap between the "haves" and the "have-nots" to widen. Yes, if we are willing to modify our excesses and to accept a better life for all of us. I desperately hope that it will be the latter.

By coincidence, I bring this memoir to an end just after the Allies of

World War II celebrated the fiftieth anniversary of D day. I stood on English soil that morning watching a massive array of ships and planes headed toward France. Before the day was over, thousands of American soldiers my age would be dead. Their lives ended that day, mine went on. I could not bear to watch the anniversary ceremonies without tears flowing down my face, but neither could I walk away from them. In that time of peril, Americans stood together even at the cost of their lives. How is it that we find it so difficult to care for one another in times of peace?